KEEPING CHILLY

GENEVIEVE MCKAY

STONEPONY STUDIOS

CHAPTER 1

BREE

"*C*an't you two keep your hands off each other for two seconds? We're trying to win a horse show here. I could use a little help getting Dragon ready."

Nicholas and I broke apart, laughing, and I turned to face Chloe's outraged glare. She stood in the doorway of our makeshift tack room with her hands on her hips and a murderous expression on her face.

Patience, I reminded myself, squashing down my annoyance. *She's been through a lot lately.*

Outrage seemed to be Chloe's mood of choice over the last few months. Even though her life looked golden to me, she'd been simmering with anger ever since her mother had kicked her out of their home.

And her crankiness reached whole new heights when our working student Jeremy was around. Which, since we all lived on the same property, was *all the time.*

"It was just a kiss, Chloe," I said, ignoring Nicholas's snicker behind me. "It wasn't like we were auditioning for adult movies or anything. We've been working hard all morning so we snuck away for a quick break."

"We're here to help," Nicholas added, plucking some stray bits of hay out of my hair. "What do you need?"

"I need a new life." Chloe's shoulders sagged. "And I need a horse who will listen to me and not try and leap out of the ring as soon as I let my guard down."

I looked at her in surprise. Dragon was feisty, beautiful and talented. But she was also quirky and independent. And those were all reasons that Chloe loved her. I'd never heard her complain about anything Dragon did before. Not once.

"Is she acting up" I asked, frowning. "She seemed relaxed all morning."

"No, not yet. But it's coming. I have a bad feeling about this show."

Uh-oh, that's not good. I looked at Chloe worriedly. Dragon was an incredibly sensitive horse who was easily set off. Especially if the humans around her were too focused on themselves to pay attention to her. She was capable of brilliance … when she felt like it. But she could also be dangerous and unpredictable. You had to be on your game when you handled her. Something I knew all too well.

I reached down and laced my fingers with Nicholas's as we trailed Chloe outside into the glare of summer sunshine, trying to think of the best way to calm her down.

Stepping outside was a sharp contrast from the cool shadows of the tack room. The air was so hot out here that it almost hurt to breathe. I'd already changed out of breeches and into shorts, but it hadn't made much of a difference. It was just past lunchtime and the asphalt parking lot beyond the stable block was shimmering with heat.

All the horses, except for Dragon, had already finished their rides, been cooled out and had cooling liniment baths to help beat the heat. So far, they seemed to be handling the temperature okay.

I winced as a screaming child ran past, pulling five wildly bouncing balloons on a string behind her. She, and the harried looking father who hurried after her, looked completely oblivious to the fact that horses might not appreciate balloons.

Normally, dressage shows didn't attract quite this many spectators, but it was a long weekend and there was a fair going on just down the road, complete with an ancient roller coaster that we could hear rattling around in the distance. Excited screams and tinny carnival music were a constant background noise.

People wandered around everywhere carrying cotton candy and wearing face-paint. Kids squealed and ran around out of control, high on sugar and desperate to pet the horses. It was the most festive dressage show I'd ever been to. But the atmosphere was a little crazy.

"How long until you ride, Chloe? Lorne and Julie should be around here somewhere. I know Julie wanted to help with your warm up."

"I'm on in an hour, but Dragon really needs to get out and start walking around the grounds. I don't trust her around this much chaos. It will take her a while to settle down. And Julie and Lorne are watching Jeremy ride that chestnut," she added darkly.

"Lauren's horse?"

"Yes." She scowled and grabbed Dragon's leather halter off the hook on the mare's stall door. "Although I don't know how they're supposed to even get close to him with his permanent fan club swarming around. I can't believe he's conned those desperate women into letting him ride their horses. He's such a faker. One of these days …"

She broke off and disappeared into Dragon's stall.

"What does she have against Jeremy?" Nicholas whispered in my ear.

I rolled my eyes and shrugged in answer to his question.

"I honestly have no idea."

Jeremy, who was in his mid-thirties, was on the older side to be one of our working students, but his lilting Scottish accent, ice blue eyes, and air of mystery had quickly gained him a following on our small local show circuit. And it was a bonus that his riding skills were beyond decent. His fans mostly consisted of single, or not so single, show moms who followed him around like an adoring flock of starlings.

He'd already gained three new horses to ride and show in addition to ours, something that drove Chloe wild with jealousy. The chestnut he was showing today, Sassafras, was actually a pretty incredible horse.

It was true that I hadn't trusted Jeremy very much when he'd first arrived at our farm, either. He'd been aloof and not overly friendly. We'd even suspected him of having some dark secret past that he was keeping from us.

But as the months passed, it was like his guard dropped and whatever chip he'd been carrying on his shoulder had just sort of melted away. He'd become more and more friendly with all of us and the horses loved him.

The only one completely immune to his charms was Chloe: her hatred and suspicion of him grew with each passing day.

"It's just so unfair that he wrapped Lauren around his little finger like that," she said, pulling off Dragon's summer sheet and folding it over the door. "She's loaded with money and has all these amazing horses. And all her rich friends want Jeremy to ride their expensive horses for them now, too. You know he's going to drop us and ride for her the second his internship here is over, right?"

"He hasn't said anything about leaving," I said firmly, "and he's free to go anytime he likes, Chloe. Why are you acting so jealous? You have nice horses to ride, too."

"I'm not jealous," she said quickly. "I'm just mad that he's fooled everyone into thinking he's this great person and a hotshot rider when he's not. And speaking of lying traitors, that stupid Maisy is doing some sort of Grand Prix freestyle demo with Thor in a few minutes, too. I get to share the warm-up ring with my two least favourite people on the planet."

"His name's Titan," I corrected automatically but Chloe just rolled her eyes and shrugged.

"He'll always be Thor to me," she said firmly. "She doesn't deserve him."

I frowned and glanced around quickly to make sure nobody was in ear-shot as she ducked down to fuss with Dragon's legs.

Chloe was one of my best friends but she was opinionated, and *loud*. Which was fine most of the time but not *here*. Not when she was saying bad things about other riders. The horse community wasn't very big and rumours spread like wildfire. I didn't want the October Horses name to get mixed up with anything negative.

"Who is Maisy?" Nicholas asked. "And why does Chloe hate her?"

I sighed and shook my head. Why did Chloe hate anyone?

"Maisy owns that farm up the hill from us with the dressage ring," I said in a low voice. "We ride the trails past her place all the time. I've never met her but I've seen her ride and she's pretty amazing. I have no idea why Chloe hates her but I think it has something to do with Titan."

"Her horse?"

"Yeah, he's this fancy Friesian-Warmblood cross that Maisy competes on. Apparently, Chloe knew him when he was a baby, back when his name was Thor, and she wanted to buy him. Only, Maisy's parents bought him first; they offered the seller more money and Chloe's deal fell through."

"Ah," Nicholas said, "the bitterness makes more sense then."

"I guess it does. But it happened like seven years ago. Chloe was a little kid for heaven's sake. It doesn't do her any good to have this chip on her shoulder all the time. It's the same way she hates Jeremy. She just can't seem to let anything go."

We cut our conversation short as Chloe led Dragon out.

The mare looked alert but relaxed. Her bay coat gleamed with good health and constant grooming. She stood with her head up, boldly surveying the showgrounds as if she was the rightful queen of everything.

She stood rock-still as Chloe ran a final polishing brush over her and then tacked her up carefully. Dragon's braids were miraculously still in place and she looked every inch the professional show horse.

I added a coat of hoof polish to her dark hooves, wiped the corners of her mouth clean and then stepped back to admire her.

"Stay right there, I'm just taking a picture for the blog," I said, shifting around to catch them from a few different angles. Chloe's somber expression lifted and for a second, she looked like her old self again.

A burst of loud clapping and excited chatter carried across from the ring and Chloe's smile fell away as quickly as it had arrived. Moving to the mounting block, she swung up onto Dragon's broad back.

"I can't believe he's convinced all those owners to hire him," she said darkly and I knew it must have been the crowd of Jeremy's owners and followers congratulating him on his ride. "He's such a lying suck-up."

"Chloe," I said in warning as I glanced over at Dragon. "You'll upset her."

I looked worriedly at the big mare, waiting for her to pick up on Chloe's agitation and start to act up. But, despite Chloe's dark mood, Dragon actually seemed in good spirits. She stood like a rock with her ears pricked toward the ring, her eyes bright with excitement. Which could be a good thing or a bad thing depending on what she was thinking about.

"Yeah, yeah, I know." Chloe sighed and patted Dragon's shiny neck. "I'm being an idiot."

"Just a little," I said, laughing. "This is supposed to be fun, remember. We're just getting experience and miles for the horses. There's no pressure. And you're not competing with Jeremy … he's on our team."

She wrinkled her nose in distaste.

"Right." She took a deep breath. "He just … ugh, I don't know. I'm always worried that if I don't start doing better on Dragon that I'm going to lose her. That Lorne is going to decide to give her ride to Jeremy."

"Oh." I stared at her in dismay. "Is that what you're worried about? Chloe, Lorne would never …"

She shook her head, giving me a bleak look. "Don't be so sure, Bree. Jeremy is doing his best to get this mare away from me, I just know it. Eventually he'll wear Lorne down."

I opened my mouth to protest but she shook her head and nudged the mare toward the warm-up ring.

"We'll be over there in a second," I called after her. "We'll watch your warm up."

Chloe just raised a hand in acknowledgement and rode away without looking back.

I watched her for a moment, feeling a cold wiggle of worry shiver in my belly. Dragon looked mellow for now, but I knew from experience that that could change in an instant.

Dressage was not her favourite thing at all, and we'd had a tough time convincing her that dancing in a ring was a good idea. Dragon was a superstar when she was out schooling on a cross country course, but she didn't have the patience or the desire for dressage. Her scores were very slowly improving but she thought nothing of throwing off a series of bucks when asked to halt or to rear if she had to stand still for more than a second. And she'd bolted right out of the ring more than once. She was definitely a work in progress.

"Want me to grab us something from the food truck before the line gets too long?" Nicholas asked.

"Yes." I brightened at the thought of food. "Extra gravy on the fries, please. We can find a table by the warm-up ring and watch Maisy's demo. I'd love to take some pictures of her and Titan."

"You got it, boss." He gave me a mock salute as he left and I couldn't help but grin as I watched him walk away. We'd only really gotten involved this past winter and I still had to pinch myself sometimes to make sure I was awake and not dreaming. I knew that I liked him way too much for my own good, but I just couldn't help it.

A year ago, I'd been certain that I was on my last legs, about to die from the disease that had taken hold of me and nearly finished me off. So, any thought of a relationship had been out of the question.

It had been a miracle that I'd not only survived but had created a whole new life for myself. I was the co-founder and social media coordinator of our October Horses project, which helped retired racehorses find new homes. And I'd found a second family in everyone who lived on the farm.

The farm, the horses, and my mind-bendingly popular blog were all a dream come true. My blossoming relationship with Nicholas, my boss Julie's son, was just the icing on the cake. I'd had a couple of boyfriends in the past but I'd never experienced this level of trust before. Certainly not with my last boyfriend Duncan, who'd thought it would be a good idea to sleep with my sister while I was in the hospital.

Nicholas felt like he was an actual part of me. Like he was my soul-mate or something ridiculous like that. And I was pretty sure that he felt the same way.

I dragged the ancient, leaky hose from a nearby water spigot and fed the end through the bars of Ace's stall, turning on the nozzle. Water suddenly spurted up at me and the hose jerked in my hand spattering liquid in an arc across my face and the walls of the stall. I'd forgotten about the faulty hoses here; the water lines were full of air bubbles and you had to hold onto them tight or they'd leave you soaked.

"Gross," I said, wiping a hand across my dripping forehead. "Sorry, Ace." That would teach me to daydream while I was doing chores.

Ace nickered at me sleepily from the back of his stall, not bothered at all by the commotion or the water now dripping into his bedding.

"Not much longer, buddy," I called to him, moving on to fill the rest of the buckets, too. We only had Dragon left to show that day and then we were free to go home and finish all the chores we had left undone on the farm.

Adie, our youngest working student, was away visiting her family for a couple of months so we'd all been stretched pretty thin. We had five horses showing that day, plus Jeremy's client's horses that he needed to warm up and ride.

And back home, we'd just had two new horses sent to us by the October Horses board of directors. They'd shipped us two horses instead of the single one we'd requested. Which meant we currently had more horses than we had stalls. Luckily it was summer so some of the horses were taking turns staying outside in the paddocks overnight. But we'd either have to sell someone before winter, or build more stalls.

I finished filling the buckets and checked all the nets to make sure they were still full of hay.

"Nipper, you're hardly eating," I said, frowning at his unfinished breakfast. He wasn't usually the type of guy to turn down food. But now the big brown and white pinto had left his net to stare wide-eyed through the bars, looking anxiously toward the show rings where a crowd had formed. Music was playing and I guessed that Maisy was probably starting her freestyle demonstration.

I studied Nipper worriedly but, other than his half-finished hay net, he looked fine. I'd just cleaned out his stall and I'd seen him drinking water so I was pretty sure he wasn't colicking.

I'll ask Julie to check on him later, just in case, I thought, pushing down my worry. I had a tendency to overthink things and expect the worst since the whole almost-dying-thing. But I was working on it.

"All right, everyone, be good. I'll be right back," I told the horses, turning eagerly toward the ring to find Nicholas and my lunch.

I hadn't taken more than two steps when the crowd around the ring began to gasp and then dozens of screams erupted.

CHAPTER 2

BREE

I froze for a second, trying to figure out what could possibly be wrong. There was lots of shouting and the sound of pounding hooves and multiple horses squealing and snorting. An anxious father ran past me, clutching his sobbing little girl to one shoulder.

"Loose horse!" somebody yelled. "We need an ambulance. We need a vet."

Cries rang out from all directions. Hooves thundered directly toward me and suddenly I wasn't frozen anymore.

"Whoa, Dragon," I said firmly, stepping out in front of her. "Whoa, good girl. You're all right."

She could have trampled me. She thought about it, if her rolling eyes and half-rear were any indication, but then she slid to a halt instead, blowing hard with the sharp, cracking sound that usually was the warning that a horse was about to explode.

"Pretty girl, smart girl," I said soothingly in a sing-song voice, taking hold of her broken reins that were dragging on the ground. "Please don't have hurt Chloe too badly. Come on, Dragon. Let's go to your stall and get some lunch. There's a good girl."

She listened to me for once, dropping her head and stuffing her nose roughly into my armpit as if for comfort.

Sirens cut through the sunny afternoon, sounding horribly out of place on such a nice day. Dragon threw her head up again, letting out an ear-piercing bellow and dancing away from me, dragging me sideways a few steps. I took a deep breath, planted my feet, and willed myself to be calm.

I wanted nothing more than to race to that warm-up ring and make sure that Chloe was okay, but Dragon was my first priority right now. I could feel her whole body shaking with agitation, and I knew that at any second, she could whirl around and take off again.

Step by step, talking to her the whole time, I guided her firmly into her empty stall and rolled the door back with trembling hands.

"Easy girl," I crooned, wincing when I saw the drops of blood that had oozed from the corner of her mouth. She must have stepped on the reins and caught herself in the mouth somehow along the way.

She let me take the bridle off but, the second she was free, she shot backwards, spinning around to pace anxious circles around her stall like a tiger, her sky-high adrenaline telling her that she needed to keep moving.

"All right, good girl," I said, "easy buddy. You're all right. I really should have taken that saddle off first, before I took your bridle off, hey?"

I just kept talking to her, saying nonsense words until her inside ear flicked at me and she huffed out a deep breath, slowing a little. She finally stopped at her water bucket and plunged her nose inside to suck up the water greedily. It was just enough time for me to unbuckle her girth and pull the saddle off. I backed hastily out of the door, locking it tightly behind me before I dumped her tack in our makeshift tack room and took off toward the ring at a run.

The scene was pure chaos when I got there. Two ambulances, and people yelling and scuttling around in all directions. Maisy's happy, upbeat freestyle music was still playing, layered over the cheerful sounds coming from the carnival, and it was all a sharp contrast against the disaster that was unfolding here.

"Where is everyone?" I said out loud, desperately looking around for my crew. I felt a stab of relief as I caught sight of Julie and Lorne in the warm-up ring and I broke into a run as I headed toward them. They were both kneeling down next to a slumped figure on the ground next to three ambulance attendants in high-vis vests.

"Oh, Chloe," I said, bursting into tears when I saw her pale face smudged with dirt. She was awake but one eye was nearly swollen shut and she looked like she was trying not to throw up. The attendants were moving her gently from the ground onto a stretcher and she cried out with pain as they swiftly strapped her down and maneuvered her toward the ambulance.

"Where's Dragon?" she called weakly, catching sight of me.

"She's fine, I promise. She's back at her stall. Are you all right?"

Stupid question. Of course, she wasn't *all right* if she was being loaded into the back of an ambulance.

"It wasn't her fault," Chloe said. "It was Thor ... I mean Titan. Dragon saw him fall. The other horses bolted and she just panicked."

Titan fell? I thought, looking around, but the crowd was too thick to see anything of what was happening in the other ring.

"I'm going to ride in the ambulance with her," Julie said, squeezing my arm. "She took a really hard fall. I'm sure her leg is broken. They'll do x-rays to make sure it isn't something worse. You can get everyone safely home? You can manage the horses?"

"Yes, of course," I said. "Jeremy and Lorne can drive the trailer. And Nicholas has his car here. We'll meet you at the hospital once everyone is home."

She nodded and gave me a quick hug before climbing into the vehicle after Chloe.

My throat closed up as I watched the ambulance pull away.

"She's okay," I said out loud to reassure myself. I looked around, wondering where Lorne had disappeared to. And where was Nicholas? And Jeremy? He had just finished his ride on Lauren's horse so he must be around here somewhere.

Titan fell, Chloe had said. But what did it all mean?

The edge of the main arena was packed with people. Little kids were crying, and some adults were, too. Some people just stared in shock and the rest of the crowd was buzzing with horrified whispers. And beyond them, above all the noise, I heard someone wailing. An agonized cry of loss and bewilderment that cut through me right to the bone and made the hair on the back of my neck stand on edge.

I'd done my time in palliative care and I was no stranger to what the aftermath of death sounded like. The haunting, anguished sound brought tears to my eyes.

Numbly, I pushed my way to the front of the crowd, dreading what I'd see. But I felt called that way for some reason. I wanted to help if I could.

"Don't look, Bree," a voice said and Nicholas was there, putting his arms tightly around me and trying to turn me away so he could block me from seeing the terrible scene. Which was sweet of him. But, considering that I'd dealt with more death in my short life than most people ever did, it was also totally unnecessary. I was much stronger than I looked.

Before I could tell him any of that, I caught sight of the horrible scene in front of me.

An ambulance was parked in the middle of the ring with all of its doors open. And so was the familiar truck of our farm vet, Dr.

Anderson. A handful of people were gathered close together nearby, holding up coolers and sheets to block the crowd's view of the disaster scene.

But nothing could block out the hysterical sobs of Maisy.

"Did Titan … die?" I asked, my voice coming out a squeak. I knew it must be him. It was the only thing that made sense. But it was hard to associate that crumpled black heap on the ground with the proud and beautiful horse that I'd seen standing regally in his pasture so many times. "What happened?"

"I don't know," Nicholas said, "she was cantering out on him and he just dropped like a stone. She's lucky she jumped clear when he fell. She could have been crushed."

"Heart attack, most likely," an older woman next to me whispered. She ducked her head right next to mine, her moist breath uncomfortably close to my ear. "I've seen it happen before. Tragic."

"An aneurism could do that, too." A woman in a blue jacket turned around, overhearing our conversation. "Sometimes the vessels in their brain just rupture. Such a shame, too. I heard she was supposed to go to Europe next month with that rider development program."

"Maybe it was drugs," a sharp voice said, rising above the others. "Considering the crowd she ran with, I wouldn't be surprised. I told the vet right when he got here that the horse should be tested. There's probably a lot of insurance money involved."

I swivelled around in astonishment, surprised by the venom in her voice. Her appearance didn't match up with her bitter words at all. She was much younger than she'd sounded, probably fifteen or sixteen, but she had a sour, embittered look about her. Her heart-shaped face and elegant blonde hair pulled back in a bun would have been pretty if she hadn't worn a murderous expression.

She glared at me and then her eyes widened as she noticed

Nicholas. Colour stained her cheeks and she tucked a flyaway strand of hair behind her ear.

I resisted the urge to roll my eyes. Girls looking at Nicholas like he was next on the menu was something I'd reluctantly had to get used to.

I glanced downward at the girl's dusty breeches and tall boots. She had her phone in her hand, held out at a strange angle as if she'd just lowered it.

She hadn't been … she wasn't *videoing* this, was she?

The girl caught my eye and then looked abruptly away, pressing her lips together.

"Now, now, Peyton," the first woman said. "That sounds like sour grapes to me."

"She used to ride with that coach, didn't she?" someone beside her asked. "The one who got the suspension for drug use and for hurting the horses. Didn't he do jail time or something? Wasn't he caught selling drugs to kids?"

"He did way worse than that." Peyton kept her eyes fixed on the ring and her mouth twisted into almost a snarl. "Maisy was one of his best students at the time. I bet the apple doesn't fall far from the tree. He probably taught her everything he knew."

"We don't know that," the first woman who'd spoken said firmly. "We shouldn't gossip when we don't know the facts. It's obvious she loved that horse."

The blonde girl rolled her eyes and made a disapproving noise in her throat.

"Well, there was a reason Lauren fired Maisy from riding her horses and hired that Scottish guy instead. I heard …" Her lecture was cut off abruptly by the sound of shouting from the ring.

I peered through the throng of people to see a tear-stained and disheveled Maisy standing between Titan and Dr. Anderson. He was a vet who'd come to see our horses often at the farm. He was normally a nice, cheerful guy but he wasn't smiling now.

"Get away from him," Maisy yelled, holding her arms out to

the side as if she was herding a rogue cow. "I want my *own* vet to look at him. Don't you dare come any closer."

"What is she doing?" the woman beside me whispered but I just shook my head. I had no idea.

The vet lowered his voice and said something I couldn't hear but Maisy's already anguished face flushed a deeper red and she was breathing so hard that it looked like she'd pass out. She shook off the first-aid attendants who were trying to escort her to the waiting ambulance, flailing out wildly with both fists until they left her alone.

I looked around the crowd, wondering where her family and friends were. Why was she all alone? Didn't she have anyone to help her? The people who were holding the blankets around Titan's body looked uncomfortable, like they definitely wished they had not volunteered for the job.

"Come on Bree, we should get the horses home. We can't do anything more here." Nicholas tugged gently on my hand.

I didn't want to go. I couldn't shake the feeling that Maisy didn't have anyone there for her. But what could *I* do? She would hardly appreciate a stranger stepping in at the worst moment of her life. Would she?

I wiped my eyes and heaved a shuddering breath as we walked back to the stalls. That was the thing about loving people and animals. Sometimes you had to let them go.

As if he'd guessed my thoughts, Nicholas suddenly stopped and pulled me up against his chest, wrapping his arms tightly around me.

I let myself lean against him, still marvelling at the fact that I had someone in my life that I could be this close to. That I could trust and let myself go with. I always felt like I had to be so strong and stoic around everyone else, because any sign of weakness might mean that my disease was coming back.

But not with Nicholas. He was like being around the horses; I could just be myself around him and not worry about weirding him out.

"We should go," I said finally.

He kissed the top of my head, laced my hand in his and together we headed back toward our stalls.

CHAPTER 3

BREE

*L*orne and Jeremy were already silently packing all our things into the trailer's small tack room. The somber mood was much different to how happy we'd been when we arrived at the show grounds early that morning. It felt like a lifetime ago.

Jeremy didn't look up at any of us while we quietly finished loading all the gear into the truck and trailer; he just worked with a grim look on his face, ignoring us all.

"Are you okay to leave?" I asked him quietly. "Your owners don't mind?"

"No, they agreed that it was best to leave." He cleared his throat, looking at me as if he were startled to find himself not alone. "My last horse is young and he was already upset with everything going on. No point in pushing him."

"Yeah, good idea." I nodded. That was one thing about Jeremy. No matter how gruff, and sometimes insensitive, he was around people, he wasn't that way about the horses. Their needs always came first.

"Lorne and I will drive the horses home," he said abruptly. "You and Nick here clean the stalls out, and collect the ribbons and prizes from the office. We'll meet you back at the farm."

Nicholas made a low grumbling noise at being called Nick, a name he hated, but didn't argue. Jeremy was bossy, and he was good at rubbing people the wrong way sometimes, but now wasn't the time to remind him that we weren't his servants.

"All right, fine," I said quickly. "We'll see you back at home."

I didn't care about collecting my own ribbons but some of those were Chloe's from her morning rides on Nugget, and I knew she'd want to have them. And we had to strip our stalls clean, or the show management would levy us with a fine.

We helped Lorne and Jeremy load the horses back into the trailer. All of them practically leapt inside, eager to be home. Even Dragon was on her best behaviour.

We waved them off and then I grabbed a wheel barrow so Nicholas and I could set to work pulling all the shavings out of the stalls and taking them over to the giant manure pile on the edge of the show grounds. With two of us working, it didn't take us long, even though I was distracted and kept staring over toward the arena where the crowd was slowly drifting away.

I couldn't see from this far away, thank goodness, but I'd overheard someone saying that some heavy machinery had arrived to put Titan's huge, limp body onto a flat-deck trailer and take it away.

I wondered what they did with horses when they didn't die at home. Did they get cremated like people? Were there horse graveyards somewhere?

"You doing all right, Bree?" Nicholas asked softly.

"Yeah, all right. You?"

"It was pretty shocking, actually. I've never seen anything like that."

I reached out and grabbed his hand, giving it a tight squeeze. "Come on, let's get our ribbons and test sheets and then get out of here. I want to go home."

We kept our hands linked as we went up to the show office, which was packed with people wearing tear-stained faces and gripping fist-fulls of Kleenex.

"He was such a nice horse," somebody said as we slipped in the open door. "She'll never get another like that."

"Maisy has lots of faults," another lady said bluntly, "but she loved that animal. This is going to devastate her. That's the end of the road for her."

"Oh, don't say that," someone else said, "I'm sure she'll get back on her feet once she's had time to grieve ..."

"Nope, I heard a rumour that they're out of money. Bankrupt. That's the last horse like that she'll sit on. That's for sure."

"Quiet now, that's just gossip," the girl behind the desk said sharply, "now is not the time. I'm sorry loves," this part was directed to me and Nicholas. "What can I get for you?"

She quickly gave us the stack of test sheets and ribbons that Chloe, Jeremy, and I had earned.

"Don't forget Chloe's saddle pad and her gift certificate to the tack store, dear. She was reserve champion in her division with that nice grey. Do you know how she's doing yet?"

I felt the interest in the room shift toward us as everyone turned in our direction.

"No," I shook my head, feeling the heat rising in my cheeks. "I think her leg is broken but that's all I know. Julie went with her to the hospital."

"Poor thing. Well, a broken leg isn't so bad. She can spring back from that soon enough. I suppose that means Jeremy will pick up the ride on that nice bay mare you have then."

"Oh, I ... I'm not sure," I said, gulping. But suddenly I knew that's exactly what was going to happen. And having Jeremy ride Dragon would hurt Chloe much more than a broken leg. It was the thing she'd feared the most, her worst nightmare come true. It would devastate her.

"We have to go." I turned and hurried back outside, pushing through the crowd, dragging Nicholas with me.

I took a deep breath when I was back in the sunshine, away from that claustrophobic office. The adrenaline of the day seemed to wear off all at once, leaving me exhausted and a little sick to my stomach. It didn't help that I hadn't eaten anything since our pre-dawn breakfast of oatmeal and coffee.

"Come on." Nicholas wrapped an arm around my shoulder and steered me toward his car. "Let's get you home."

Our drive back was mostly silent. I stared out the window, struggling to process everything that had happened. How could a day that started out so full of sunshine and promise end up so badly?

The horses were already unloaded and put away by the time we got back and Jeremy had brought in all the boarders as well. Everyone was bedded down eating a late lunch or maybe an early dinner. Our two new young racehorses, Poppy and Jet, were out in their paddocks munching on hay nets.

"Julie called. Chloe has gone in for surgery," Jeremy said gruffly from where he was brushing Dragon in her stall. I could see a blob of cream at the side of her mouth where he'd already treated her cut. "Lorne wants to head up to the hospital whenever you two are ready to go."

"You're not coming with us?" I asked slowly, noticing the sort of possessive way he'd draped an arm over Dragon's back.

"No, I don't do well with hospitals. Besides, Chloe doesn't need to see me. You can text me to let me know how she's doing. Lauren called and invited me to their barn dinner tonight. It's for the whole team to celebrate their wins."

He didn't meet my eye when he spoke and I felt an uneasy churning in the pit of my stomach.

"You're going out for dinner to *celebrate?*" I said incredulously. "While Chloe is in the hospital having surgery?"

"Yes, yes I am." He ran a soft-bristled brush down Dragon's neck slowly. "It's been a long day and I need to blow off some steam."

He can't be serious, I stared at him in bewilderment. But apparently, he was.

"Right, let's go then," Nicholas cut in before I could argue any further. "Lorne will try and drive himself if we don't head him off soon."

"Fine," I said, leaving the barn with a reluctant backward glance at Jeremy.

He was working a brush through Dragon's unbraided mane, talking to her in a low, soothing voice. Looking at her like she was already his horse.

The important thing to think about right now is Chloe, I reminded myself.

I would have to worry about Jeremy's strange behaviour later.

CHAPTER 4

BREE

*W*e had been right to not let Lorne drive himself. He was more upset than he'd let on earlier. He twisted his cap between his hands the whole way to the hospital, his face white and his lips pinched tightly together like he was in pain. I wasn't doing much better honestly. Part of it was worry about Chloe. But the other part was that I didn't want to step foot in a hospital again for a long, long time. I knew that Lorne felt the same way.

I'd nearly lost my life here. And Lorne's wife and soulmate, Gretta, had passed away when we'd been in the nearby palliative care center together. It wasn't a time either Lorne or I wanted to remember.

Nicholas met my gaze in the rear-view mirror and sent me a reassuring smile.

The parking lot at the hospital was full so we had to find a spot in a far back corner and walk all the way to the front door.

I knew Lorne was in a hurry but the closer we got, the

slower his feet went, the less he spoke and the more he hunched his shoulders into a protective curl. Which was alarming since he was usually full of vigor and sass. Not much usually got Lorne down but this whole accident had clearly shaken him.

"Lorne, you know Chloe's going to be okay, right? It's just her leg," I said, attempting to sound like I knew what I was talking about.

"It was a bad fall, Bree," he said quietly, pulling his cap off and gripping it between both hands. "Dragon tripped when she spooked. She fell right over on Chloe. For a second it looked like …." He broke off and I reached out and took his arm, squeezing tightly.

I could imagine what it had looked like. Especially if Chloe had blacked out for a second.

"Dragon spooked when Titan fell?"

"Yes, he made this horrible sound when he went down; I've never heard anything like it before. All the horses nearby were terrified and a few of them bolted. Which upset Dragon. Another horse nearly ran into her and that's when she leapt sideways and fell."

"That's awful."

"Titan was a good horse." Lorne shook his head, looking a little like his old self again. "It's a real shame his rider lost him like that."

I was about to answer but just then the front doors whooshed open and that antiseptic hospital smell hit me. I gulped, suddenly needing all my wits to focus on not throwing up or bolting outside. Only my grip on Lorne's arm anchored me down.

Luckily, Nicholas took over, marching us up to the desk and finding out exactly where we needed to go to find his mom and Chloe.

"Third floor," he said, herding Lorne and I to the elevator.

We saw Julie the second the elevator doors opened. She was

halfway down the hall sitting on a plastic chair, a cardboard cup of coffee in her hand and a magazine spread open on her lap.

She broke out in a relieved smile the second she caught sight of us.

"She's going to be okay." Julie stood up, stretching her cramped muscles. "She's already out of surgery. The break was clean, they just had to reset it. She'll be in a cast."

A wave of relief shot over me and tears stung my eyes.

"Can we see her?" I asked, struggling to keep my voice steady.

"Yep, if we wait an hour or so, we can. But she won't be up to much conversation. Are you guys okay waiting that long?"

"Of course, we are," Lorne said. "I want to see that she's okay with my own eyes."

"Are her parents here?" I asked.

Julie's expression fell and she made a disapproving noise in her throat.

"Her dad is out of town right now and her mom ... her mom said she wasn't going to come."

"Seriously? She really holds that much of a grudge?"

Julie shrugged and looked away.

Chloe's mom was kind of an intense woman. She'd practically disowned Chloe for putting off university until next year in order to focus on riding. That's why Chloe had had to move in with us in the first place; her mother had kicked her out. Chloe hadn't seen her mom or her little brothers in months.

"She made sure that Chloe was going to be okay and that we were taking her back to the farm with us," Julie said slowly. "But, no, she's not coming to see her."

I gritted my teeth and shook my head. My own parents had been amazing when I'd been in the hospital; they'd barely left my side and had been my strongest advocates. I couldn't imagine my mom *not* dropping everything to be there if I was hurt.

"Maybe we should all get something to eat while we wait,"

Julie said, "I remember how fantastic hospital food is. It will be just like old times."

She grinned at us and we all groaned.

Julie had spent her own terrible time at the hospital many years ago when she'd been in a car accident that had ended her riding career. She'd also lost her husband, Nicholas's dad, in that accident. That had been when Nicholas was a kid but I knew that they both still carried the scars from it. Even after many surgeries, Julie still had burn marks across her body, including her face and arm. I barely even noticed them anymore but new people often gave her a surprised second glance when they first met her.

We filed downstairs to the cafeteria and, despite my anxiety at being in this building at all, my stomach rumbled in anticipation as soon as I smelled food. This hospital actually had a pretty good head chef and their kitchen team made it their mission to make the food as tasty as possible. Unfortunately, I'd been too sick during my extended stay here to appreciate that very much.

"Carbs," I said, my mouth watering, "I need carbs now."

I ordered whichever pasta had the cheesiest sauce on the menu, a side of garlic bread and chocolate cake for dessert. I felt like I hadn't eaten in years.

I was too focused on food to join in on the conversation but I half listened as Julie and Lorne talked about the horse show and how we'd done that morning before the accident. Nobody talked about Dragon or what was going to happen to her now that Chloe couldn't ride.

The problem was that Dragon was a heck of a lot of horse. Too much for me or Adie to ride. Unless we wanted to take on another rider then Jeremy was the obvious choice. But we all knew how badly Chloe would react if it came to that.

. . .

We were back upstairs before the hour had passed, waiting anxiously outside Chloe's door until a slightly irritated nurse ushered us inside.

"Just a few minutes," she told us. "She needs to rest. You can pick her up tomorrow."

We filed up to Chloe's bedside and I gulped to see how pale and small she looked in the hospital bed. Like a little kid.

She shifted as we approached the bed and her eyelids drifted open.

"Hey, Chloe," Julie whispered. "How are you doing, girl?"

"Hi," Chloe smiled sleepily at us and waved a languid hand in our direction. "Is Dragon here?" She asked dreamily. The pain medication was apparently in full force.

"She's safe at home," Lorne said gruffly. "Eating her body weight in hay."

Chloe laughed and her eyes fluttered shut again. "Don't let Jeremy ride her, okay? I'll be back tomorrow. Promise me."

Lorne patted her hand gently. "Just go to sleep now; we'll worry about that later."

"Promise me." She frowned even though her eyes didn't open. Her grip on Lorne's hand tightened.

But luckily, he didn't have to answer because Chloe yawned and snuggled deeper into her pillow before beginning to snore softly.

"I guess we should go," Julie said. "We'll pick her up tomorrow."

The second we were out of the hospital I took a deep cleansing breath of fresh air and wiped my damp palms on my jeans. I felt like I'd escaped from a prison somehow, even though it was a perfectly nice hospital.

Around me the others were doing the same and I guessed that it was nearly agony for any outdoorsy type of person to even think of being stuck in a bed for longer than a day. I never wanted to go back there again.

Visiting that place had reminded me of how lucky I was to be alive. It was a good reminder of how I had to live each day fully and not take a single second for granted. Chloe's accident could have been much, much worse.

CHAPTER 5

MAISY

I wouldn't let those idiots take me to the hospital. I wasn't hurt. Not in the broken bones and blood sense anyway. I was fine on the outside.

It was the inside of me that had been carved out, hollowed, stripped of everything that was good and right with the world. Only an agonizing dark void was left. There was no doctor's cure for that.

My bond with Titan, the best friend I'd had in this world, had been severed without a second's notice. Nothing. No warning. Just there one second and then, *blam*, gone. Like the best part of me had been brutally erased.

I couldn't even comprehend what had happened at first. It felt like a joke, a prank someone was playing on me. *Ha ha, your horse fell in public and nearly crushed you. That* I could have handled. I kept expecting him to get up. To lift his big, beautiful head and lumber to his feet like he did after a good roll.

But he didn't. And all those people were screaming and point-ing. And I couldn't think. It felt like there was something I should be doing to make it better. Some magic words or a talisman I could use to bring him back if I only knew how.

But there was nothing. Just this unbreaking loneliness.

I was glad when I could take out my anger on the ambulance attendants who came to hover around me. I was glad when I could rage at the bumbling vet and tell him to get the hell away from my horse. Anger felt so much better than the bewildered hurt.

It was a relief when everyone finally left me alone. I didn't have anyone with me at the show that day. I had been doing a simple demonstration. It was supposed to be a quick hour out of my day. A goodwill gesture to do something about rebuilding my shoddy reputation after my old coach, Dirk's, public downfall. It was one of the conditions of me staying on the European Devel-opment Team. I had to do all this public outreach crap to prove that I wasn't a terrible person.

Not that what had gone down with Dirk had had anything to do with me. Sure, I'd ridden with him for years but he hadn't done anything shady to me or Titan. And I hadn't seen him do anything to the other horses, or the riders, either. Not really.

I hadn't even boarded at his barn. I'd trailered in for my lessons and trailered out again. I'd been completely focused on my own riding and career. When the group launching the complaints against him had asked, no begged, me to testify, I'd turned them down flat. It wasn't that I'd been protecting Dirk; the whole thing was just none of my business and I'd tried to stay out of it.

That should have been the end of it. But it wasn't. By the time the gossipy horse community was done with me there had been nothing left of my reputation. There'd been nobody left to stand with me at all.

Which meant that there was no one around to back me up when I wouldn't let that hack vet near Titan. He was trying to be helpful, on some level I knew that, but he wasn't my *own* vet. He didn't even know Titan or care about him. And, on a more basic level, he wasn't the guy who knew what to do with the insurance company when a beloved, but high priced, horse died. There were forms to be filled out properly and calls to make. And the only one I trusted to do that right was my own vet, Monica.

This is the end of my dream, I thought bleakly. Titan had been a one-shot gamble for our family. And unless I found an owner willing to take a chance on me, or bought a foal and waited the six years it took to get it going properly, then my dream was dead in the water.

All those thoughts whirled frantically through my head while I waited crouched down beside Titan. Guarding his still body like a tiger protecting her cub until Dr. Patel arrived and I could finally let down my guard. I knew I looked like a crazy person to the audience of people still milling around. But I didn't care. Titan was all that mattered.

Monica Patel had known me my whole life, so the second she arrived she took two steps toward me and then wrapped me in a tight hug. I sagged against her for just a second, silent sobs wracking my body. The relief of being in the presence of someone who was definitely on my side was almost overwhelming. She knew how much I loved this horse.

"Go home, Maisy," she said gently. "I'll take care of him from here."

"There will be an autopsy?" I asked in a raw voice, wincing at the thought of my beautiful partner being laid out on a table somewhere to be cut open.

"Yes, a truck is coming to take him back to the hospital. Don't worry, we'll find out what happened to him. I'll call you tonight or tomorrow morning at the latest. Maisy, I'm so sorry this happened to you."

That nearly undid me again. I knelt down one last time to wrap my arms around his beautiful head and kiss him softly in that hollow spot over his eye. The spot I knew so well.

"Goodbye, sweet boy," I whispered. None of this was real. This must all be a dream. I could hardly force myself to walk away from the body. Some part of me was screaming that this was all wrong, he wasn't really dead, and I shouldn't be walking away from him. Surely, it was some sort of joke and he'd pop up any second, giving himself a good shake, and march back to the trailer with me.

Sorry for scaring you, mom, his expression would say. *Can we go home now?*

I packed the trailer like a robot, snarling at anyone who tried to break through the fragile wall I was trying to build up around myself. Whether they were well-meaning or not, I couldn't take a second to think about what was happening back at that ring or I would stop functioning completely.

I couldn't think about the sound Titan had made as he fell. The breath that had whooshed out of him. The utter fact that there had been nothing I could do to save him. No last minute life-saving measures I could fix with money or a phone call to friends or by begging the vet. Nothing. He was there and then he was gone.

Gone. How could Titan be gone? He was everything.

I focused on the road, coaching myself through every little step I needed in order to get home safely. Put the key in the ignition, Maisy, not too much gas, blinker on. This is a stop light. I drove carefully, like there was still a horse in the trailer who would care if I drove too fast or took the corners too sharply.

Step by step I made my way home. To my farm, which wasn't a home at all without Titan.

Rory, my ancient childhood pony, bellowed from the driveway as soon as he saw the trailer and my heart seized in my chest. How would I explain to Rory that his best friend hadn't come home with me? Would he think I'd sold Titan? Had forgotten him somewhere? Had I betrayed the deal we'd all had to be together forever?

Forever. Just this spring I'd refused another good offer on Titan. One I was crazy not to take. Even my parents had urged me to consider it. But I couldn't do it. He was too much a part of the family to just sell. And now...

Ignoring Rory's neighs, I unpacked the trailer one item at a time. I couldn't remember who'd taken off Titan's saddle and bridle. Even his boots. There was a lock of tail hair in a plastic bag. When had that happened? Who had put them back in my trailer?

I threw the saddle on its rack without even checking it over. It was an expensive gift from one of my sponsors. It had been custom made for Titan's broad back. Maybe the tree had been broken in the fall but I didn't care. It would never fit another horse like that again.

I threw my saddle pad and his travelling rug in a heap in the corner, tossing his brushes after them, hard enough that they hit the wall with a thud.

"Shut up, Rory," I said dully as he bellowed another neigh. Wearily, I tossed him a flake of hay over the fence to distract his anxious pacing and high-pitched calling.

It worked. He shut up instantly. Rory was the crankiest, most ornery pony on the planet, and he'd loved Titan. But his life was completely ruled by food. If there was anything edible around then he'd stand there until it was finished, no matter what was happening around him.

He'd been a terrible children's pony and we'd only won so many championships together because I'd been a stubborn, determined little child who had matched him perfectly in temperament. Also, he'd loved showing. His sour little person-ality would blossom into a model pony whenever we trotted down the center line. The balking, bucking monster who gave me hell at home would transform into a forward, flowing little prince with pricked ears and a sweet expression. All lies.

"Titan's not coming home," I told him as he ate his hay.

He snorted, not looking at me, but he seemed contented enough so I left the truck and trailer connected and headed slowly up to the house.

The closer I got though, the harder it was for me to breathe. My chest felt tight, like a giant weight was pressing down on me.

Am I dying, too?

Panic shot through me in waves. My stomach heaved suddenly and I doubled in half. I stumbled the few feet off the driveway into the woods and dropped to my knees to let my body do its thing. Retching, I threw up my lunch into a patch of ferns.

When my body stopped convulsing, I turned and sat with my back up against a tall Cedar, shaking slightly. My body did feel a bit better, lighter. But the numb cocoon that had been protecting me from my own feelings since the accident, was wearing off and I could feel the ocean of panic crashing around underneath it.

I can't handle this, I thought suddenly, as my heart rapidly picked up speed and my breath caught in my throat again. *I don't know what to do.* I was pretty sure that people were supposed to sleep after a trauma. But that was the last thing my body wanted. Adrenaline raced around inside of me, looking for an outlet. I needed to call my parents to let them know. I had to call my contact, Etienne, on the development team. If I couldn't go to Europe then all my flights needed to be cancelled.

Titan's death meant too many things to me. There was the loss of him, the dark abyss that yawned at my feet. Too big to be dealt with. But there were other things, too. Future things that pushed in on me. For the first time since I was eight years old, I didn't have a horse. My entire life was geared toward training and showing and caring for a horse. All my connections were horse people. I could not, not for one second, imagine a life without horses.

CHAPTER 6

MAISY

I pushed myself slowly to my feet and headed inside.

I used the back entrance, the one that led to the separate suite that my parents had set up for me downstairs when I'd decided to keep living at home to cut the costs down. It wasn't big but it had a bedroom with an ensuite, a small sitting area, and a kitchenette. And down at the far end was the door to the full-sized workout room my parents had set up for me long ago.

But as I stepped inside, I realized that it was also a sort of shrine to Titan. His beautiful framed portraits hung on nearly every wall. He was … he had been … a stunning horse and the camera loved him. People sent me prints of photos they'd taken of him all the time. Plus, there were the official show pictures and then some fun ones of us galloping on the beach or candid shots of us hanging out at the barn. There were even two sculptures we'd commissioned of him. Memories of us were everywhere and right then I could not handle looking at his face.

I marched to my room to strip off my breeches and change them out for shorts and a tank top. I didn't shower. I didn't think I could stand being alone with my own uninterrupted thoughts for even ten minutes.

I dashed upstairs the second I'd changed. My parents decorating tastes were decidedly less horse-obsessed than mine. It was a little like stepping into a museum. All modern sculptures, uncomfortable furniture and abstract paintings of ocean scenes.

I took a deep breath and headed to their big den area where there was a pool table, an oversized television and the much-needed liquor cupboard. I wasn't much of a drinker at all, maybe a glass of wine here and there when we were celebrating, but right then all I could think of was finding something, anything, to buffer these waves of misery crashing around inside of me.

I opened the big cabinet and stared at the shelves, looking unenthusiastically at the rows of dusty bottles. I actually had no idea what most of them held. My parents weren't really drinkers either but people gifted them expensive bottles on every holiday so they now had quite the collection.

All I knew is that I wanted something that tasted good and that I could drink right out of the bottle.

There, perfect, I thought, reaching in to grab a pale pink bottle with a hand-drawn picture of a plum on the label. *Plum Port. I think that's kind of like wine, isn't it?*

My aunt Rachel liked to make weird fruit wines and stuff and bring them to us every time she visited. Which lately had been a lot. And my parents never had the heart to tell her that they didn't like the sweeter, fruity stuff. They just dutifully stuffed the bottles on the shelf and forgot about them.

At least they wouldn't care how many bottles I took.

Whoa, that is strong, I thought as the cork finally came free with a pop. The fruity smell made my eyes water but the scent was also strangely delicious.

I tilted the bottle back against my lips and took an experimental sip. I couldn't help but gasp as the burning liquid seared its way down my throat. But then, just as quickly, the burn turned into a sweet, smooth sensation that tingled all the way through me. And the taste was incredible. Light and sweet. It was like spring time and happiness.

I sighed in relief as the anguish inside of me receded just a smidge, leaving a small buffer around my aching heart.

I picked up the bottle and made my way to the couch. I turned the television on to distract myself and sat curled up in one corner sipping away until some of the tension eased out of my shoulders. I grabbed the soft, decorative throw rug off the back of the couch and wrapped it tightly around myself and then picked up my phone.

I had to tell my parent's first. Even if it put a damper on their world cruise. They were Titan's actual owners on paper and they needed to know what had happened before they heard it from anyone else. Not only because they'd loved him too but also because of the insurance.

I took another swig from the bottle for courage and hit their number before I could change my mind.

But the second I heard my mother's voice on the line, sounding far-away like she was truly on the other side of the world, all my resolutions to be as to the point and factual as possible melted away and I began to sob. It took forever for me to get the story out properly, taking restorative sips of the mystery wine for courage when I stumbled over the most awful parts.

"Oh, sweetie, we are so, so sorry," my mother said and I could hear my dad saying similar things from right beside her since they were both sharing her phone. "That lovely, wonderful horse. I wonder what on earth happened."

"I have no idea," I said miserably. "But I don't know what to do without him."

"I know, sweetheart. We know how much you loved him. And

he loved you."

Those words were meant to be so kind but they left me feeling awful. Titan loved me. And it had been my job to protect him. And I hadn't.

"Are you there, Maisy?" My dad asked, sounding worried. "This connection isn't the best."

"Um, yep. Still here. I'm not sure what to do about the insurance. He … his body … is with Dr. Patel right now, but is there someone we need to call?"

"We'll do that, darling. We'll handle that end of it. Have you talked to Etienne yet?"

"No, I guess that's all over now, isn't it? I can't go to Europe without Titan."

Etienne was my liaison for the development team, and he had gone to bat for me when I'd been dragged into Dirk's very public disaster. I'd nearly lost my spot on the team during the scandal and it was only Etienne's networking on my behalf that had saved me. I was pretty sure there was nothing he could do for me now, though.

"Well, call him and let him know. Maybe there is a horse you could lease or a young horse that needs more experience that you could borrow."

"Maybe," I said dully. I couldn't imagine getting a new partner at this late hour. And the development team wouldn't want me to ride a young horse. They wanted solid Grand Prix horses and riders who just needed international exposure. And I could never afford a horse of that caliber now. We might be well off by some people's standards but we couldn't blow a quarter million dollars, or more, on another horse.

"Don't rush into anything," my dad was saying. "Another horse is out there waiting for you. But you need to take time to grieve for Titan."

"Even if we could afford it, there will never be another horse like Titan," I agreed. "I suppose we could get a foal. I could start over again."

There was a very long silence on the other end and then my father cleared his throat a few times.

"It's probably not the time to discuss anything serious," my dad said, "you've had a huge shock today. You rest and recover and we'll talk about things when we get back to Canada."

"But darling," my mother broke in, "you know that we discussed that Titan would be our last investment into horses."

"I know," I said quickly, "I wasn't saying—"

"It's just your father and I are ready to take a new direction in our lives. We've enjoyed our life in the country of course, and we don't regret a single day of supporting you with the horses. It's just—"

"What your mother is trying to say, is that we've decided to sell the farm. We wanted to wait until you and Titan were in Europe. You could have stayed over there permanently to train. We've actually already spoken to Mary at the real estate office. She thinks we could get a great price for the property. And you know Abigail said she'd take Rory on as a companion to her horse."

I sat there frozen and the only thing I could hear was a roaring sound in my ears.

"Darling? Are you still there?" My mom's voice was tight with anxiety.

"I'm here," I said weakly. "But look, I'd better go. I'll call Etienne right now and let him know."

"All right, get lots of rest and take care of yourself, dear. We'll be home in another month or so. Unless you need us to come home early."

"No, no, of course not. Thank you both," I said woodenly, trying to keep any trace of anger and betrayal out of my voice as I hung up.

It was *their* farm after all, and they'd supported me for all this time. I had no reason to complain at all. But how could they even think of selling this place? I loved this farm like it was a piece of me. I'd spent some of my best moments here. It was a sanctuary from the outside world, a place where I could just be myself with the horses, without pressure. I couldn't imagine living anywhere else. And I'd assumed my parents had felt the same way.

I took another sip from the bottle, feeling the flush already heating up my cheeks. The liquid didn't burn this time. Just went down sweet and smooth.

Etienne answered on the third ring, which was unexpected. I didn't even know what time it was in Belgium or Germany or wherever he was.

"Maisy," he said in his booming voice. Day or night, the guy radiated enthusiasm. "How is my shining star?"

That would have been more flattering except I knew he said it to everyone on the team. We'd done a few group zoom meetings to get acquainted so I'd figured out by now that he just liked to throw out the compliments like candy. Not that I was complaining.

"Um, I have bad news," I said. And then I told him quickly, skipping the most painful details to get right to the point.

He was silent for so long that I thought he'd hung up.

"Oh, Maisy, this is not good. I'm so sorry."

"Thanks." My throat closed tightly in response to his sympathy. "This means I'm off the team, right?"

"Well, I'm not sure, honestly. It doesn't give us much time to see if we can borrow a substitute. Grand Prix horses don't grow on trees, you know."

"I know."

"But, don't despair yet. We have lots of friends and connections here. Let me ask around and see what we can come up with. If we find something suitable then you'll have to come out early to start training."

"I can do that," I said quickly. Soon there wasn't going to be anything left for me to stay for anyway.

"Right, well let me work on it and I'll call you back. Give me a few days. No promises, though."

"Of course not. Thank you for trying. It means a lot to me."

"Take care of yourself," he said and then he was gone.

I set my phone down with a sigh. I'd already muted it against any texts or phone calls that might come in. I could see dozens of notifications blinking on my screen but I was too exhausted to respond to anyone's questions or sympathy, whether it was real or fake, yet.

I had no more calls to make. There were no friends I wanted to reach out to for comfort.

I stood up restlessly and walked around the living room, unable to avoid the damn tributes to Titan even here. My parents had had these huge paintings made of him a few years back. They were stunning, really. There he was, neck arched and veins bulging, mouth dripping frothy foam. His wise, kind eyes looking right into my soul …

Pain hit me hard then, unexpectedly, like a swift punch to the gut and I doubled over crying out from the shock of it. I hadn't known that grief could be a physical thing. That it could suck the air out of you and dig its claws in under your collar bone, burrowing straight for your ravaged heart.

I had to get out of there.

I couldn't go downstairs to my suite. I couldn't face that yet. I wanted to be away from here, away from this house and all its memories. I needed to be somewhere that I could forget myself. Even just for a little while.

I went down the hall to our guest room and pushed open the door. Aunt Rachel had stayed here for a few weeks last month, when she'd had her latest bad breakup. She didn't have the best track record with relationships. And whenever she was feeling blue, she liked to come stay with her sister, my mom, to recover.

Which pretty much meant she shopped heavily during the day

and went out to dance clubs and bars nightly until she felt better. With any luck she'd left some of her clothes behind in our closet. She stayed here often enough that she usually needed a second wardrobe.

Yes. I flicked through the sea of slinky dresses until I found something that I wouldn't be embarrassed to wear. It was a silky sort of pantsuit with a plunging neckline, dark blue and probably plain by Aunt Rachel's standards but on me it worked well enough.

She'd left her bathroom stocked with make-up and I put on the bare minimum, concentrating on making my eyes look a little less red and puffy. I pulled my hair back into a messy bun and fixed some silver clips in place to keep the stray bits contained. I stared at my reflection in the mirror, trying to feel anything but depressed.

It didn't work. Sighing, I found some black flats, because there was no way I'd be able to manage heels, grabbed my car keys off the hook in the hallway and made my way to the little red convertible.

It was only when I fumbled getting the door open that I remembered all the alcohol I'd taken down. I was probably more than a little drunk. Driving right now would be crazy. Dangerous.

I don't care, I thought, suddenly furious at the world, *so what if I crash? I welcome it. Anything would be better than feeling like this.*

I glared at my car for another minute and then sighed. Even drunk, even with this whirlwind of pain and rage churning through me, I knew better than to risk hurting, or killing, another person. That was a line I wouldn't cross.

I slammed the car door again and fumbled for my phone. We didn't have anything like uber out here in the country so I googled a local taxi company and made the call.

Then I slumped down against my car tire to wait. I put my

head in my hands and closed my eyes, wishing I could sleep for a year and wake up when this was all over.

From far away, Rory neighed, and I looked up with a stab of anxiety. Had I even fed him?

Yes, I had a vague memory of throwing him a flake of hay. That hadn't been very long ago. He'd be fine.

Before I could change my mind and go check on him, tires crunched up the driveway and a yellow car stopped a few feet away from me.

CHAPTER 7

MAISY

I pulled myself upright and tried not to look like a drunken psychopath as I headed toward the taxi and slid clumsily into the back seat.

The driver looked at me warily in the rear-view mirror, his fingers tapping on the steering wheel.

"Where are you headed to?" He asked finally.

"Um …" At that point I realized that I had no idea where I was headed to. Where did people go in this town to forget that their best friend had just died in front of them? I should have called Aunt Rachel for advice.

"I just need to get away," I said, my voice slurring a little. "I need to forget this entire, crappy day. Is there like a bar or something you can take me to?"

I knew I sounded about twelve years old right then. What single girl in her mid-twenties didn't go out partying every weekend with her friends? Other girls would already have their favourite bars mapped out, one to suit every mood.

But not me. I rode, I trained, I studied. And I planned for my future. That was it.

"Ah …" His lips tightened and I cringed at the trace of pity in his eyes. "I understand that. How about the casino then? It's safe and well-lit. And you can have some friends meet you there, yes?"

He was looking at me with real concern now and I wondered just exactly how bad I looked.

"Right, the, um casino then, thanks."

I'd never been there in my life but it sounded much better than sitting at home. He was probably paid by the casino to bring tourists there or something but right then I didn't care.

Despite the alcohol, my body was jittery with anxiety, like there was a wolf inside me that was trying to tear its way out. I wanted to scream and do something violent. And also, to run and run until I left all this grief and horror behind. But I did none of that, just sat there staring blankly out the window.

It turned out that the casino was only about fifteen minutes from my house. A huge brick and glass building that I'd barely even noticed before. Even though it had a flashing neon sign overhead.

"Here is my card," the driver said unexpectedly when I paid him. "You can call me when you're ready to go home."

I hesitated, frowning.

"I have a daughter your age," he said softly. "And I worry about her. It would be nice if you could have some friends meet you here, but if not, then I'd like to make sure you get home safely."

His concern brought tears too close to the surface and I turned away abruptly.

"I'm fine," I said firmly. "I can take care of myself. But thanks." I took the card and shoved it into my purse, not looking back as I stumbled toward the casino door.

The cool air steadied me a little and I was able to get through the security at the front door easily. They barely even looked at my ID.

The second I stepped inside, though, I froze in confusion as the wall of noise hit me. There were people everywhere and some sort of party was happening on the level above me. I could hear a muffled voice talking through a microphone and every time the speaker stopped there was loud laughter and applause.

Lights flashed, bells went off from the casino floor to my right and the whole thing was completely overwhelming, especially in the state I was in.

Right, so let's figure out how this thing works. I edged myself in beside a tall potted plant so I could stealthily check out the scene.

The wide-open area in front of me was divided into different sections. Tables for card and dice games on the left and banks of whirring, blinking slot machines on the right. I couldn't see a bar but servers were walking around with loaded drink trays everywhere so I assumed that you just asked them for something if you wanted it.

A huge curved stairwell ran up the middle of the room directly across from me and the whole upstairs was full of people. The laughter and applause came from the darkened area on the upstairs right. On the left was a restaurant and some sort of sports bar where people were yelling and cheering at a bank of oversized television screens all broadcasting something different.

I narrowed my eyes as I caught sight of the horse race being broadcast on the one nearest me.

Was there nowhere in this world that was free from seeing or thinking about bloody horses? I blinked hard and turned toward the slot machines, putting the galloping racehorses firmly behind me.

With all the fresh air and excitement, I'd assumed that my alcohol buzz was done but now it seemed to come back all at once. A strange feeling of being drunk enough to curl up under a table to nap but also really vibrantly aware of everything. The lights, the colours, and the noise all swirled around me touching my skin and making me feel like I was walking through a dream.

I swayed between the double rows of machines, entranced by the laughing people, the music, and the bells and lights going off all around me.

Finally, I stopped in front of an old-fashioned looking slot machine decorated with a jungle scene with snakes and an Indiana Jones-type man swinging from a vine across a raging river. He had a scantily clad woman tucked under one arm, but instead of screaming in terror, she was staring boldly out of the picture. A heavy revolver in one hand pointed directly toward me.

"This one will work," I said out loud, only slurring my words a little. "I want to face the world just like that. With a cold look and a big gun."

The sweaty, disheveled man sitting at the machine beside me glanced my way and laughed, shaking his head.

I stared hard at the machine, trying to figure out how it worked. *Right, money.* I needed money. I dug out my wallet and miraculously found some cash. I didn't even know why I had it in there since I used credit cards most of the time.

A memory flashed; the horse show, I'd packed money so I could buy lunch at the food truck. Titan.

I made a strangled sound as the pain stabbed through my gut again and then I shoved my twenty-dollar bill into the machine. It made a whole bunch of bleeping noises; wheels began to spin, and it played some sort of swashbuckling theme song.

I stared at the flashing buttons in front of me and tentatively pushed the middle one. The whole machine began to pulse and whir and then suddenly the wheels stopped and the pictures on the screen lined up to show three revolvers side by side.

The word *Winner!* flashed up on the screen and I nearly fell out of my seat.

"How much?" I stumbled over the words. Images of a trip to the Caribbean and fistfuls of cash swam before me.

The guy next to me leaned over, his beery breath hot against my neck as he stared down my cleavage. "Hey, high-roller," he said, "looks like you made yourself a fancy five-dollar bill."

"Oh."

"It's a nickel machine, you know. But keep playing. You might get a good payout. Here, I'll get you a drink."

"Okay, thanks," I said, feeling much happier.

I wasn't sure how long I sat there playing my jungle game or how many drinks I took down, but there was a moment where I finally relaxed and let go. No more harrowing memories of that afternoon. No terrifying worries about the future, or the bleak knowledge that I'd just lost everything I'd worked so hard for.

Everything blurred after that. I had a vague memory of winning more things. Of moving with a group of people, my new nameless friends, to the card tables. I was rolling dice, kissing someone's hand for good luck, cheering madly along with everyone else.

There was singing, too. The whole floor joining in. And for a few minutes, I was pulled up onto a table to dance with some drunken, glittery girls. Who were these people? I had no idea, but they were a heck of a lot better than the friends in my real life right then. I couldn't remember a time where I'd had so much fun.

"Oh my god, is that Maisy?" a sharp voice said. "She has some nerve to show her face here."

I was back down on the floor by then. And in front of me was a crowd of people that, even in my drunken state, I recognized very, very well. It was like I was the equestrian version of Ebenezer Scrooge being haunted by the ghosts of horse shows past. But why were they all here now in one place?

"Maisy?" My old boss, Lauren's, face swirled into focus, looking concerned. "What are you doing here? Are you all right?"

Ah, it was one of Lauren's famous parties. That explained all the horse people.

A pang of sadness hit me. This time last year it would have been me having fun at this party. Lauren had always been nice to me. When I'd stopped riding her horses, we'd parted amicably despite what the gossip in the horse community said.

"Sweetie, can I get you anything? You don't look well."

I couldn't answer her. My tongue felt thick and I just wanted to get away. I turned and other faces swirled in front of me. Hands reaching out to touch me. Words firing at me on all sides.

"Oh, you poor thing, we were so sorry to hear about Titan. You must be devastated."

"You're not still going to Europe without a horse, are you?"

"It's too bad you've had such luck. First your coach, then this. It's like you're cursed."

I could feel the words like cuts across my skin, opening me up and leaving me feeling raw and exposed. I couldn't think of how to answer.

I looked up and saw a pair of piercing blue eyes watching me from a nearby table on the outskirts of the group. I recognized him right away as Lauren's new Scottish rider. The one everyone was talking about. He had a drink in his hand and was studying me with a look of … was that *pity*?

He raised his eyebrows and suddenly a sea of anger washed over me, drowning all my reason and good sense. How dare he sit there and judge me like that? He didn't even know me. None of them knew me.

As irrational as it was, all I wanted to do was march over there and punch him in the throat.

I clenched my fists and took two steps toward him. I wasn't sure if I was actually planning on hitting him. But, before I could do anything too stupid, a wave of nausea shot over me and I stumbled, clapping a hand over my mouth.

The alcohol, the trauma and the lack of food, had finally

caught up with me and my body was rejecting it all. I had to get out of there.

"Watch out," someone said helpfully, "she's going to be sick."

I turned and plunged in the direction of the bathrooms, pushing through the crowd in my desperation to get away.

"Look at how drunk she is," a sharp voice said, "disgusting."

The voice was familiar but I couldn't stop. I needed to find … It was too late. I would never make it to the bathrooms in time. I veered toward one of the gigantic potted palms dotting the lobby and threw myself down, heaving into its decorative pot.

There were gasps of alarm around me and one woman shrieked as if she'd been stabbed. A man walking by laughed and a few people made sympathetic noises as I retched and groaned over and over again. Tears stung my eyes and I wanted so badly to get out of there, but my body was not letting that happen.

"Whoa there. You're all right, I've got you." Hands twisted my hair gently out of the way as I abruptly heaved again.

"Everyone's watching," I whimpered as I rested my forehead against the floor. I could feel tears of embarrassment soaking my cheeks.

"Don't worry about that. I'm sure it's nothing they haven't seen before. We've all been there."

"Have we?" My arms shook as I pushed myself weakly into a crouch. "This is a first for me."

I kept my eyes fixed on the carpet, too mortified to look at him.

"Are you ready to stand up?"

"I think so," I said hesitantly, wobbling to my feet with his help.

As I stood up, I realized that there was still a crowd of people around us, staring at the scene with glittering, greedy eyes. They weren't there to make sure I was okay, they just wanted to watch me fall apart.

"Don't pay attention to them," the man said quietly in his

lilting accent. It was Lauren's rider. The blue-eyed man who'd been judging me earlier.

I pulled away abruptly, or at least I tried to, but I completely misjudged how out of control my body was.

"Easy, girl," the guy said, grabbing at my arm again. "You're all right."

Easy, girl? Like I'm a horse? I made an angry sound in my throat and yanked my arm out of his grasp.

I shouldn't have pulled away so hard because it turned out that he was the only thing keeping me upright. My momentum sent me backward and I went down like a toppled tree in the forest, hitting the ground with a thud that shook every bone in my body. My teeth snapped together as my skull smacked the floor and I tasted blood in my mouth from where I'd bitten my lip.

I saw stars and then blackness. And although I could hear people moving around me and voices calling out, it seemed like it was from light-years away. I didn't even bother to open my eyes.

"Does she need an ambulance?"

Somewhere near me, I heard somebody laughing and a bright flash made me squint my eyes even more tightly shut.

"Don't worry, I'll drive her home," a calm voice was saying. "It's okay, I'm her neighbour."

CHAPTER 8

BREE

"Should we wait for Jeremy to get back?" I plucked my tea mug off the table and carried it to the living room where we were holding an emergency meeting. "This mostly concerns him after all."

"Oh, I don't think he'll be back before late." Julie frowned. "From what I hear, Lauren's parties are pretty legendary."

"Besides, we know what he wants," Lorne added. "He wants to ride Dragon."

"I know," Julie sighed. "Chloe is going to hate that so much, though. I wish there was another way. But it makes the most sense. We'll have to ask Jeremy to give up his outside clients, though. It will be too much if he picks up rides on Dragon and Nugget. There are the young horses here now, too. Plus, Follow."

"That wouldn't be fair to ask him to give up his clients," Lorne said slowly. "He's made commitments to them. And it wasn't his fault there weren't quite enough horses for him to ride here when he arrived."

"But now there *are* enough," Julie said firmly. "We have to come first for him, Lorne. He's our working student after all. Not that he's much of a student. His clients will understand."

"I don't like it," Lorne frowned and took a gulp of his cooling tea.

"I could call Adie and ask her to come home early," I said, curling up into the same corner of the couch where Nicholas was sitting. "And I could take on more horses. My riding has improved quite a bit. I could definitely handle Nugget."

"Nope," Julie shook her head abruptly and then her expression softened, "I mean, yes, absolutely, you're improving. You're on your way to being a great rider. And you could easily take over riding Nugget if you wanted to. But I think two horses to ride is plenty. You do a lot of the barn work, plus all the blogging and networking, Bree. It's enough. Last year you were on the brink of death. I'd rather not have you running ragged. Give it until next year before we increase your workload. Okay?"

I sighed but didn't argue. Secretly I was glad that I didn't have to ride more horses. I loved my lessons and trail rides on Ace and Nipper, but I wasn't like Chloe. She could ride eight horses a day and it still wouldn't be enough. She'd resented sharing any of the rides with Jeremy, thinking she could handle the whole lot of horses by herself. And maybe she could have if we had a staff of grooms and stable help to take on the rest of the work. But we didn't, everyone had to pitch in where they were needed. Mucking stalls, cleaning paddocks, wiping tack, and feeding. All the nitty-gritty details beyond riding that went into running a barn full of horses. The thoroughbreds and the seniors were just a lot of work.

Nobody had the luxury of being able to focus *only* on riding without doing the other work, too.

"And Adie needs to spend all the time she can with her family before her dad takes the older kids back on tour. She'll be starting school in the fall regardless so she won't be able to help as much anyway. I'm not sure how long it will be before Chloe is back on her feet."

"Months," Lorne said gloomily. "This is terrible timing."

"It always is. And we're overflowing anyway. We'll have to sell another horse soon if we don't want someone to spend a winter in one of the outdoor paddocks. We don't have the space."

"Or we ask a senior to leave?" Lorne looked at Julie with his eyebrows raised.

She tilted her head to one side, considering, and then sighed. "I suppose we could, but I'd hate to do it. That herd is so happy. I know their owners would like to see them all end their days here peacefully. It would be a shame to ask them to leave out of the blue."

Lorne nodded. Nobody wanted to see any of the older boarders go.

"We'll advertise Nugget up for adoption in the next couple of weeks," Julie said finally. "He's ready. We've given him a great start and he's kind and uncomplicated. Are there any applications on him already, Bree?'

"Lots. Although some of them are pretty old. I can go through them tomorrow and see if the applicants are still interested in meeting him."

I respected our decision to make sure the horses were going well under saddle and exposed to shows, trails and all sorts of things before rehoming them. We wanted to give them the best chance to succeed in their new homes. But it meant that people originally interested in adopting would have sometimes moved on by the time the horses were ready. It was a trade-off.

"Timely is going well too, but I'd like to keep him longer for Jeremy," Lorne said. "He's signed up for that event on the mainland next month."

"Definitely." Julie nodded. "Dragon and Timely are going to be our big-ticket sales for sure once they're ready. But we need to make sure we finish them both properly, with no holes in their education. Dragon especially. If we can attract more donors to the program with some high-profile sales then might be able to expand in the future."

I looked up in surprise. This was the first time Julie had said anything like that. We had plenty of work to do around here without thinking of expanding.

But she had this look in her eye, an inspired sort of gleam that told me she was envisioning a whole different future for the program.

Lorne nodded quickly but he had a similar look of excitement in his eye and I wondered if they'd been making secret plans without me.

"So, that's Jeremy riding Nugget, Dragon, and Timely for now. Plus starting Poppy and Jet in the next couple of weeks. And Bree to continue on with Nipper and Ace plus keep on with Chilly's rehab and whatever it is we do with Follow."

"The vet said Chilly can start going for longer walks. And we can add in some trot works in a couple weeks. His leg is holding up really well so far," I said. "And I think Follow is just enjoying being a horse for now. She's not ready for much else yet."

Julie sighed and nodded but she didn't look overly happy about it.

Chilly had arrived at our place with a badly bowed tendon. And Follow was the most complicated of the horses we had in the program. Physically she was in great shape but mentally she was a bit of a mess. She'd come a very long way from the terrified filly she'd been when she'd arrived, though. We could at least lead her out to the pasture without her panicking, and we could brush her and take her for short walks as long as she had a friend with her. But she was an anxious girl and any change to her routine sent her in a bit of a tail spin. We weren't really sure yet what her future would be like.

"Still, I should start taking her into the ring and doing some groundwork with her," Julie said. "Maybe this week I'll concentrate on getting her and the babies out on the lunge line and doing some work in hand. That will give Jeremy some time to figure out how he'll work them all into his schedule."

I sent her a sidelong glance, trying not to look too surprised. Julie sometimes lunged the horses, and she gave the rest of us lessons all the time, but other than that, she was pretty hands-off on training.

She hadn't ridden since her horrible accident had torn her family apart. But she was brilliant with the horses. Maybe working with them on the ground would lead to her finally wanting to ride again.

But I knew better than to bring it up. I just crossed my fingers for luck when she wasn't looking.

"I could ask your dad about putting off my summer school internship for a few weeks until we have stuff figured out," Nicholas said quietly.

"No," Julie and I said at the same time.

"You're looking forward to that internship," I told him firmly, "and my dad is way too excited to have you there. He'd be crushed if you gave it up."

My dad was a teacher at the university and he also ran an advanced summer school program to earn some extra money. He'd arranged for Nicholas and some of the older senior students to help him out with some classes as part of an internship. Nicholas wanted to be a history teacher like my dad so this would be a great experience for him.

"If you're sure." He looked at me doubtfully.

"I'm completely sure." It wasn't quite a lie.

Of course, I wanted Nicholas to be here all day, everyday. And I was slightly irritated that my dad had interfered with my summer plans by taking Nicholas away. But I wasn't selfish enough to say so.

"It will be all right," I said, snuggling closer so my shoulder was leaning against his. "You can do my stalls on the weekends if you really want. I'll save you the worst ones."

"You'd better," he said, reaching out to playfully pinch my ear. "I don't want to miss out on all the fun."

Lorne went back down to his cabin shortly after that and Julie went to bed not long after. It had been an exhausting day for everyone.

"Are you staying up for a bit?" Nicholas asked.

"I don't think I'll be able to sleep. I'm still wired from everything that happened. I wanted to do some research on Follow anyway."

"Always the research," Nicholas said, laughing as he pulled me to my feet. "I think you should go into investigative journalism or something. Your talents are being wasted here."

"Says you. I'd much rather be spending all day with the horses than stuck in an office somewhere." I shivered at the very thought of being trapped inside all day.

"I know, I know. I was joking. Come keep me company while I fall asleep then. I always sleep better when you're around."

"Okay, I'll grab my laptop then and be right there."

I went and changed into leggings and a tank-top for sleeping in and then brushed my teeth and grabbed my laptop before tiptoeing down the hall to his room.

It wasn't like we actually had to hide anything; Julie knew we were dating. But there was a certain level of awkwardness that just happened when you were living in the same house with your boyfriend's mom. Or maybe it was just me. Nicholas didn't seem bothered by it at all.

He was already in bed when I got there and I scootched in beside him, nestling myself into his shoulder as he draped one arm over me.

"All right, what are we researching tonight?" he asked,

yawning and leaning his head against mine as I fired up my laptop.

"Follow. I want to see if I can find anything in her past that explains why she is the way she is. I know it's a longshot, but I thought that if I could talk to the breeder then maybe I could get some insight into what she was like when she was little. If she was always neurotic like this then maybe we shouldn't even try to ride her. Maybe she'd be better off as a companion horse somewhere."

"But if she was a normal foal—"

"If she was normal once then we know that it was probably some sort of trauma that made her like she is. And trauma can usually be worked through."

"Interesting," he said, his breath tickling my neck.

Shivering a little I turned a pretend glare on him.

"Are you going to be distracting?" I asked him, trying my best to sound irritated. "Because I thought you were going to fall asleep while I worked on this."

"I'm suddenly not that tired anymore. I have the feeling that I'm going to be very distracting tonight."

"Oh really?" I said, raising an eyebrow. "I think you lured me in here."

"You're probably right. I'm terrible that way."

Laughing under my breath, I shut my laptop and set it on his bedside table.

Then I half-turned to face him, watching the shadows play across his face in the low light. I sighed contently as his lips trailed up and down my neck.

"Well, I suppose my research can wait a little bit longer then."

His laugh rumbled against my skin, as he reached up across me and flicked the lights off.

CHAPTER 9

MAISY

*B*urning thirst was the first thing I was aware of. Followed by the painful pounding of a large drum somewhere behind my right eyeball. And then, finally, the horrifying realization that I'd not only let a complete stranger drive me home, but that I'd drunkenly clung to him, sobbing all over his shirt while he'd awkwardly patted my hair.

I had some vague, disunited memories of being carried inside. After that I couldn't remember anything else.

Maisy, what have you done? My cheeks burned with shame as I forced myself to sit up and open my eyes. The light stabbed into me and I could barely see through all the squinting. Okay, I was in my parent's bedroom for some reason. But I was alone at least, that was one thing. And I hadn't been kidnapped or hacked to pieces by a stranger so that was another good thing. How could I have been so careless and stupid? I was so lucky that I hadn't been hurt.

My stomach rolled as I crawled to the edge of the bed and

gingerly stood upright. I looked down, realizing that I was wearing a pair of my mom's fuzzy pajamas; the blue ones with the ducks all over them. Had I been drunk enough to put these monstrosities on? Or had the *stranger* had to undress me?

Horror after horror.

I looked around for the borrowed pant-suit from last night but there was no sign of it.

The house was utterly still and I wished, not for the first time, that our family had a dog. A big, protective one with lots of teeth.

"Hello?" I called quietly, as I made my way into the hall and then to the kitchen.

The place was empty but there was a handwritten note on the kitchen table propped up against a bottle of Worcestershire sauce. And my phone was there too, right next to my purse.

Morning sunshine, hope you're feeling better. Add a splash of this and some salt and pepper to tomato juice and chug it down. Best cure for a hangover I know. Trust me. Here's my number if you need anything else. Your keys are under the mat.

I squinted at the phone number and the illegible scrawled signature beside it and then crumpled the note up in a tight ball and tossed it in the garbage can.

"Thank you, stranger," I said out loud, "but I hope I never see you again. I just want to forget last night ever happened."

I checked my phone to make sure it was still working and rummaged through my purse to check that all my cards were there. Everything seemed to be there so at least he hadn't robbed me while I'd been passed out.

I stumbled to use the bathroom and rinse my mouth out with water, wincing at my reflection in the mirror. The combination of my puffy, blotched face, matted hair sticking up in all directions and those awful pajamas was a sight I could have lived without ever seeing.

I needed to change and brush my teeth but I wasn't quite ready to go down to my own suite and face reality yet.

Ignoring my pounding head and sore, bruised body I lurched back to the kitchen. Against all odds, I was starving. I made myself a bowl of cereal, taking it into the living room where I sat cross-legged on the couch to eat.

I flipped through my phone as I ate, carefully checking out my social media pages just in case I saw anything about me or Titan. Or anything about my behaviour last night.

After a few minutes I breathed a sigh of relief and let myself relax a little. So far there was nothing obvious that I could see. Just the usual updates from online friends and strangers on how perfect their lives were. How nice for them.

Bits of the night floated back to me and I groaned, hardly able to believe that that had been me. I was usually so reserved. Who had that laughing, drinking person been? Someone who felt at home with strangers. Someone who had vomited in a plant.

And while part of me was mortified with how I'd behaved, another part of me felt like it had happened to the heroine in a movie rather than to me. And, the weird part was; I almost envied that girl.

Yeah, well, that girl passed out in a stranger's car and is lucky to have made it home alive, I reminded myself.

I looked down at the blinking notifications on my phone and sighed. I hadn't opened up a single text or message the night before but I supposed that there was no time like the present.

Half of the messages were from people I knew from showing and riding and there were a few from people I'd gone to school with. It was a small city and word got around fast when something tragic, or gossip-worthy, happened.

I tapped on the most recent one, from a girl I'd hung out with at shows a few times. But instead of a sympathy note there was a short message with a video attached.

Hey, Maisy. I really don't know if you'll appreciate me sharing this with you but if was me, I'd want to know what was going on and what

people were saying about me. I'm so sorry about Titan and for well...
this. Let me know if you need to talk or need any help. Rylan.

I stared at the message with a sinking feeling in my gut.

No, this isn't happening again, I thought desperately, staring
blankly at the attachment icon for the video, *it can't be. Why now?*

Last year, after the thing with Dirk blew up, there were some
people who thought that I was lying to protect him. Or that I'd
refused to testify because he'd paid me off or blackmailed me.
And one person, or a group of people, in particular had sort of
made me their personal punching bag.

First, it had started with comments on my public pages. Nasty
comments and name calling. And, while it had been shocking, it
wasn't anything I couldn't handle. I'd just closed or moderated
the comments sections for my public posts and stopped sharing
anything too personal.

Instead of stopping though, it had only escalated. Someone
had started making these crazy, awful videos about me and
posting them all online. They'd also figured out how to send the
videos to everyone on my contact list. The content was pure lies;
things accusing me of being Dirk's accomplice or that I was mean
to Titan or a drug addict. Stupid stuff. But the videos were really
well done, very convincing, and some people started to believe
them.

And when they'd gone out of their way to send the videos to
Etienne and the entire board of the development team, it had
almost cost me my spot. I think only Etienne fully believed that I
was innocent. The rest of the board wanted to kick me off, but
Etienne had stuck with me and convinced them to give me a
second chance.

And now, as if Titan's death had triggered something, it
looked like the nightmare was starting all over again.

My finger hovered above the screen and then I forced myself
to hit play.

The video started with a black screen with words scrolling

across it. Dramatic music played in the background. Lots of screeching violins like in a horror movie.

Who is Maisy Fletcher? It said at the top and the next words flashed up one by one. *Spoiled. Rich. Brat. LIAR. Drunken Horse Killer.*

Then there was a short clip of me and Titan doing an extended trot. It must have been from years ago, early on in our career when I still wasn't in control of my body and I hadn't learned how to sit Titan's expressive gaits yet. My hands bounced all over the place and, even in that short clip, I'd caught him in the mouth more than once. Where had this video even come from?

Then the clip stopped abruptly and there was a close up of the corner of Titan's mouth to show where it was trying to open against the bit, and then a close up of my dressage whip in my hand. Which was completely unfair because, even back then, I'd never used it on Titan as a punishment.

My eyes blurred with tears as the video abruptly switched to another, more recent, scene. Again, it was at a horse show, this one on the mainland. And I remembered exactly the moment it had been taken. I'd been leading Titan by the bridle to go somewhere or other when he'd suddenly thrown his head up and neighed at a nearby horse. The sound and the abrupt jerk on the reins had scared me and I'd spun around and snapped the reins a couple times to get him to pay attention to me again.

At the time, the incident had been over in two seconds, and both Titan and I had forgotten it. But obviously someone had remembered. They'd slowed the video down to show the anger on my face. It had been fear really, but in the video it looked like I'd wanted to kill him. And it zoomed in on his face too, his look of alarm as I'd jerked on the reins.

I felt like a sharp knife had wedged itself between my ribs and I curled in on myself, hardly able to breathe.

And there ... there it was. The next scene showed the moment

Titan fell. *Murderer.* The words popped up, bright red slashes across the screen.

I shut my eyes tight, not able to watch another second. I didn't know if I could survive any more of this. But the music changed and my eyelids popped open involuntarily.

The video had switched to the casino.

More words sprung up on the screen.

This is how much Maisy cared about her horse.

And there I was, standing on a table with some people I didn't know, rocking out and singing along to the music that was loudly playing. And then it switched abruptly to the one part of the night I clearly remembered; vomiting into a plant while a perfect stranger held my hair.

RIP Titan, the words read, *You deserved better.*

And then it ended.

I stared down at the black screen, numb with shock, my breath coming out in short, sharp gasps.

What type of person hated me this much to torture me like this? Who could have twisted the love I'd had for Titan to make something this depraved? Someone wanted to hurt me. Badly.

My hands shook and I nearly dropped my phone when it began to ring.

This isn't happening, I thought as I saw Etienne's name pop up on the screen. *I'm not awake yet. This is all a horrible dream.*

But it wasn't.

"Maisy, we need to talk," he said as soon as I answered. But he didn't sound like the usual fun-loving Etienne. He sounded cold, distant and business like. "I'm so sorry but the board has decided to cut you from the team. It's nothing personal."

"You saw the video," I said dully.

"We did. It was sent to every member on the selection committee first thing this morning."

"I... I loved Titan." It was the only thing I could think of to say. Somehow, it seemed more important to convince Etienne that I was a good person than to stay on the team.

"I know you did," he said, his voice softening. "But, in this case, image is everything. We let you stay on the team after the last incident but we can't let this one slide. I'm sorry but that's our final decision."

"But—"

"Best of luck with everything, Maisy. Maybe we'll see you out there competing one day. Goodbye."

And just like that he'd hung up.

I leaned back on the couch with a small whimper of pain, my breath coming out in hitches. I was dying. My world was over. There was nothing left for me here.

My gaze drifted over to the half-empty bottle that I'd left on the side table the night before. I hadn't even put the cork back in the bottle. With shaking hands, I reached over and wrapped my fingers around it, pulling it closer to me as if it could offer me some sort of comfort.

Closing my eyes, I took a drink.

CHAPTER 10

BREE

"Careful, Chloe, don't fall over," Lorne said helpfully as we escorted her gingerly inside to the couch.

It was early morning, still dawn really, when the nurses had sent her home. The hospital was crowded and they needed the beds so she had to go. She'd only been given a brief lesson on how to use the crutches and a few minutes to get used to them before the nurses had shooed us out the door.

She looked awful, her face lined with pain and exhaustion. Wincing and groaning, she sank gratefully onto the couch with a deep sigh.

"That was the longest twenty-minute car ride of my life. I can't believe how tired I am. And how sore. I feel like I've been hit by a truck."

"You had a nasty fall, Chloe, and going under anesthetic can be rough on your system," Julie said, tucking a fleecy blanket over her knees. "You need to rest now."

"I just can't believe this happened. What rotten timing. I was hoping to go to that event on the mainland. Now Dragon will have to wait a whole other year before she goes."

Lorne and Julie exchanged a quick look but said nothing.

"I don't even remember what happened." Chloe rubbed her temples. "There were all those people yelling, horses bolted, and then Dragon just sort of leapt out from underneath me."

"You don't remember about Titan?" I asked cautiously.

"Oh, right. He fell or something. I couldn't see what was happening. Is he okay?"

I gulped and looked up at Julie but she just shrugged.

"I'm sorry, Chloe. He died," I said, getting it all out quickly. "He had a heart attack or something. It was awful."

"He's…. dead?" Her face turned even more pale if that was possible. But then two spots of colour began to stain her cheeks and her eyes blazed with anger.

"It's that idiot's fault. That Maisy. She never treated him right. She probably drugged him or something trying to make him perform better."

"Chloe, that's not fair," I said firmly, "you didn't see it. Maisy was devastated. It was just an awful accident. The whole thing was horrible. I hope I never have to see anything like that again."

"Fine, believe whatever you like." She closed her eyes and sagged back against the couch, looking more exhausted than ever.

"Lie down and rest," Julie said gently. "You need to take it easy."

Chloe nodded and slowly eased herself backward until she'd stretched out full-length, her head resting tiredly against the pillow.

We'd decided to set her up in the living room until she was strong enough to manage the steep staircase to her bedroom. Julie had draped the couch in soft blankets and the fluffiest pillow she could find. The table beside it was loaded with bowls of snacks and a glass of water and some of Lorne's old horse magazines. I'd set Chloe's phone and tablet out beside them. Everything she could want was at her fingertips. Except her health and Dragon, of course.

"Do you want me to make you some breakfast?" Julie asked, staring at Chloe's pale face anxiously. "You must be starving."

"No thank you." Chloe heaved a weary sigh. "I'm going to just rest for a few minutes and then go down to the barn. I need to make sure Dragon is all right."

"Well, that's a terrible idea," Lorne said, breaking off in a grumble when Julie made a face at him.

"I'm just going to rest my eyes," Chloe mumbled and then, just like that, she yawned loudly and was out cold.

"Poor kid," Julie said softly. "She's had a rough time."

We left Chloe snoring softly to herself and went quietly to the kitchen. Lorne sat down heavily at the big wooden table while Julie and I started putting breakfast together. I wasn't a great cook, but toast and scrambled eggs I could handle.

"No Jeremy this morning?" I asked, glancing over at Lorne.

"No, he didn't make it home until early this morning. I told him he could take a couple days off anyway so he's probably sleeping in. He's due for it."

I sighed heavily, thinking of all the chores still left to do down at the barn. It looked like Julie and I were going to be on our own today once breakfast was done.

Not that I could fault Jeremy, not really. He was entitled to a few days off after all but I wished he could have taken his vacation later once we'd found someone to replace Chloe.

It took a while to eat, clean up all the breakfast things and get changed into barn gear. So, it wasn't until I was coming back through the living room to head outside that I checked on Chloe again. To my surprise she was no longer sleeping.

She was sitting upright, looking bright and alert for the first time since the accident, with her tablet clenched between both hands; her gaze fixed fervently on it.

"What are you looking at?" I asked cautiously. I didn't like the expression on her face. Her cheeks were flushed and her eyebrows were drawn in as if she were angry but she also had a weird little smile on her face. She looked a bit deranged to tell the truth.

"Are you okay?" I tried again when she didn't answer. "Chloe?"

"It's nothing," she said sharply, tilting her tablet away from me. "Just sweet, sweet karma in action. That's all."

"What do you mean?"

"Oh, Bree, you're too nice to understand these things. But here, I guess it wouldn't hurt to show you. The truth will be out there for everyone to see soon enough."

"What truth?"

"Look." She turned her tablet around and hit play on the video cued up on her screen.

I came closer, sitting down on the coffee table beside her so I could watch.

My heart sank as words scrolled across the screen and then it sank even further when the photos and videos appeared. I had only seen Maisy ride a couple of times but she seemed like a quiet, kind rider, and Titan always looked happy and proud. This video made her look like a monster.

I raised my eyebrows when we reached a bizarre scene that looked like it was taking place in a casino. I reached out and shut it off quickly before I could see any more.

"Chloe, that is horrible. Who would post something like that? Poor Maisy just lost her horse."

"Poor *Maisy*?" Chloe asked incredulously. "No way, now the public finally gets to see what she's really like. A spoiled, drunken brat who wasn't good enough for that brilliant horse."

"That is a terrible thing to say. But I don't understand who would go to all this trouble. A lot of work went into making this."

"Not really." Chloe shrugged. "It would take two seconds to

edit the images together and add the text and music. And throwing it online would be easy. Anyone can do it. The hardest part would have been getting the pictures and the videos in the first place. You have to admit, the whole thing was pretty brilliant."

I looked over at her sharply, not liking the proud tone in her voice. I knew Chloe had an irrational hatred of Maisy over something that had happened years ago. But was there any way she could be involved in making this video somehow?

I was on the edge of asking and then I changed my mind. Of course, Chloe wouldn't have had a chance to do this. She'd been at the hospital up until a couple of hours ago. And she might be angry but she wasn't malicious. Was she? It was probably the pain medication making her talk like this.

"Well, I'd better get started on cleaning stalls," I said finally. "Do you want me to help you down to the barn now? Or would you rather go later?"

"Oh, later," Chloe said, staring back down at her tablet. "I want to see what everyone is saying about this video. That witch is going to go right down in flames. Burning."

She didn't even notice when I headed out the front door. And she didn't mention visiting Dragon at all.

CHAPTER 11

BREE

*T*he next two days were full of work with very little time for riding. Nicholas was doing his internship in town, Jeremy was still on his mini-holiday, and Chloe was firmly out of commission. So that left me to do morning feeds on my own.

The early morning air was fresh and sweet when I rolled the barn door back and was greeted by an excited chorus of neighs and nickers. Even more excited than usual.

"Well, good morning, everyone, are you all extra hungry this morning? What's with all the noise?"

Snorts and more neighs. Someone banged a hoof against their stall door, most likely Dragon, but then another took it up and then another.

"Okay, okay," I said, looking around in surprise, "simmer down, everyone. What's the matter with you all?"

A row of faces looked at me expectantly, eyes bright and noses bobbing, like they were encouraging me to figure out what their problem was.

I looked up and down the aisle carefully but I couldn't see anything out of place. Shrugging, I went to the hay room and started doling out flakes to everyone, taking a second to study each horse to make sure they were all eating properly and there weren't any signs of colic or injuries.

They all tucked into their hay happily but they still weren't quite settled.

Dragon looked to the back door of the barn, which was still rolled shut, and let out a ground-shaking neigh, snaking her head back and forth in irritation.

A tiny, unfamiliar, neigh answered back.

What in the world?

I marched down the aisle and rolled the door partially back to see a small golden pony face staring back at me about an inch from the door.

"Oh, hello," I said reaching out to gently pet him, "aren't you cute...ow!" I yanked my hand back quickly as his ears flattened and he reached out faster than I would have thought possible and nipped me sharply on the hand.

"Hey, you stop that. Bad pony." I waved my hands at him to get him to back out of my space, glaring at him.

He glared right back at me before sighing and backing up two reluctant steps. He dropped his head and sulkily began nibbling at a few blades of grass growing next to the barn.

"Well, aren't you a prize specimen," I said, staring ruefully down at my thumb. He hadn't broken the skin but the nip mark was red and angry-looking. It was going to bruise for sure. "You're a pretty rude house guest, you know."

I studied what I could see of him, taking in the burrs in his mane and the scrapes on his nose and chest. One side of his neck was plastered in a layer of dirt. He'd obviously been on an adventure but he looked fat enough. Although, he kept gazing into the barn over my shoulder to where the other horses were eating their hay.

"You stay here and I'll get you some breakfast. Then we'll figure out where you belong. Although, I doubt they're missing such a bad pony."

The people up the hill from us, the Plekowski's, who owned the fancy eventing barn, had a few ponies, although this fellow didn't look posh enough, or well-behaved enough, to have come from there. His coat was shaggy and he looked kind of old.

I rolled the door back into place behind me so he wouldn't sneak in and then grabbed a small flake of hay and filled a bucket half-full of water for him.

His little nose, and teeth, were pressed right at the door when I eased it back again.

"No, get back," I told him firmly, and he shifted backward about a foot before diving toward my hands. I was about to push him out of my space again when I noticed how his gaze was fixed on the water, not the hay. As soon as I set the bucket down, he plunged his nose into it, making desperate little glugging noises as he swallowed.

He slurped the bucket up greedily, half-closing his eyes and taking the water down in deep gulps until the entire pail was drained. Even then he didn't start eating, just licked the bottom of the bucket as if he could make more appear.

"Poor thing," I said reaching out and stroking his neck. He didn't try to bite me this time. Just sighed heavily and lipped half-heartedly at a few whisps of hay.

I walked gingerly around him, keeping my distance since I half-expected him to try and kick me, so I could get a better idea of his condition. He wasn't skinny at all but there was enough grass growing wild out here on the hillsides to feed a whole herd of ponies. From what I could see, he was just filthy, thirsty and full of small cuts. They looked harmless enough until I came around and saw the gash on the back of his front leg. It looked ugly and deep. Blood stained his fur right down to his fetlock and I could see now that, compared to the other ones, his whole front leg was swollen badly.

"Don't worry friend, we're going to help you," I told him.

I pulled out my phone as I went back in to get him another bucket of water.

Lorne answered on the second ring, sounding groggy and disoriented.

"Hey, Lorne, sorry to bother you so early but we have a bit of a situation here. Would you mind sending Jeremy down? I know it's his day off but we have a minor emergency."

I quickly filled him in on our new houseguest.

"We'll be right down," he said, suddenly not sounding sleepy at all.

The pony drank half of the second bucket of water in deep, satisfied gulps but finally he sighed happily, snorting and rubbing his nose on me in an appreciative sort of way before turning to eat his hay properly.

The rest of the horses were quiet, not restless at all now that I'd figured out their mystery.

I put a pot of coffee on, then mixed everyone their buckets of grain and supplements and fed them slowly, thinking the whole time.

It wasn't until I reached Nipper's stall that it came to me. I knew who the pony was. He was the scruffy little senior who'd lived with Titan. We'd trail ridden past his farm dozens of times. I just hadn't really paid much attention to him since we'd always been busy ogling Titan when we'd passed.

The poor little thing, I thought, *he's all alone. He must have broken out to be with the other horses.*

Tears stung my eyes as I thought about Titan's huge body lying motionless on the ground. I wondered where Maisy was and how she was doing. The memory of her screams and her broken expression still haunted me.

Jeremy strode into the barn, looking grumpy, and Lorne limped in right behind him; they must have driven down together.

"Sorry about wrecking your day off, Jeremy," I said right away. "I'll make it up to you, I promise. But I just need someone to hold this pony so I can get the senior horses outside and free up a stall for him. I want to clean up his cut and call the vet. I put on coffee. Extra strong just for you."

I said this last part hopefully. Jeremy made the grossest coffee I'd ever tasted. He added double the number of scoops you were supposed to and it was basically like noxious tar that you had to add half a cup of cream and sugar to in order to make it taste decent. Only he didn't drink it like that; he drank the awful brew black.

He stared at me blankly and then his lips curved up slightly at the corners.

"That will do for a start," he said, heading to the coffee pot. "What's all this about a pony?"

"I think he's Maisy's," I said, "you know, Titan's owner from the show. He's cut up pretty bad and he was so thirsty. He must have hurt himself breaking out of his place. He probably misses Titan. What?"

Jeremy had swivelled around to stare at me and his expression was a mixture of anger and concern.

"Maisy has a pony?"

"Yes," I said slowly, "he's Titan's companion. Why?"

Jeremy swore under his breath and took his coffee down in one gulp.

"Right, let's get him inside then. I'll deal with Maisy once we've had a look at him. You get to do my chores tomorrow too, though."

I narrowed my eyes at him, not sure if he was kidding or not. With Jeremy you never could tell.

CHAPTER 12

MAISY

*S*omewhere in the house a phone was ringing. Not my familiar ring-tone but the loud, shrilling of my parent's land-line that only telemarketers used.

I groaned and rolled over, keeping my eyes tightly shut against the sun streaming in through the window.

What time was it? What day was it?

Muttering, I pushed myself to my knees and crawled off the bed, pressing one hand against my throbbing head as if that would keep the rest of me from falling apart. At least I was in my own bed this time. And I wasn't wearing duck pajamas.

Bathroom. Water, brush teeth, shower. In that order. I would deal with whoever was burning up my parent's ancient phone later.

My throat was so dry that the first gulp of water almost sent me to my knees. I made a little whimpering noise under my breath and forced myself to keep taking it down. Then I stumbled to the shower and stood under the steaming water with my eyes closed, half-asleep as the water washed part of the misery of the weekend off of me.

I felt brittle and hollow, like an old dried-up husk of myself. Slowly, I lowered myself to the shower floor and curled up in the corner with my arms around my knees, letting the water pour down over me.

I had no idea how long I sat there. Long enough for the water to go from hot to lukewarm and finally to cold before I staggered to my feet again and shut it off.

The phone was still ringing from deep in the house but this time it was accompanied by a relentless thumping sound on the front door.

What the heck was going on?

I started toward the stairs before remembering I was just wearing a towel and had to double back to throw on a t-shirt and shorts.

"I'm coming, just shut up for two seconds," I muttered as the banging on the door got louder and louder the closer I got to it. My head still felt like it was splitting in two.

"What?" I said, wrenching the door open so hard that it smacked into the wall, leaving a slight dent where the handle had hit the drywall. A few flakes of paint drifted to the floor.

Crap, my parents are going to kill me, I thought and then remembered that I was not alone.

"You're alive? You didn't answer your phone," the man in the doorway said in a lilting Scottish accent, glaring down at me.

"Excuse me, do I know you?"

But even as the words left my mouth. things fell into place and my cheeks began to burn. I hadn't recognized him when he wasn't all dressed up. The stranger from the bar who'd helped me home and watched me make a fool of myself was now dressed in jeans and faded green t-shirt with a cartoon deer on it that stretched across his muscled chest.

In the light of day, I could see that he was a few years older than me. His features were all sharp angles; planed cheekbones and a nose that looked like it had been broken at one point. Probably more than once. He was deeply tanned, with laugh lines that fanned out away from a pair of piercingly blue eyes. He wasn't laughing now, though.

"Yes, we met while you were vomiting into a plant," he said impatiently. "Did you lose a pony, though? Yellow. A bit of a biter."

"Oh my gosh, Rory," I said, putting a hand over my mouth. My stomach gave a lurch like I was about to lose whatever food I'd last had. Just how long had I been out of commission? It had just been a day, right? I'd only missed giving him breakfast, hadn't I?

Time was all mixed up and blurred together. My eyes began to burn.

"He's at our place," the man said shortly. "He must have broken out. He's hurt himself. I'll drive you over."

A wave of nausea swept over me and whether it was leftover sickness or the guilt of forgetting about Rory, I turned around and made a run for the bathroom before I could vomit in front of this guy. Again.

I will never, ever drink as long as I live, I vowed as I lay weakly on the cold bathroom tiles and stared miserably up at the ceiling. I closed my eyes, content to just fall asleep there and never move again.

I heard the bathroom door creak open but I didn't have the energy to anything but stay exactly where I was.

Water ran in the sink and the next thing I knew a cool cloth was pressed against my forehead. I flinched away and then relaxed into it.

"I didn't thank you for saving me last night," I said, sighing.

"That wasn't last night," he said quietly. "It was three nights ago. Have you been in here all this time? Who was taking care of the pony?"

I kept my eyes shut tight to block out his piercing stare.

"Is he … is he okay?" I asked, my voice cracking on the last word.

There was a long pause and I looked up at the man in alarm, fearing the worst.

"He's dehydrated and he has a pretty good gash on his leg. The vet is coming."

He was looking at me so kindly that I could hardly stand it.

"Why are you being so nice to me?" I mumbled, reaching up and taking the cloth from him.

"Because I've been where you are," he said quietly. "And I know what it feels like to lose something good."

I took a deep breath and sat up slowly, rubbing my face with my hands.

"I don't remember much about that night. Did we … I mean, did anything—"

"No." He cut in. "I just dropped you off. I guess I should have checked on you again, though. I thought you'd be okay."

"I'm an idiot," I muttered.

He didn't disagree.

"I'm going to leave you the farm address on the table, all right? The vet is coming for the pony in an hour. You'll be there?"

I gulped and looked down at the floor, not meeting his gaze. "I'll be there."

"Good."

When I looked up again, he was gone.

I forgot to ask him his name. I pulled myself to my feet and made my way to the back door, slipping my barn clogs on over my bare feet and walking down to the paddock.

I held onto the fence and stared bleakly at the place where Rory should have been. Where Rory and *Titan* should have been. The big water tub was on its side, not a drop of moisture left in it. There was no hay, of course, and the little grassy paddock had been grazed right down to nothing. I could see where Rory had pawed the dirt near the fence in places to try and reach the grass on the other side. I climbed slowly over the fence, guilt and sadness tightening my throat until I could barely breathe.

The fence had been broken at the far end of the paddock. Not the top rail, but the bottom two. The middle one had been knocked from the post at one end and there was fuzzy palomino fur stuck to the roughened edge.

I could fully imagine Rory sticking his head through to get at the grass on the other side and then pushing with his chest until the whole thing broke. He'd actually been quite the escape artist when he was young. But he'd given it up after he'd retired, content to stay at home with his buddy.

There was a dug-up area on the other side of the fence where he'd scrambled through but any hoofprints that might have given a clue as to what he'd done next were lost on the grassy meadow. I'd seen enough anyway. It was enough to know that he'd been hungry and thirsty enough to run away. That he'd been abandoned by Titan and by me and had gone to find himself a new home.

I righted the water tub on my way back and turned on the tap, glumly watching the water swirl up the sides. I knew I was wasting time so that I could put off facing the people who'd found Rory. Put off apologizing or making excuses.

Still, I felt better when the tub was full, a little more like a responsible pet owner and less like a drunken girl who vomited on strangers and abandoned her childhood pony.

Maybe that video was right, I thought miserably. *I am spoiled. I am a terrible horse person. I should probably give it all up and go into accounting or something.*

I went back to the house and threw on a pair of dark fitted jeans and a clean polo shirt. I tugged my hair into some sort of order and put on a bit of make up; not that it helped much. I looked exactly like I felt. Like a gross, bad person.

I settled an oversized pair of sunglasses on my head, grabbed the address and my car keys off the kitchen table and, gritting my teeth to make sure I didn't chicken out, I headed out to my car.

The drive was way too short.

"Oh, it's this place," I said out loud as I matched the address up with the numbers on the fence post to my right. "The October Horses place."

I'd been passing this farm for years and had hardly given it a second glance but last year even I couldn't help but notice a lot more activity happening there. The barn had been spruced up and the fencing repaired. More paddocks and pastures had been made. And I was pretty sure they'd added a second house halfway up the hill.

I didn't know anything about the people who owned it. After the whole Dirk incident, I'd stayed far away from local gossip. I just kept my head down and focused on my own self without bothering much about anyone else. But the October Horses sign had intrigued me when I'd first seen it. I'd half-wondered if it had been turned into some sort of new-age horse lady retreat or something.

I was about to find out.

I took a deep breath for courage and exhaled slowly, listening to the sound of my tires crunching up the driveway over a new bed of gravel.

There were a few horses in the small paddocks that ran alongside the barn next to the parking lot. A fine-boned, slender grey filly fixed her big eyes on me as I drove up, letting out a piercing whinny. An old horse stood in the paddock next to her, his once bay coat frosted mostly white with age. He glanced up from his hay net and then went right back to calmly eating.

"Hey there," I said to the filly as I shut off the car and climbed slowly out. I grabbed Rory's halter off the passenger seat and looped it over my shoulder. The horse gulped at me as I approached, her eyes wide and anxious. There was a groove worn in her paddock where she'd tramped up and down the fence line. I wondered what had caused her to be so upset.

"Hello," a friendly voice called from behind me and I spun around to see a girl, a bit younger than me, with shoulder length brown hair and a kind expression on her face. She walked toward me, smiling.

I looked at her warily, wondering if the guy who'd rescued me had already told her what I'd done to Rory. Was she secretly judging me? I couldn't tell if her smile was genuine or not.

"I'm Bree," she said encouragingly. "Welcome to October Horses."

CHAPTER 13

MAISY

"Your pony is in the barn," she added when I sort of just stared at her. My brain was still foggy with whatever alcohol I'd tried to poison it with over the last few days.

"His name is Rory," I started to say but the filly let out a piercing neigh behind me and I jerked in surprise as the lingering headache behind my eyes sprang to life again.

"Sorry," Bree said, "she's only been here a few days so she hasn't settled in yet. Sometimes it takes them a while to decompress, especially if they've come straight from the track. Others just walk off the trailer like they've lived here all their lives."

"She was a racehorse?" I asked incredulously, looking over at the delicate filly. "She can't possibly be old enough."

My voice came out sharper than I'd intended and I saw Bree's smile slide a little.

"She's three, so that's old enough. She trained at the track and had a couple of races but it wasn't for her. She's too anxious for a busy environment like that. As soon as she's a little more settled she can go out in the pasture with the others. Do you want to see your pony, er, Rory, now? The vet should be here any minute."

The firm way she said it didn't leave any room for more discussion. I nodded and followed her into the barn, resigning myself to the fact that I'd probably already rubbed her the wrong way. I had a real gift for that.

Rory was standing with his head over a stall door, looking perfectly content and unharmed. He gave a low, greedy little nicker when he saw me, arching his neck like he did when he thought treats might be coming.

Despite the smug look on his face, I felt tears of relief sting my eyes. If anything had happened to him, I wouldn't have been able to forgive myself.

"Hello, stinker," I said, coming up to scratch his neck and place a well-timed kiss on his cheek before he could nip me. "I'm so sorry, buddy."

"That's a great nick-name for him," Bree said, laughing. "He has a pretty strong personality."

"Strong is not the word for it." I cleared my throat at him in warning just as his upper lip began to twitch in the direction of my arm. He sighed instead of biting and lowered his head dejectedly, ears drooping. "He was a terrible child's pony. But once we got to know each other, he became a real friend. He's sort of fallen back on his old ways since he retired, though. I think he loves being naughty more than anything else."

"Yeah, we noticed that. You should look at his leg, though; that's why the vet is coming."

Right, I shook my head to clear it of the lingering fog. He looked so much like his usual self I'd totally forgotten that he was hurt.

I slid the stall door back and ran my hand gently down the pony's neck, scratching my nails through his mane in that way he liked. My hand stilled though as I caught sight of the state of his leg.

"Oh no." I'd actually never seen swelling like that before. His entire knee was the size of a grapefruit and when I ran my fingers over it gently, the skin was hot to the touch. "Have you given him anything for it yet?"

"No." Bree shook her head. "We thought we should wait until we found his owner, er, you, or the vet got here, just in case. The swelling has pretty much doubled in size since we brought him inside so we're worried about infection. He can walk on that leg, although it's tender, and he ate and drank fine. He was just really dehydrated."

I winced, thinking of the empty overturned water bucket. How long had Rory been thirsty before he'd had to break out in desperation? A horse couldn't go without water for very long. If he hadn't have broken out of his paddock then he could very well be dead right now. I could have literally killed him.

Guilt and remorse swept over me, pressing down on my shoulders until I could willingly disappear into the ground. I was an ambitious person but I'd always prided myself on taking good care of my horses. This … this was unforgivable.

"Hey," Bree said, clearing her throat awkwardly. "I just wanted to say how sorry I am about Titan. I was at the show when … when it happened."

Her kind words caught me off guard and I sucked in a breath of air, feeling like I'd been punched in the gut.

"Don't talk about it," I said, closing my eyes. "Please. I can't right now."

"Okay, I won't. I'm sorry. I know." Her words came out in a rush.

How could she possibly know, though? How could she know what Titan's silky coat had felt like after he'd been standing in the afternoon sun? Or the way his wise, brown eyes would stare at me so kindly, so lovingly from across the field. How he'd follow me around sometimes because he wanted to be there, not for food, not because I had treats but because he just wanted to hang out beside me.

How he hated peppermints but ate up his joint supplements like they were candy. How could so many complicated, wonderful things that made up the soul and *essence* of Titan suddenly be snuffed out? Just extinguished like nothing?"

I opened my eyes slowly, realizing I was clutching Rory's tangled mane in my fist and that Bree was still watching me kindly.

"Sorry," I whispered, keeping my eyes fixed on the pony's swollen knee. Shame burned through me. I was such a mess.

"I spent a long time in palliative care." Bree's voice was so quiet that I had to strain to hear her. "I understand what it's like to lose an important part of you that you love."

"Were you sick?"

"Yep, I nearly died. I never in a million years thought I'd make it out of there alive. But I did. It was a miracle. Either of science or the universe; I don't know. I don't take a single day for granted anymore."

Before I could ask her more questions, the rumble of a truck pulling up outside cut me off.

I turned to look down the aisle and my heart sank when I recognized the vehicle. Dr. Anderson. The short, grumpy vet from the show grounds who'd tried to take Titan's body before my own vet could get there. Who'd said that horrible thing about needing to test Titan's blood as soon as possible. As if he'd automatically expected to find drugs in my horse's system. He'd looked at me as if I was trying to cover up a murder. As if I would purposely drug or hurt my own horse.

But now he bustled toward us, whistling under his breath and waving happily at Bree. I shrank back into the stall before he could see me and busied myself putting Rory's halter on. It seemed to take forever for my shaking hands to get the buckle done up.

"Do you want me to take him?" Bree asked quietly and I silently, gratefully, handed her the lead rope while I stayed back in the shadows like a coward. I couldn't hide forever, of course, but I was willing to take all the extra seconds she could give me to compose myself again.

I watched through the bars as the vet gently poked and prodded around the wound behind Rory's knee, then palpated the swelling that had surrounded the entire leg.

"I think it's just a soft tissue injury," the vet said slowly. "But I could x-ray to be sure if you like?"

Bree glanced toward me and I nodded.

Rory stood relatively well for his x-ray, although he kept reaching out his little nose to snatch at the vet's green overalls. Bree was ready for him every time, though.

"Well, there are no bone chips that I can see, and no fractures," the vet said. "The wound is too wide to suture but it doesn't look overly deep. With something like this we just keep it clean and support it until the tissue granulates in on its own. It will leave a scar, but I'm guessing this old fellow's showing days are over."

He sounded so kind and so much different than when I'd met him at the show that I started to step forward, ready to ease myself into the conversation. But he went on without looking up.

"This poor old guy looks like he's had a rough time of it lately. It was nice of you to give him a soft landing. The old fellows get neglected all the time. He'll need stall rest for a week."

I froze and Bree looked at the vet in alarm.

"Oh, he's not a rescue," she said quickly, "more of a boarder. But we can do stall rest for the week, for sure. No problem."

I melted back into Rory's stall while Bree and the vet continued talking, too mortified to say anything in my defense. Sure, Rory looked a little banged up and dirty now. But normally he had a great life at our farm. Okay, maybe he didn't get brushed as often as he should but he was well fed and up to date on his feet and his vet care. What more did this guy want?

My face felt hard and hot as I sank down in the corner of the stall, the drama of the last few days catching up with me again. I was pretty sure that I was having some sort of breakdown. Normal adults did not behave like this. I should be striding up to that vet and defending myself. But I just didn't have the energy right then.

Hooves clopped and Bree put Rory back in with me, his knee now wrapped in a brightly coloured bandage. She shot me a quick glance but stayed silent as she shut the door behind her and walked off with the vet, still talking about the care Rory's knee would need.

The pony gave me a suspicious glance and dove on his hay, swishing his tail at me in irritation. His patience with humans ran out at about the same time as the treats in their pockets did.

Come on, pull yourself together, I told myself fiercely. I wiped my eyes and shakily pulled myself to my feet. Then I yelped and jumped backward as I realized that another face was staring in at me. The guy from the casino. I didn't even know his name.

"Hello?" he said, raising an eyebrow at me. "Is your pony okay?"

"Um." I cleared my throat and made some effort to appear like a stable human being. "Yes, I think so. He will be."

"Well, that's good. He's quite the character."

He grinned at me and I couldn't help but smile back a little bit. "He's awful, but he's pretty funny when you get to know him. And smart. When he's feeling better, I can get him to show you his tricks. He can bow and say yes and no and spin. He could even sit down on command, but he's too old for that now."

I broke off, realizing that I'd been babbling.

"I look forward to seeing that," he said, raising an eyebrow. Then he turned and walked down the aisle without saying another word.

"Wait, what's your name?" I called at his retreating back.

He turned around and gave me a lopsided smile.

"Jeremy. Jeremy from Scotland."

And then he was gone.

I stared at the spot where he'd been and sighed.

He'd gone out of his way to help me not once but three times. And he'd held my hair while I vomited in public. I probably needed to buy him a thank you card and a gift certificate or something. Did thank-you-for-saving-my-life cards even exist?

"Well, that's good news," Bree said, appearing in front of me. "You must be relieved. I hope you're okay with him staying here for a few days."

She looked at me questioningly and I nodded obediently. I'd actually zoned out while the vet was going over patient care and didn't really know what Bree was talking about.

"Of course," I said, clearing my throat a few times. "Did the vet bill you or something? I need to pay you for that, and for board."

"He'll email me an invoice this afternoon and I'll get it to you. Do you want to see the rest of the horses?"

"Um, sure?" I really didn't want to but I couldn't see a polite way around it. Horse people always assumed that everyone wanted to see their precious babies. Bree was nice, though; I hated to disappoint her.

"Come on, they're mostly out on pasture now."

Great, a hike was just what I wanted after a life-altering trauma and three (or was it four?) days of heavy drinking.

But my grumpy mood lifted a little when she rolled the back door open and I followed her out into a sloping pasture.

The whole valley opened up below us and the purple mountain range in the background was streaked with sunlight, making the whole scene look a little magical. Back before my life had been consumed by horses, I'd loved to read, especially fantasy books. This looked like a scene right out of Lord of the Rings.

"Wow, we don't have a view like this from our place," I said. "Too many trees around."

"I love riding in the woods past your farm. It always looks so tidy and cozy. And we always admired …" she broke off and looked away. "The horses."

We walked in silence after that and I closed my eyes and sighed, feeling the warmth of the sunshine on my face and the good smell of fresh pasture grass around me. It truly was a magical spot.

"Here they are," Bree said quietly and I opened my eyes to find myself in the middle of a big herd of horses.

My first impression was that they all looked a little crocked, hairy, and flabby, and then I realized that many of the horses around me were actually ancient. A white mare close by lifted her head and stared at us with grass hanging out of her mouth. She snorted and then made her way purposefully toward me, not stopping until she was nearly standing on my toes.

"Hi." I laughed, reaching out a hand for her to sniff.

"This is Slate," Bree said, reaching out to hug the mare fondly around the neck. "She's my second favourite out of the seniors, next to Bear. He's the gelding you saw when you first arrived. We have a mix here of senior boarders and the thoroughbreds who are part of our program."

"Oh," I said, nodding. "You retrain racehorses?"

"Yep, this is our first year but it's going really well so far. I love working with them."

I made a non-committal noise in my throat, trying to look at least slightly interested. Thoroughbreds weren't my thing. I'd only ridden a couple but they were too spooky and quick on their toes for my liking. I preferred a nice, solid, earthy horse like Titan.

"This is Ace," Bree said enthusiastically, gazing at the small, unremarkable bay gelding like he was made of gold. "He's my special project."

"Nice," I said, petting him a couple of times to be polite.

I half-listened as she introduced me to a handful of other horses, nodding and immediately forgetting their names the second she moved onto the next one. I wondered what sort of convincing excuse I could give for escaping this little interlude. My head was killing me.

"Well, I guess I'd better …" I started to edge backward and immediately came up against something warm and solid directly behind me.

"Gah." I spun around to find a pair of alarming blue eyes looking directly into my face from about three millimeters away. "What on earth?"

"Oh, sorry, that's Chilly. He has no personal space."

"Yeah, I can see that." The horse had a white face that was divided neatly at the top by a jet-black forelock. His blue eyes were uncanny. I backed up a few steps and he followed me instantly, walking toward me until his head butted up against my chest. "What is he doing?"

"Um, he wants a hug," Bree said, trying unsuccessfully to stifle her laughter. "Sorry, Adie taught him that. He loves attention. He's the biggest suck."

"I'm not going to hug you," I told him firmly, backing away again. But the animal was like glue. He just kept coming until I tripped and had to grab onto his big face to keep from falling over. He didn't startle at that, or react at all. Just sighed heavily when my arms wrapped around his jaw, closed his eyes and leaned into me.

Um, well, this is weird, I thought, smiling a little despite my irritation at his bad manners. Horses weren't supposed to just invade your space like that. And yet, I didn't get any threatening vibes off of him. He was just … odd.

He was some sort of paint horse; bay with jagged white irregular markings all over his body. He was solidly built and tall, too.

From the little I could see of him, he looked decently put together.

He was so warm and solid that, for just a second, I leaned my forehead against his and felt a slight lessening of the pain and guilt in my chest. Something shifted inside, a small chink in my emotional armour breached, and I pushed away from him abruptly before I could start bawling again.

"I'd better go," I said quickly. "I have some phone calls I have to make."

"Sure, of course. What time are you coming back to take care of Rory?"

"Coming back?" I said, frowning. "I can pick him up in a week, right?"

"Well, yes, but he needs his wound taken care of twice a day, he needs to be cold hosed and given his medication. Normally, I'd say we could do it but Adie is away and Chloe broke her leg so we're short-staffed."

"Right," I said. I hadn't thought about any of that, not having really paid attention to anything she had told me earlier. "I'll come tonight then, I guess."

Bree frowned at my unenthusiastic response.

"All right then," she said slowly, "well, if you come after dinner then I can show you what to do and what to give him. Do you want to bring his grain or would you like us to feed him? We can work it into the board."

"I can bring his stuff," I said quickly. "I'll bring some hay, too. And his fly sheet. Bree, thank you for everything. And for dealing with the vet, too. I appreciate that. This weekend has been … hard."

I said this all in a rush, trying to make up for all my unappreciative moments in one run-on sentence.

"I understand," she said, laying a hand gently on my arm. "Don't worry, I know."

Before I could second-guess myself, I pulled her into a quick hug, suddenly overwhelmed with gratitude for how kind she'd been to me. I had grown out of the habit of trusting people, especially horse people. But she seemed like a genuinely nice person. I wished I could have a friend like that in my life.

I let her go abruptly; turned and rushed for the parking lot without looking back, not even pausing to say goodbye to Rory.

CHAPTER 14

MAISY

I'd only been gone for an hour but, by the time I got home, I felt exhausted; like I'd been away for weeks. And like I'd been dragged under a bus and stomped on by elephants for good measure.

I dragged my feet down the hall in the direction of the kitchen. I wanted nothing more than to eat something unhealthy and then curl up under the covers and sleep for another few hours.

I changed my mind when I saw the state the room was in; empty bottles everywhere, frying pans, plates and cutlery all over the counter. A congealed mess of what looked like maybe, *hopefully*, half-cooked egg crusted to the stove.

"Good grief," I said, tossing my purse down on the table and making my way slowly through the house.

My parent's room was a mess. My discarded clothes lay on the floor along with more bottles, and an assortment of crumb-filled plates I didn't even remember using. The stale smell of too much alcohol, sweat, and sadness hit me in the face like swamp gas.

"So gross," I said out loud, throwing the comforter onto the floor and stripping the sheets and pillow cases off the bed. I held everything out at arms length as I marched to the washing machine and dumped it all inside, adding extra soap and changing the dial on the machine until it read "heavy load." I pushed the button for extra rinse.

The bottles and the plates were dealt with next and then I had to go get cleaning products to work on a sticky stain on the carpet that I hoped was from the empty can of root beer lying near by.

That was one thing done. Already exhausted, I went to the kitchen and loaded all my dirty dishes into the washer and scrubbed the counters. There was a half-burned frying pan on the back burner with some sort of mystery sludge congealed on the bottom. I had no memory of using the stove at all. Had I made *pancakes* at some point?

I was lucky my parents weren't here to see this. My mom was a complete neat-freak. I would have to go over the house carefully before they got back to make sure I hadn't missed anything. She had eagle-eyed vision when it came to mess in her house.

After that, I made sure the guest room was in order and then I went downstairs to tackle my own suite.

It actually wasn't so bad. I had done most of my damage to the upstairs and had apparently only come down here to sleep the last of my hangover off.

I kept my eyes fixed downward as I worked, avoiding seeing all the memories of Titan that surrounded me on all sides.

Tomorrow, I'd take it all down and pack it away carefully in boxes. If the house was going up for sale, then I'd have to take it all down eventually anyway. It would be easier to go on functioning if I didn't have reminders of what I'd lost constantly surrounding me on all sides.

When I was one hundred percent sure that the house would pass my parent's inspection, I went wearily back upstairs to make myself some tea.

I curled up on the couch in front of the television to find something to distract myself with. But after a few minutes I got up again, restless. I felt exhausted but also like there was this current of nervous energy running through me that wouldn't let me relax. It was the same feeling as right after Titan had passed, like there were prickles of electricity under my skin that wouldn't let me stay still.

"I might as well pack up Rory's stuff," I said to the empty house. It was funny; I had spent many days and nights by myself in this house and it had never seemed like such a lonely place before. Now, just without Titan's presence on the property, it felt like a stranger's house, like I didn't belong here anymore.

I slipped my barn clogs on and grabbed my truck keys. It was still hitched up to the trailer where I'd left it and I took a few minutes to carefully back the trailer up to its spot beside the barn and unhook everything properly. Then I pulled up next to the hay room and slid out of the cab slowly.

This place felt so sad without any horses here to greet me.

Come on, let's get this over with. I dropped the tail gate of the truck and made myself march to the hay room and grab a few bales. Rory loved his food but he wasn't a big guy so I only needed a couple of bales if he was going to be there for less than a full week. I threw four in just in case and then I went to the feed room to grab his grain, his minerals and arthritis supplements.

At the last minute I threw some brushes into a bucket and brought that along too. I might as well clean him up while I was there tonight.

As soon as the truck was loaded, I drove it to the house as quickly as I could. It felt like I'd held my breath the entire time I was in the barn, the oppressive feel of the place had weighed down on me until I could hardly get any air in at all. Which was dumb, because I loved that barn. I remembered when my parents had built it when I was just a kid. It had been a dream come true at the time.

I couldn't think about that anymore, though. That life was gone. I sat back down in front of the television and turned it up loud, ate a sandwich, drank my cold tea. Anything to distract myself from whatever it was I was feeling.

My phone buzzed beside me and I glanced over to see a text notification pop up. And it wasn't from a number I recognized.

I looked at it warily, feeling my heartrate begin to climb.

Don't open it, I thought just as my finger hit the icon.

Just four words. *Karma Is Coming, Witch.*

And below that was a video.

I can delete it, I thought, panic racing through my veins. *I can ignore the whole thing and pretend it's not happening. I'm already off the team, what more do I have to lose?*

I hovered for a second and then tapped the video.

CHAPTER 15

MAISY

*W*ho *is Maisy Fletcher?* The text read, superimposed over a picture of my head. It was the most unflattering photo possible. Obviously taken at a horse show after I'd just taken off my helmet and was all sweaty and red-faced. I was talking to someone just outside of the photo but with the sun in my eyes, my mouth open and my eyes all squinty I basically looked like I was giving someone hell.

Spoiled. Rotten. Monster.

The text was black with red streaked through it. The photo switched to one of Rory and I when I was just a kid. We were walking back to the barn after a test and I could tell that he'd just reached out his nose to bite me. And I had a warning look on my face and my hand raised up to swat his nose away. At least that's what I knew was happening but to anyone who didn't know us it looked like I was about to punch him in the face for no reason.

Horse Abuser. Murderer.

A photo of Titan popped up with the image of a tombstone beside him.

Sign the petition to stop this menace to society from ever owning another animal again. If you love animals, then you HATE Maisy Fletcher.

A box popped up on the screen with a link to an actual petition that people could sign.

Gasping, I threw the phone to the far end of the couch and stared at it in horror. My breath came out in erratic jerks, my ribs spasming from the effort just to get air in.

Am I dying? I wondered. *Am I having a heart attack?*

I had no idea, but gradually my panicked breathing slowed and I was able to think a bit more clearly.

This was escalating. I knew I needed to tell someone. But who would I tell? The police? My parents who were a thousand miles away taking their dream cruise? Would anyone be able to actually stop something like this?

No, my first instinct had been right. This was just a nasty prank. Surely, if I just ignored it, the whole ridiculous thing would die down eventually. How many photos and videos of me could these people possibly have anyway? Surely, they'd run out of them at some point. Where had they even gotten them from in the first place?

Part of me wanted to click on the link and see how many people had signed the petition, but my better sense kicked in. I shut off my phone instead and tossed it on the table with a thump. I could live without it for the evening. I needed a break.

I wanted to be out of this house. I was practically counting down the seconds until the time I was supposed to go and see Rory again.

It took forever but finally, thankfully, the sun drifted through the trees and six o'clock came.

The truck keys were still in the ignition, and I burned down the hill, anxious to put my own sad home far behind me.

The barn was full of horses eagerly waiting for their dinner when I walked in. Excited nickers filled the air and far down the aisle a horse was banging a hoof against their stall door.

I paused in the open doorway, not entirely sure of my welcome.

"Stop that, Dragon." A girl on crutches came out of what must have been the feed room, clutching a bucket determinedly between her fingers.

"Do you want help with that?" I asked quickly, watching her struggle to keep hold of the bucket while she maneuvered her crutches down the aisle.

"Oh," she startled slightly, then her expression darkened when she got a good look at me. She seemed vaguely familiar but I couldn't think of her name. We'd probably met at a horse show or something.

"Hi, I'm Maisy," I said awkwardly when the silence stretched out uncomfortably. I had no idea why she was staring at me like that.

"I know who you are," she said stiffly.

Um, okay.

She turned away, nearly tripping in her haste to get away from me.

"Are you sure I can't help?" I asked.

"No, I can do it myself." She hoisted her bucket higher and thumped down the aisle.

Suit yourself, I thought, taking a stab of pleasure in watching her struggle to open the stall door. I was used to some of the local riders being a bit standoffish to me. Even before the whole lawsuit and criminal charges thing, my old coach, Dirk, had been pretty cutthroat. He'd encouraged us to just focus on showing and ignore everything else.

"These people are not your friends, they're your competition," he'd say. "They will stab you in the back the second you let your guard down."

It was just the way he'd talked: I'd never bought into any of that stuff, although I knew that some of his students did. But his very presence at a show had been enough to keep people away.

After the videos started last year, things had gotten so much worse. I didn't even trust the people who tried to be friendly anymore. It was too hard to tell who was sincere and who was pretending. It was easier to just keep to myself.

"You must be here to see your devil of a pony," a dry voice behind me said, and I turned to see a woman with long blonde hair coming out of a stall. My eyes leapt to the scars on her face; she'd obviously been in a fire or an accident at some point and the pale marks stood out against her otherwise tanned face. I forced myself to focus on her warm, green eyes instead.

"Yes, thank you for looking after Rory," I said.

"He's quite the character. I'm Julie, and this is Lorne." She motioned to an older man who hobbled out of the feed room with a smile on his face.

"Good to meet you," he said, reaching out and shaking my hand firmly. His calloused hand surrounded mine in a warm clasp and I couldn't help but smile back at him.

I studied them, liking the look of both of them instinctively. They just had the aura of good people and I relaxed a little bit.

Nobody mentioned anything about Titan, for which I was grateful. Bree showed up a few minutes later and told me where I could put all Rory's things. She even put the kettle on so I could soak his alfalfa pellets. He was such a greedy little thing that he'd eat up anything mixed in with mushed up pellets, even his supplements and medications.

The little stinker was already eating hay but he looked up and nickered pitifully when he caught sight of me and, more to the point, the bucket in my hand. Like he hadn't been fed in years.

"I hope he eats his dinner with all that medication in it," Bree said worriedly.

"Rory lives for food," I assured her. "He'd probably just eat the medication without the food if you handed them to him like a treat."

True to his nature, he plunged into his feed tub nearly up to his eyeballs the second I stepped away.

"Wow, you weren't kidding," Bree said. "Come on, you have to meet the rest of the thoroughbreds."

She led me down the aisle, pausing in front of each stall to introduce the occupants and forcing me to admire them.

They were decent enough horses, I supposed. They had beautiful, elegant faces and intelligent expressions. But I'd seen a lot of animals over the years, and it took something special to impress me now. These horses were too fine-boned for my taste. I liked a huge, broad-chested massive horse that reeked of power. One like Titan.

Only the giant mare, Dragon, came close to the body-type that I liked and she had an awful personality. She pinned her ears at us and shook her head, guarding her food.

"She's all show," Bree assured me, "she doesn't really mean it."

"Sure she doesn't," I said, raising an eyebrow and stepping back well out of the mare's way. Life was too short to handle horses like that when there were plenty of good, sweet horses like Titan in the world.

"And you remember Chilly," Bree was saying, leading me to the next stall.

I smiled despite myself as his goofy face popped up over the stall door, trailing a mouthful of hay. He nickered eagerly when he saw me and something in my chest loosened a little at the sound.

"So, why is he here?" I asked curiously. "He's not a senior and he's not a thoroughbred, so what's his story?"

"Believe it or not, he is a proper thoroughbred," Bree said, laughing. "He even raced. He has the frame overo gene, which is a really rare colour mutation in thoroughbreds. We were so surprised when he stepped off the trailer. We thought they'd shipped us the wrong horse. You should see his followers on the blog, though. Everyone loves him."

"Hey, friend," I said, reaching out and letting him nuzzle my fingers. He lipped gently at my empty palm and then wiggled his nose sideways in little circles, working his way from my hand to my wrist and then up my arm right to my shoulder and back down again.

"What is he doing?" I asked.

"I have no idea. Sorry, he's a bit weird. Sort of marches to the beat of his own drum."

I stayed still as he worked back up my arm again until his nose was resting on my chest, just below my collar bone, over my heart. He stayed that way, not moving. And then he gently blew out a puff of warm air.

Moving slowly, not wanting to break the spell Chilly was casting over me, I reached up and touched his face, running my free hand down his broad forehead. He sighed happily and closed his eyes.

I don't know how long we stood there. I probably would have stayed locked that way forever if I could have. But somebody, most likely the cranky girl on crutches, slammed the feed room door and the spell was broken.

Chilly snorted gently and went back to his hay, and just like that, he was a normal horse again and I was just another human. I looked up to find Bree studying me quietly.

"What?" I said, surprised at the croak in my voice. I hadn't realized how close to tears I'd been, and it took me a moment to compose myself.

"When I was in the hospital, I dreamt of horses," Bree said unexpectedly. "Right before I nearly died, it was a horse that came to me."

"Oh." I swallowed hard. I wasn't sure what else to say.

"I didn't even like horses before that dream. I didn't know

anything about them." She paused and looked down at the concrete floor for a minute, thinking about what to say next.

"Some people see horses just as pets or livestock, or as partners, or as sports equipment. And, it's true, they can be all those things. But sometimes it feels to me like they are something else, too. Something deeper. "

"Deeper?" I asked, wrinkling my forehead.

"Yes," she went on determinedly. "I don't think about this stuff all the time, but sometimes, like that moment you had with Chilly right there, I feel that there is something more to horses. Something we humans haven't even begun to explore yet."

She paused and looked down at her hands. "Sometimes when I'm with them, I feel like the layers of the normal world peel back and reveal the *other* for a second."

Her cheeks flushed and I could see that she was a little embarrassed to have revealed her inner workings to me like that.

"What do you mean by *other*?" I asked slowly, struggling to understand.

"Well, I don't know what else to call it. But I had a lot of time to think about things when I was recovering in the hospital. Things I'd never thought of before my dream. Sometimes, I get the feeling that there's more to life than what we see. Sorry, I know that sounds weird."

It did. It sounded really weird. I didn't like things that were outside of my comfort zone like that. But Bree had been so nice and helpful to me that I didn't want to hurt her feelings.

"Don't apologize," I said quickly. "Thanks for sharing. So, can you show me what the vet wants me to do for Rory's knee?"

"Sure," Bree said, sighing softly. She looked disappointed that I had nothing else to add to her philosophical conversation, but I didn't think I could handle talking about anything profound right then. I was barely holding myself together as it was. "I'll get the bandages."

I watched carefully as she syringed a weak mixture of betadine and water over Rory's wound to clean it and then carefully patted it dry and applied an antibiotic cream before wrapping it again.

Rory was so focussed on his food that he didn't even put up a fight, and I was relieved that he didn't seem to be in too much pain.

"The vet said to do this for the first five days and after that we can start airing it out between treatments to encourage the tissue to granulate in. We just need to worry about preventing infection at this point. He's lucky the cut was so shallow; it didn't hit anything important. Do you know how he did it?"

I thought of the empty overturned water bucket and felt my face flush.

"He broke the fence," I said. "He was upset to be alone, I think."

Not really the truth, but it was as close as I was going to get right then. I wanted to keep her from hating me as long as possible.

"That makes sense. He probably was searching for other horses. Do you know … do you know what your plans for him are yet? Do you think he'll try and break out again once you have him home?"

"Oh, I hadn't even thought of that. He was supposed to go stay with a family friend, Abigail, when I went to Europe. She has an older horse that she wants a companion for. I guess I should call her and see if she wants to take him earlier. He'd be miserable at our place all alone."

"Oh, that's good," she said, looking relieved. "He seems like a social guy. I was worried he wouldn't do well on his own. I wasn't sure if you were planning to buy another horse or …"

"No," I said sharply, cutting her off. "I have no plans."

"Right, sorry." Her cheeks flushed as she silently gathered up the old bandage material and I cursed myself for snapping at her. She was only trying to help.

"Well, I guess I'll see you tomorrow," I said finally.

"Yeah, you should come for breakfast. We always have lots to go around."

"Um …" The thought of eating breakfast with a group of strangers was strangely appealing compared to being alone in my own house, but I shook my head. "Thanks, but I think I have a couple of online meetings tomorrow. I'll come around ten though, if that's okay."

"Sure, of course." If she was offended by my rejection, she didn't show it. "We'll be riding by then, but I'll make sure to come help you with Rory if you need it."

"No, I'll be fine. I've treated lots of wounds. Now that you've showed me once, I know how to do it. I don't want to interrupt your day. Thanks, though."

"All right, see you around," she said and walked into the feed room.

I said goodbye to Rory and hurried out of the barn. When I reached the end of the aisle though, something made me turn around. And there was Chilly staring at me with his strange ice-blue eyes. He didn't move, just kept his unblinking gaze fixed on me.

"Goodbye," I said to him quietly, then turned around and hurried to my truck without looking back.

CHAPTER 16

MAISY

The one good thing about Rory running away was that I had no reason to go into my depressingly empty barn anymore.

I went straight to the house and got changed into shorts and a tank top and made myself a sandwich for dinner. I ate it while I slowly walked around the house, trying to find a place to settle.

I wanted to do something. I wanted to ride, which was what I always did in the past when this restless, anxious feeling churned around inside of me. The house felt like it was pressing in on me and I needed to get out.

I wasn't much of a jogger; I normally worked out in our home gym a couple days a week only because I had to do it to stay in shape. Not because I wanted to. But now I threw on my running shoes and headed outside.

It was a perfect summer evening; the sky was streaked with pink clouds and the air smelled fresh and cool after the heat of the day. I walked for a while and then broke into a trot, surprised at how good it felt.

My feet ate up the ground as I fell into a steady rhythm down the road, the motion soothing me.

Our farm was on a dead-end road at the top part of a long, steady hill that sloped downwards toward the busier road down below. The neighbourhood was a mix of large family homes and horse farms of all sizes. I passed the Plekowski's massive stable with the indoor next door to us. A place I'd never been invited to ride even though my parents knew the owners. The big family kept to themselves for some reason.

Must be nice to have a whole farm of back-up horses when you lose one, I thought resentfully. There would never be a horse to replace the bond I'd had with Titan. I wouldn't even try. But I still wanted to ride. It was so much a part of my life that I couldn't imagine giving it up.

By the time I passed the rolling farm, there was a stitch in my side, but I didn't stop or take a break. Just pushed on through the pain.

I did pause when I saw the driveway for October Horses down below, though. It would seem to weird to run past their place, like I was stalking them or something, so I turned around and headed back up the hill.

But going uphill was a little different than downhill. I was tired and I found my pace lagging until I fell into a brisk walk. I wiped the sweat off my forehead and let my aching lungs recover before pushing on again.

Footsteps sounded behind me and I whirled around to see another runner gaining on me.

Good lord, this can't be happening, I thought gloomily, *this guy is everywhere.*

"Need some help?" Casino guy grinned at me and I was caught again by how nice his eyes were. The blue was much lighter than mine, like the shallow parts of the ocean that I remembered from our family trips to Mexico. They crinkled up the corners, laugh lines fanning out.

My gaze drifted down to his abs, outlined by his tight shirt, and I forced myself to look back up again. He obviously took working out more seriously than I did.

"Not unless you want to carry me," I said, stepping away a little just in case he thought I was serious.

"You look like you're doing fine on your own. First time running in a while?"

"Ah, yeah, it's been a while," *Since like high school when I was forced to run laps.* "Does it show that badly?"

"No, you're doing great."

All lies but I appreciated it.

"Look," I said, taking a deep breath, "I never thanked you properly for helping me out that night at the casino. And then, well, afterwards. I know how stupid I was and how badly it could have ended if you hadn't been there."

He looked at me sympathetically and nodded.

"You're welcome."

There was an awkward pause.

"So, um, you're riding for Lauren now, are you? Isn't Sassafras fantastic?"

He stopped walking and stared at me, looking startled.

"I hope I didn't take any rides from you. Lauren said her old rider had left."

"Oh, no, don't worry about that. Lauren and I are good. I was supposed to be heading overseas so I'd already given notice. You just showed up at the right time. I know there are these rumours going around that she fired me but it wasn't like that. I honestly don't mind."

"Are you sure?"

"Hey, you saved my life. I don't think I'm allowed to be

annoyed at you. Speaking of that, can you please let me know how I can make it up to you?"

"No need for that," he said, waving a hand in my direction. "It's what any decent person would have done."

"No, seriously though. And there's everything you've done for Rory, too. Please."

"Well," he studied me for a minute. "How about dinner?"

"What? Like a date?" I asked, my cheeks flushing and my heart speeding up just a little bit. I hadn't dated anyone in a long time; I really hadn't trusted anyone enough to let my guard down since that whole thing with Dirk.

"Not if you don't want it to be," he said, misinterpreting my hesitation. "How about more like a working dinner. I have some ideas to run past you. I'd like to invite Lorne and Julie, too."

"Oh." Definitely not a date then. "What kind of ideas?"

I really hoped they weren't going to ask me to ride any of their straight-off-the-track crazy thoroughbreds. As much as I wanted to ride, I had enough self-preservation not to go down that road. Yeah, I was a decent rider but I wasn't a fan of getting bucked off or run away with.

"Now, now, that's cheating. If I tell you what my ideas are now then you might not like them and you won't come to dinner."

I shook my head as he grinned at me.

"You're tricky, aren't you?"

"Very. So, you'll come?"

"I will. Thank you. I could use a distraction from, you know, life."

"I hear you. Okay, tomorrow at seven then. Meet at the barn."

"All right." Before I could say anything else he turned around and jogged away, heading back in the direction he'd come.

I stared after him for a moment feeling a strange fluttering inside my chest that I pushed down resolutely.

He was just being nice, I told myself firmly. *Not a date.*

With a sigh I headed home at a walk, too tired to break into more than a shuffle.

I was strangely excited over being invited to dinner. So far everyone but the girl on crutches had seemed nice. And really, would it be the worst thing in the world if they wanted to offer me a job riding their horses? I didn't have any other prospects at the moment and it was going to take me a while to figure things out.

If Dirk hadn't gotten himself suspended then I could have turned to him for answers. He knew everyone in the horse industry and could always pull a miracle out of thin air by calling in some favours.

He hadn't been a super nice man, and he'd had a temper, but he'd always known how to get stuff done. And boy could he ride. Despite all his personal flaws, he'd been a great coach for me. He'd had a way of teaching that just worked for my brain. True, he'd yelled, a lot, and he often outright insulted his students, but if you ignored all that, then he was brilliant.

He'd made me and Titan the unstoppable team we'd become. It wasn't my fault if not everyone appreciated Dirk's unconventional methods.

When I finally made it back to the house, I locked the door firmly behind me and padded into the kitchen. The silence of the house pressed in on me. I wished I had a dog or even a cat to keep me company. My parents hadn't gotten a new dog after our old rottweiler, Smudge, had passed away and now there would be no more pets if the farm was going up for sale.

I was still sweaty and gross after my almost-run so I chugged down two glasses of water and made a bee-line for the shower.

My muscles ached, but in a good way, and I felt like the alcohol was finally out of my system.

Even though it was still early, I crawled into my bed and snuggled down under the covers. All my troubled thoughts about

Titan and the videos and Rory came flooding into my brain but I resolutely pushed them away.

I was too tired to deal with any of that. It had been a long day and my worries would still be there tomorrow. With that thought, I fell asleep.

CHAPTER 17

BREE

"$\mathcal{D}$ o you think Poppy is ready to go out on pasture with the senior group?" Julie asked, setting the basket of hot, fragrant toast down in the middle of the table.

I paused, surprised that she was asking me. I was one of the least experienced horse people here, even though I'd been working with them for over a year. I always thought of myself as a beginner compared to everyone else. Not the one to make herd decisions.

"Um, sure. She's settled down a lot. I think being out with the other horses will make her happy."

"That's what I thought, too. Okay, go ahead and turn her out with them this morning. She'll fit in well with that group. Who do you want to leave in with Rory?"

I thought about it for a second, considering everyone. "How about Follow? She could use some one-on-one time; she's been a bit neglected since Adie's been gone. And she doesn't mind hiding in her stall."

Follow was one of the thoroughbreds from the first group we'd brought in. But, while the other horses had blossomed in their new life here, Follow had continued to be afraid of pretty much everything.

We had no idea if something awful had happened to her in her past or if there was just some faulty wiring in her head. We'd run bloodwork and had massage and chiropractic done and a full work-up from the vet. But everything pointed the fact that she was a healthy horse that should be thriving when she clearly wasn't.

She'd actually come a long way in some areas. She used to launch into a blind panic every time we tried to lead her out to pasture. She'd spin and bolt back to her stall and then stand and shake there for hours. She'd hated to be brushed or even touched and she hadn't trusted any of us.

Gradually that had changed, though. She could lead nicely to the field and seemed to enjoy her time out there with the other horses. She loved to be brushed now, especially when Adie groomed and fussed over her. And she could pick up her feet perfectly and had even started going for walks around the property.

But she was far from being a riding horse; nowhere close to being adoptable. At this rate, I couldn't guess what her future would look like at all.

"Good idea," Julie said, "you can always switch her up with someone else in the afternoon."

I nodded, concentrating on my breakfast and half-listening for the thump of Chloe's crutches coming down the stairs. Despite how hard it was for her to navigate an entire flight of old, wooden steps she'd insisted on sleeping in her own room after her first few nights on the couch.

She was so stubborn that she'd hardly let anyone help her. I mean, I was all for pushing through when things got tough, but there was a time to admit that you needed a bit of help too. Chloe had long gone past that state.

"Have you decided what we're going to do about Dragon?" I asked in a low voice.

Julie sighed and shook her head. "Yes and no. Unfortunately, the mare needs to stay in work. She can't sit around for months while Chloe heals. Jeremy is the obvious choice, but I know how much Chloe is going to hate that."

Hate was probably an understatement.

"What about Maisy?" I asked. Although Chloe seemed to dislike her equally, I wasn't sure if she'd be much of an improvement over Jeremy.

"Yeah, that's probably the direction we'll go first. Lorne and Jeremy are having her for dinner at their place tonight."

"Oh?" I looked up in surprise, a little stung that I hadn't been invited.

"We'll just keep Chloe occupied while they present Maisy with the idea. She might not want to ride here. No need to upset Chloe before we have to."

"Right," I said slowly. I didn't like the idea of going behind Chloe's back on this; not even for a short time. But I also saw the sense in what Julie was saying.

"The truth is that somebody has to ride Dragon," Julie said, frowning. "So, at some point, Chloe is just going to have to be okay with that."

She broke off as that tell-tale thumping of Chloe's crutches started down the stairs.

~

We spent the rest of the day working hard with the horses. All the seniors needed to be groomed before turnout a few days a week and today was the day.

Chloe helped as best she could but she wasn't able to pick out feet of course and not all the horses appreciated her new crutches so close to them.

Jeremy and I turned out everyone who wasn't being worked with that morning.

He hesitated when he came to Dragon.

"She should be worked today," he said as she circled her stall like a tiger, pawing up the bedding in her impatience to be outside and doing something. "She has too much pent-up energy, she's going to hurt herself."

"No, she won't," Chloe said loudly from where she was brushing Bear in his stall. "She can wear off her energy in the pasture."

"She's not that type of horse," Jeremy said flatly. "She needs work."

Chloe made a face at him but said nothing. Despite her stubbornness, she must have known that Jeremy was right. While some horses could be perfectly happy to be turned out for the rest of their lives, Dragon needed focus and a purpose to channel all her wild energy.

"Well, just turn her out for now," Lorne said from the folding chair where he'd settled himself just outside of the tack room. "We can decide all that later."

I moved Follow over into the stall beside Rory and then finished turning everyone else out.

"Are you ready to go out, sweetie?" I asked the little grey mare, Poppy.

She tugged against the lead rope eagerly, excited to be heading outside.

Now that she'd settled in, her personality was much calmer and kinder than when she'd first arrived. Without the anxiety, it turned out that she was a really sweet horse who loved being around people.

"We're going to have to start your training soon, little one." I said, running a hand down her neck to steady her excited prance. The original plan had been to add the mare to Chloe's riding string, but now it looked like Jeremy would be picking her up as well, along with Nugget.

Which meant that he was officially over-horsed. Between our crew, his client horses and the barn work, he wasn't going to have time to sleep.

I led the filly carefully through the gate, waiting until she'd settled a little before unbuckling her halter and stepping away.

She made an excited little squealing sound under her breath and whipped around, breaking into a gallop from a standstill.

I watched her go with my heart thumping a little. I never got tired of watching these beautiful horses run.

Humming under my breath, I walked back into the barn to see who was left. Nipper and Ace were still inside finishing their hay. I had a lesson on Nipper booked for later on that morning and I was planning on schooling Ace in the ring.

Timely and Nugget were waiting for Jeremy. Follow had been stationed next to Rory. And then there was Chilly.

He had his head hanging over his stall door and his gaze fixed on the end of the aisle toward the parking lot. His ears were pricked as if he were listening, waiting for something.

"She's not here yet," I told him quietly, looking around to make sure nobody was around to hear me. "Let's get you outside, buddy. We'll take you on your walk later this afternoon."

He lagged back when I tugged gently on the lead rope, turning again so he could peer out the big front door. Finally, he sighed and followed after me.

"You are a strange fellow," I told him. "But you're right to be so nice to Maisy. I think she could use a friend right now. Maybe you're the right guy for the job."

I didn't really think he could understand me, or at least not everything. But it was my habit to talk to all the horses like they knew what my words meant. Sometimes it even seemed like they were paying attention to me.

When I came back in, my gaze landed on Follow and I bit my

lip, thinking about how I would tackle our session today. I hadn't had much luck on finding any more information about her. I'd sent emails and left messages for the breeder listed on her papers but so far had heard nothing.

Eddie, one of the founders of October Horses and my sister's boyfriend, had put me in touch with Follow's last trainer but he hadn't been able to be much help, either.

"She was like that when she came to us," he'd said, "we couldn't do anything with her without keeping her drugged. She never even raced with us. It was a shame, really, she had the bloodlines to be a talented horse."

And that was as far as I'd gotten. I'd been too busy on the farm to do much else.

"I guess I'll brush you and take you for a walk," I told her, going into the tack room to get a box of brushes.

Follow skittered back to the far corner of her stall and I waited in the doorway, keeping my breathing easy and calm until she swivelled and took a few steps back in my direction.

It was like that every time anyone tried to interact with her. Her automatic response was to run far away from humans.

But gradually, her recovery time had become shorter and shorter. Where once she would have shivered in her stall for an hour. Now she could come out of her corner and see what I'd brought her.

"Carrot," I said, holding it out to her.

She stretched her nose out as far as she could until her lips flapped against the carrot and then she grasped it between her sturdy teeth.

"There you go, good girl."

She stood still while I slipped on her halter and began to run the curry comb over her shoulders in small circles.

She shuddered once and then closed her eyes and sighed happily. Grooming sessions seemed like the one time when she could set her fears aside and just enjoy something.

I brushed her carefully from head to toe, running a soft goat-hair brush through the fine strands of her mane and forelock. Then I clipped on her lead and walked her firmly out into the aisle, not hesitating or looking back.

Getting her to leave the barn was always tricky. But if you pretended that you were in charge and knew exactly where you were going then she'd usually follow.

If you showed any hesitation though, she'd often just spin around back to her stall.

Today she was in an extra mellow mood. She followed me along happily enough out into the sunshine, and I took her up to the ring to do a circuit in there, and then down past the barn toward the trails.

When I'd first started doing this with her, she'd refused to go more than twenty feet from the barn. But now she could go all the way to the bridge and back again and spend five or ten minutes in the ring without freaking out.

She still had a long way to go, but the fact that she could leave the barn and the other horses at all was encouraging. She'd come a long way even if it had taken a very long time.

"We just need to find out what makes you tick," I told her, gently running a hand down her neck. "Somewhere out there is that one puzzle piece that will click into place and make all your weird behaviour make sense."

She snorted and itched her nose on my arm before turning around, gently but firmly, and heading back toward the safety of the barn.

CHAPTER 18

MAISY

*T*he barn was in a bit of chaos when I arrived the next morning to take care of Rory. Julie was in the middle of mucking out all the stalls and the aisles were full of fallen hay and shavings. Bree was tacking up that crafty-looking chestnut paint horse she liked to ride, and beside her Jeremy was grooming a rangy chestnut.

That's a nice-looking horse, I thought in surprise. I didn't remember seeing him before but then I hadn't really cared enough to pay close attention to them when Bree had given me my tour.

"Good morning," I said, feeling a little braver around him after our meet up the night before. For some reason, he didn't seem to judge me over my behaviour at the casino or for nearly killing Rory, so I was going to do my best to be pleasant. "Your horse is quite nice."

"Thank you," he said, raising an eyebrow at me.

I'd meant it as a compliment but I guess it had come out sounding a little condescending.

"No, I mean it. Thoroughbreds aren't my thing but—"

"I know," he cut in, "you mentioned that several times the night I drove you home. I seem to remember you asking why I wasted my time with them?"

"Seriously?" I winced. "I will probably be paying for that night for the rest of my life. I'm sorry if I offended you. I'm an idiot. Your horse is honestly lovely."

My words came out in a tumbled rush and to cover my embarrassment, I reached up and ran my hand down the chestnut's well-muscled neck. Admiring the way his hide rippled under my fingers.

"Everyone makes mistakes," Jeremy said quietly. "I don't think you need to punish yourself forever. This is Timely, by the way. He's a good boy."

"He's your favourite." I said, guessing by the undisguised pride in his voice.

"Actually, he is." Jeremy patted the horse affectionately. "He has a lot of potential. We'll go to the mainland next week to get some real show miles under his belt. Not too many options on the island here, unfortunately. He needs some real tracks to compete at."

"Oh right, you Event, don't you? I guess there are more jumper and dressage options here. Or Hunters, if you like that stuff."

"I like it all." Jeremy shrugged. "But I'm definitely used to a more robust show scene. I keep telling Lorne he should hook up with the people next door the ones with the indoor, and set up a proper show facility. We could really use something like that here."

"That sounds nice," I said, although I couldn't get too enthusiastic about something like eventing. Much like thoroughbreds, it was just not my thing. "Well, I'd better take care of Rory. Have a good ride."

The pony was waiting for me with his head hanging in the aisle and his little ears swivelling around like he was plotting something awful.

"What are you up to, stinker?" I asked him, rubbing his forehead and deftly avoiding his teeth as I reached over to scratch his neck. "How are you still so bad after all these years?"

He rolled his eyes at me and backed up, giving me room to enter his stall.

"It's a trap, isn't it?" I laughed, knowing far better than to trust his innocent expression. "Hang on. I'll get you an extra flake of hay and then we can get you all fixed up."

I tossed his hay over the stall door and then went back to the feed room where his soaked alfalfa cubes were waiting. I carefully mixed in his medication, reading each label to make sure I was doing everything like Bree had showed me. And then I mixed it all up with the sticky wooden feed spoon that had obviously seen better days, and headed back to Rory.

He made a demonic, low rumbling sound in his chest as he saw the bucket and hobbled over to his rubber feed tub, nickering greedily the whole time.

"Okay, don't have a heart attack," I told him, dumping the mix into his tub. I slipped his halter on him between mouthfuls and draped the lead rope over the stall door to keep it out of the way. I probably didn't have to bother with the halter while he was nose-deep in his dinner but it was better to be safe than sorry.

I carefully unwrapped the bandages, kneeling down to examine the cut on his leg to make sure it was healing. It still looked ugly but the edges were less angry-looking now and the tissue did seem to be filling in a little. I washed it carefully, squirting the diluted betadine mixture right out of the squeeze bottle in a steady flow so it cleaned what little debris there was away. I dried it carefully, making sure I didn't hurt him. Then I smeared the medicated ointment on a piece of square gauze and stuck it right over the wound. I wound the roll of light cotton bandaging around the area before adding a brightly coloured vet wrap layer over top.

"There, all finished, and you didn't even notice," I told him. But he didn't bother to look up. Just licked out the last bits of food in his bucket and plunged his nose into his hay.

I fished out a curry comb and started to work on his thick coat.

I brushed him until my arms hurt, laughing as he leaned into the pressure to get the most out of his massage. I combed out his mane and tail until he looked like a decent citizen again and then stood back to admire my work.

"There, all done. You look fantastic."

I paused for a second to study him, realizing for the first time how happy he seemed.

He was really enjoying being surrounded by all these horses and he clearly loved all the attention being showered on him.

"Have I been neglecting you a bit, buddy?" I said out loud. I hadn't really thought about how much he'd been pushed aside when he'd been retired from riding.

Sure, his basic needs were, usually, met but nobody spent hours grooming him to a high shine or combing his hair out lovingly. When I was a kid, I'd spent all my spare time teaching him tricks. I remembered how proud he'd been when he'd show off his tricks and how happy we'd been together.

It must be hard to be a horse, I thought, *you get replaced so easily when you're old or injured. People just move on to the next thing and forget you.*

It hadn't been done out of meanness, of course. I'd kept Rory all this time because I'd promised him long ago that I'd never sell him. I'd had two horses between retiring Rory and buying Titan. Both I'd shown for a couple of years and sold for a healthy profit. It's what had allowed my parents to buy Titan in the first place.

But Rory had always been a permanent fixture. The trusty companion.

I guess I'd taken him for granted all this time.

"Well, you'll get spoiled lots once Abigail comes to get you," I told him. "She's been itching for pony to love."

My happy mood faded a little as I stepped out of his stall. I didn't want to go home and face another day in my empty, lonely house. I put my things away in the tack room as slowly as I could and then soaked Rory's dinner alfalfa pellets.

I hesitated in the aisle, wondering if there was anything else here that I could do.

Maybe Bree won't mind if I go to the ring and watch her ride.

"Are you looking for something to do?" Julie asked, startling me when she popped her head out of a nearby stall.

"I'm kind of at loose ends right now." I shrugged.

"Well, grab a pitchfork. We can always use extra hands here. Especially being so short staffed right now. I'd love some help."

"Okay, sure," I said, mustering as much enthusiasm as I could manage. Mucking stalls was definitely not what I'd had on my wish list. But at least it was *something*.

I picked up a stray muck fork that was leaning against the wall, and rolled the extra wheelbarrow out from the second grooming stall where it had been parked. Then I got to work.

It wasn't like I was a princess or anything. I'd never had my own groom, or staff. I was used to cleaning my own stalls and paddocks on a regular basis. But I wasn't one of those people who got a great feeling of satisfaction from seeing a row of freshly cleaned stalls or a swept aisle. I couldn't care less about cleaning; I did it because it needed to be done. Nothing more, nothing less.

Still, it was nice to sort of fall into a rhythm, it was hypnotizing in a way. Sift, sift, scoop. Sift, sift, scoop. Over and over as I worked my way from stall to stall. I wasn't in a rush; it wasn't like

I was getting paid by the hour or anything. Or at all. And I didn't have anything else to do after I left here.

"You're a pro at this," Julie said and I looked up to see her smiling kindly at me.

"I've had some practice." I realized for the first time that I'd worked my way to the end of the barn. The sight depressed me a lot more than I'd expected. I really wasn't ready to leave. "Is there anything else I can do to help around here?"

"Want to ride a horse for me?"

I hesitated, considering the question. I'd half expected to want to say no, that the idea of riding anyone but Titan would just feel wrong. But it didn't. My relationship with Titan hadn't just been about riding. It had been about bonding with a trusted partner. That was something I'd probably never be able to replace. But riding itself? I didn't think I ever wanted to give that up. It had been nearly a week since I'd ridden and already my body was feeling it.

"Yes, okay," I said finally. "Which one?"

Anyone but Dragon, anyone but Dragon.

"His name is Nugget and he was one of Chloe's rides. He's a good boy and is pretty much ready to be adopted. But I'd like to see how he goes with someone who doesn't know all his buttons. Are you willing?"

"Sure," I said. I was pretty sure that Nugget was the small, innocuous bay that Bree had introduced me to. Shouldn't be a big deal.

"Okay, I'll go grab him for you. Do you have a helmet with you?"

"Ah, no and I'm in jeans. But I live like two minutes away. Can I run home and grab my stuff first?"

"Sure, meet me back here in fifteen minutes. I'll have him all groomed up for you and ready to go."

"Great, I'll be right back."

I drove faster than I needed to get home, feeling strangely

excited about the prospect of riding something new and different. This was probably exactly what I needed to take my mind off everything that had gone on last week.

I rummaged through my closet until I found a pair of clean full seat breeches and a black polo shirt. My boots and helmet were in the barn unfortunately so I had no choice but to go down there and grab them.

Every time I stepped into my own barn it felt less and less familiar. Without the horses it had an abandoned vibe to it. Like it was full of restless ghosts and too many memories. I grabbed my stuff as fast as I could, adding spurs and a dressage whip to my armful of things to take, and got out of there as fast as I could.

CHAPTER 19

MAISY

*J*ulie was waiting for me when I got back. And I'd
been wrong about the horse. Nugget wasn't the bay.
He was a compact grey with a friendly expression.

"Hey, handsome," I said softly, coming up to introduce myself.
I reached out my hand to let him sniff it and then gave him a pat
on the shoulder.

"He's a nice, all-around horse," Julie said as she unclipped him
from the cross-ties and slipped on his bridle. "He's uncomplicated and kind. He's not the most forward guy in the world but
he'll be perfect for an amateur to love on."

I nodded, pausing to strap on my spurs and helmet before I
followed her down the aisle and out into the sunshine. Bree and
Jeremy were nowhere to be seen when we got to the ring; something I found strangely disappointing.

"All right, hop up and let's see how you like him. He's fairly
responsive so you don't need a lot."

I nodded, only half listening to her as I tightened my girth and ran down the stirrups.

Nugget stood nicely when I got on him and I took a second to fix the stirrup length and get used to the feel of a strange saddle before picking up the reins firmly and asking him to move forward.

Nugget hesitated, arching his neck and mouthing at the bit, reluctant to move into the contact. Instead of stepping off smartly, he began to back up and it was only when I gave him a little jab in the ribs that he jolted forward.

"Okay, hold up," Julie said, stepping in front of me with a frown. "Let's remember how inexperienced he is, okay? You have to treat him like he's a baby still."

"But, don't you want him to submit to contact?" I asked in confusion.

"Well, in a way and eventually. But we're not packaging him into a shape at this stage. He just needs to go nicely forward. He's not going to the Olympics; he doesn't have FEI young horse classes coming up. We can afford to take our time with him."

I just stared at her, not really sure what she wanted from me.

"Here," she said, coming over and putting her hands gently on the reins. "Let's loosen these up a little so he can stretch down and seek the contact. You'll still have a light feel of his mouth but no constriction, okay?"

"Um, sure." I decided to just go along with it. It had been a long, long time since Titan had been young and green, and I hadn't really ridden any babies since. When I rode at Dirk's, we'd been expected to package and contain our horses from the moment they stepped into the indoor, or he'd spend the next hour shouting at us. Those horses had to be attentively on the bit at all times. Stretching and loose reins were a reward for after the work was done.

I felt a flicker of interest. This was something new and different. Even the horses I'd ridden for Lauren had been well past the baby stage.

"Okay, so let's start again. Ask him to move on but keep that same length of rein.

I asked him with my seat and then, when he didn't respond, I gave him a sharp nudge in the side that had him leaping forward into a quick march.

"Easy," Julie said. "Next time give him more time to respond. He was still processing what you'd asked him. Remember, your aids are going to be slightly different than what he's used to. And he hasn't actually felt spurs before, even blunt ones like that. You'll have to be tactful with them."

I nodded, trying to get a feel for the horse beneath me. He was so much different than Titan. So much narrower. And in one sense he seemed quick and alert and yet, he was almost sluggish to my aids. But he gradually relaxed as we walked around and began to softly mouth the bit and stretch down a little. I felt his back come up underneath me and his hind end step under just a bit more.

"Good," Julie said, "so much better. When you're ready, ask for a trot."

I made sure to be patient and have more subtle aids this time and was rewarded with him moving up into a slow trot.

And this is why I don't like thoroughbreds, I thought, sighing. The trot was fine, although nothing spectacular, but it lacked the vital power that Titan's had. That force that infused his personality into every stride. Titan owned every ring he walked into like he'd been a natural king. He went in expecting people to admire him and he never missed a chance to show off.

This trot was like a boring, watered-down version of that. I bumped my legs gently against his sides with every step, trying to build some sense of animation into him. But instead of driving him forward, his head shot up and I felt his back drop away from me. His ears swivelled around in confusion and I brought him back to a walk with a sigh.

"So, what happened there?" Julie said, moving so she was

walking beside us. She had her arms crossed over her chest and a frown on her face.

"I don't know. He just doesn't feel right. Like he's lacking power."

"Well, you're right about that. He needs to build up strength to be able to use his hindquarters properly. Remember, he's only been in steady work for a few months. We have to be patient with him. Did you have to use a lot of leg with Titan?"

I paused, caught off guard by the question. "Yes, I definitely needed spurs with him or he wouldn't settle into work. He was really powerful but also kind of lazy. He did the bare minimum until you made him do more."

"Ah, I see. Well, most of these guys aren't going to need to be ridden like that. They're bred to be more sensitive and hotter than your guy was. I know that's the fashionable thing to do now but most horses don't need to be prodded at every stride to get them to move forward properly."

"All right," I said, not liking her judgy tone. I was only riding the way I always did at home. It wasn't like I was beating this horse or mistreating him or anything. I'd just met him and was trying to figure him out.

"Okay, trot again. This time use more seat than leg. And keep your lower leg still."

The next half hour wasn't the easiest ride I'd ever had but at least it was interesting. And by the time I got off, Nugget and I had an understanding of how he liked to be ridden. Julie had reminded me a few times to stop badgering him with my legs, something I hadn't even realized I'd been doing. But, other than that, the rest of the ride went well enough.

I actually found that I'd enjoyed myself. In the past, I'd always ridden horses that suited my style of riding; I hadn't had to adapt myself so much before. It was hard work but I liked it.

I cooled out Nugget and brushed him in the cross-ties, half-hoping that Julie would give me something else to ride.

"You did good," she said, as she picked up Nugget's tack and headed toward the tack room. "Have a good dinner tonight."

"You're not coming?" I asked in surprise. I'd thought that dinner was supposed to be at Julie's house.

"No, not this time. Lorne and Jeremy are your hosts tonight. Thanks so much for helping out today. You can leave Nugget there, I'll put him outside."

And with that she was gone.

I guess I've been dismissed, I thought with a sigh. I gave Nugget a final pat, did a final check to make sure that Rory had hay and then headed out.

It wasn't until I got home that I realized that I had a couple of missed messages on my phone.

Dr. Patel. Monica. I dialed Titan's vet as fast as I could, my hands shaking and my heart beginning to pound.

"It was a rupture of the aortic artery," Dr. Patel said the second she was on the line. "He probably had a weakening of the arterial wall. Most likely a genetic anomaly he was born with. There was nothing anyone could have done, Maisy. It's nobody's fault."

I sagged back against the couch and pressed my hands over my eyes, trying to hold back tears. The relief I felt was overwhelming. Which was stupid, because knowing what killed Titan wasn't the same as bringing him back. And I'd already known that I hadn't drugged him. And yet, something deep inside of me had been terrified that he'd died because of something I'd done. Some mistake in his feeding program or his supplements. Something toxic in his pasture. Somehow it felt like it had to be my fault.

"I'm so sorry," Monica said kindly. "I know how much you loved him. He was one in a million."

"He was," I said, wiping my eyes hard and trying to pull myself together. "Thank you. For everything. You'll send it off to the insurance company, right? I don't care but it's for my parents."

"I know. You don't have to feel guilty about having him insured. It's a practical decision when you have a valuable horse. He's an investment as well as a best friend."

It made sense when she put it like that, but it didn't make me feel much better for getting money and benefitting from his death. It felt a little gross, quite honestly.

"Are you looking to buy a youngster now?" The vet asked. "I see some nice horses in my travels. I could keep an eye out for you."

"Thanks," I said quickly. "Not yet, though. I'm not ready."

"Well, you give me a shout anytime when you decide what direction you want to go next," she said, sounding a little too jovial. "My cousin breeds Hanoverians. She has an excellent program and usually has some nice youngstock available."

"Okay, I'll keep it in mind. Thanks for everything. I should go, though."

I stayed on the line just long enough for her to say a few more flattering things about Hanoverians and assure me that she'd send on the paperwork to the insurance company and then I hung up, taking some deep breaths to center myself again.

I went to find some food, mulling over everything the vet had said.

"It wasn't my fault," I said out loud, trying to convince myself that it was the truth. Sure, Titan had seemed a little tired lately. I'd chocked it up to his heavy training and showing schedule. I'd added more days-off into his routine. I'd upped his minerals, I'd gotten him a massage. He'd seemed happy enough and he'd never balked in his training sessions. But there had been something ever so slightly off about him that I hadn't been able to put my finger on.

It wasn't your fault, I told myself again, firmly. But I had the feeling that it was going to take a long, long time before I believed that.

CHAPTER 20

MAISY

I was full of nervous excitement by the time I was ready to head to the barn again that evening. I'd dressed in jeans and a somewhat decent shirt but I'd kept it super casual. I still had to take care of Rory's knee and give him his own supper anyway, so there was a chance I would have a layer of hay and pony slobber on me by the time my dinner date happened.

I'd just finished putting the final wrap on Rory's knee when I sensed someone standing nearby.

"I heard you rode Nugget today," Jeremy said in his lilting Scottish accent. "How did you like him?"

"He was interesting," I said, "I mean he was good. Not like the horses I usually ride. But I liked him."

Jeremy studied me with his head tilted slightly to one side like he was trying to figure me out.

I shifted nervously, wondering what I'd said wrong.

"Um, are we still on for dinner?" I said, picking up the used bandaging material that I'd dropped by Rory's feet.

"Of course. Lorne sent me down to collect you. Are you all ready?"

"Yep, let me just put this stuff away."

He kept watching me steadily and my heartbeat sped up a little bit as I slid past him and put my brushes away, tossing out the old gauze and bandaging.

This is not a real date, I reminded myself, *they just want you for hired help.*

I opened the bag of carrots that I'd brought with me and snapped one in two, laughing when I heard Rory's greedy little nicker. He could sense treats within a twenty-mile radius.

"Okay, piglet, here's yours." I said, coming back out into the aisle and stuffing the smaller half into his mouth, avoiding his eager teeth. Then I walked down to Chilly's stall to give him the bigger share.

"Here you are, handsome. You're so much more polite than that pony."

Chilly took his carrot gently, bobbing his nose up and down as he crunched it thoughtfully between his teeth, then nuzzled my bare arm gently, getting orange slobber all over it.

I rested my head against his for just a second and then turned to find Jeremy watching me with a strange expression on his face.

"What?" I said, a little defensively, wondering if he was one of those guys who believed that horses were working animals and not pets.

"Nothing." He shook his head as if to clear it. "You've taken a shine to Chilly, have you?"

"Yes, I guess so. He's a good soul."

Jeremy nodded and made a waving motion towards the front of the barn.

"Well, if you're all ready then let's eat."

The walk up to Lorne's house was silent and a bit awkward. Neither of us seemed to know what to say without the distraction of the horses around us so I was glad when we finally reached the little house perched halfway up the hillside.

"Maisy," Lorne said as soon as we stepped inside, "good to see you. Thanks for coming. The food is all ready so let's get started."

I sniffed the air appreciatively, my mouth watering at the good smells coming from the kitchen.

"Okay, I'll just wash my hands and then be right there."

I followed Lorne's directions to the guest bathroom and scrubbed the orange slobber off my arms and the dirt from under my nails as best as I could. I plucked a few stray bits of hay out of my hair and then decided it was good enough.

"Wow, this looks fantastic. You made all this?" I said, staring down at the platters of food laid out like it was thanksgiving supper or something. There was enough food to feed an army.

"Ah, well I'd like to lie and tell you that I'm a top chef," Lorne said, smiling at me, "but we just ordered it in tonight from one of our local restaurants. I didn't know what you'd like so I ordered a few different things."

"Oh, thank you, but you didn't have to do that. I eat anything."

"Well, Jeremy and I pretty much live on left overs and take-out when Julie isn't cooking for us so we'll have plenty to tide us over this week. Go on, help yourself. There's wine too, if you like."

I must have made a face because Jeremy came to my rescue.

"We have juice and pop, too. I like the sparkling grapefruit myself."

"That sounds great, thanks." I picked up a plate from the end of the table, eyeing up the food to see if there was any way I could fit a bit of everything on it. I'd barely eaten anything but crackers and sandwiches for the last week and my stomach was rumbling at the sight of so much actual food set out in front of it.

"Load up," Lorne said, laughing at the expression on my face. "And you're welcome to come back for seconds. You look like you could use some fattening up. Get some meat on those bones."

Why do old people always feel the need to comment on a person's weight? I thought, barely resisting rolling my eyes. I'd been to so many riding clinics where the teacher would be screaming at people for being too fat or too thin or having too much boob. As if those things were something you could change in an hour-long lesson. How about some useful advice instead?

Still, seconds and thirds sounded like a great idea. I loaded up with steak and baked potatoes and asparagus dripping in hollandaise sauce and made a vow to come back for the rest.

Since the table was full of serving trays, I followed Lorne into the cozy living room, stopping to admire the view from the huge picture window that looked down over the stable and across the fields beyond, right to the mountains.

"I bet you never get tired of looking at this," I said, sitting down next to Jeremy on the couch since that was the only free space left in the little living room. Lorne had settled into the reclining chair in the corner and the other couch was full of unfolded laundry and bits of tack. They had quite the bachelor pad vibe going on here.

I listened politely as they talked together about the farm and the new horses who had arrived just the week before. Now and then they looked over at me, trying to include me in the conversation, but I was happy just shovelling as much food in as I could, undisturbed.

This was the first real meal I'd had since Titan had died and I practically hoovered the plate down in one go. And then went back for seconds.

Gradually, any awkwardness I'd felt faded away and I leaned back against the couch, feeling relaxed and content for the first time in a while.

October Horses certainly was a very peaceful place.

"I'll get dessert," Jeremy said, taking my plate, and Lorne's, from us and disappearing into the kitchen.

'Do you need any help?" I called but he didn't answer.

"So," Lorne said, kicking out the foot rest on his recliner chair so he could get a little more comfortable. "You've probably seen how we're short a rider or two. You guessed why I asked you here."

"Not for my great company?" I raised an eyebrow at him.

"Well, that too, of course." He grinned at me and shook his head. Then he sat up a little straighter, looking more serious. "Did Bree tell you about how she and I met?"

"Uh, no." I broke off as Jeremy came back into the room, handing out plates loaded with oversized slices of black forest cake.

Lorne looked down at his cake for a long minute and then set the plate carefully down on the table beside him with a sigh.

"Bree was in palliative care with my late wife, Gretta. They shared a room. Gretta took a shine to her right away.

"She'd always say, 'there's something special about that girl, Lorne. I think she has more living to do yet'. Neither of them was expected to make it, you see. And then Bree died."

"Wait, what?" I set my fork down with a clatter.

"That's right, she died. They managed to bring her back though, just in the nick of time. Everyone said it was a miracle."

He paused for so long, I wasn't sure if he was finished with his story or not.

"When she woke up again, something had changed. She started to get better. She started to live. Gretta was so happy. She would say, 'Lorne, that girl is going to make a difference in the world and it's up to you to help her'."

Jeremy glanced over at me and smiled. I guessed he'd heard this story before.

"This project was my wife's dream that she passed on to me and Bree. It's her legacy that she left us. But it's more than that, too. The horses bring people together, strangers together. We become family here. A team. Do you understand?"

His eyes watered up with emotion and I realized for the first time just how elderly and fragile he was.

He must miss his wife so much, I thought.

"What Lorne means," Jeremy said quickly, "is that we're short-staffed right now. Chloe will be off her feet for a while and Adie won't be back for a few weeks. We have shows booked for almost every weekend for the rest of the summer and fall. We'll be hard-pressed to pull it all off without some more help."

"And you want me to be that help?"

Jeremy shrugged and then nodded. "If you're not doing anything else, then yes. You could pick up a few rides but also help out around the barn. You live nearby so it would be easy for you to hop down here."

I took a bite of cake, pretending to think it over. I'd already decided to say yes, even if it was just for a month or so. The idea of waking up every single morning just to walk aimlessly around my empty house was terrifying. And even though I'd never be able to replace the bond I'd had with Titan, I still didn't want to give up riding. It was what kept me sane most of the time.

"I'll do it," I said. "I can ride and help in the barn. Whatever you need."

"Excellent!" Lorne rubbed his hands together like I'd fallen for an evil plot or something. "Then I guess we should talk about Dragon."

"What about her?" I said cautiously, suddenly on guard. Out of all the horses, that was the one I didn't like. She was pushy and demanding. But she was also huge and powerful. Not my favourite combination.

"Well, we have a bit of a situation," Lorne said, rubbing a hand across his forehead.

"It wouldn't be a situation if you didn't cater to that girl." Jeremy stood up and took my plate abruptly out of my hands even though there was still a nice blob of icing left to scrape up. I'd saved it for the last bite. "It's your farm, Lorne, not hers."

"Yes, yes, I know." Lorne frowned. "But Chloe has been here since the beginning. Since before there was even an October Horses. She rode Dragon for me when nobody else would. And they have a connection. I feel like I need to at least respect her opinion on what the mare needs."

"Why doesn't she want Jeremy to ride Dragon?" I asked bluntly. There was no point skirting around it; if the mare was dangerous or Jeremy was a jerk to the horses or something then I wanted to know it up front.

"Chloe has an irrational hatred of me," Jeremy said, not looking particularly bothered about it. "She thinks we're in some sort of competition here. And normally I wouldn't care. I'd just say she's acting like a silly teenager. But, in this case, she's blinded about what that horse needs."

"Oh," I said, a little taken aback.

"Chloe feels that Dragon needs a different type of rider than Jeremy. She thinks he'd be too firm with the mare. I don't agree with her. Jeremy is an excellent rider. But I'm willing to humour her a bit in this situation since she's been through so much lately. And because she feels very protective over Dragon."

"You really think she'll want me to ride her instead?" I asked skeptically. "She didn't seem like my biggest fan when I met her earlier."

"Yes," Lorne sighed, "she does get some strange ideas in that head of hers. But in this case, we don't have many options. It's either you or Jeremy, and she's made it clear that she'd prefer it not to be Jeremy."

"I suppose I can try the horse if she's not dangerous," I said slowly. "As long as I don't have to jump her or anything. And as long as I'm not stepping on your toes by taking your ride, Jeremy."

Jeremy opened his mouth to answer but Lorne cut him off.

"Dragon is strong," he said, "and she needs a bit of finessing. You have to make her think that all your aids are her decision.

She's hard work but she's also a great ride. A powerful, sensitive horse. Chloe loves working with her."

Well, I understood about the power part anyway. You can't move up the levels in dressage without loving the feeling of a powerful horse underneath you. When Titan stretched out into a gallop it was like the whole world shook beneath his feet. It had taken me a long time to learn how to control that power of his though, and he'd been a nice, sweet horse who would have never taken advantage of me. I honestly wasn't sure how that would feel on a horse who didn't want to be told what to do.

"I guess I'm willing to try," I said quietly. "As long as you're certain she's not dangerous."

"Nothing you can't handle," Lorne said, waving a hand dismissively through the air. "And, if she doesn't suit you then Jeremy will ride Dragon and you can pick up another horse to work with. Chloe will just have to be on board with that."

I nodded and then remembered the thing I had planned to ask them.

"You said there were more horses that need to be ridden. Is Chilly one of them?"

"The pinto?" Lorne asked, giving me a strange look.

"Yes. Who rides him normally? I'd like to give him a try if he isn't spoken for."

Lorne and Jeremy exchanged a glance.

"Well," Lorne cleared his throat. "Bree has taken on his rehab for now while Adie is away. He's able to do short rides in the ring and on the trail. But only at the walk."

"Why? What's wrong with him?" I asked, my voice coming out harsher than I'd meant. I hadn't really examined him up close or anything, but he'd looked fine to me.

"He arrived with a pretty significant bowed tendon, unfortunately," Lorne said. "We're not sure what his long-term prognosis is. Although the vet is really happy with his recovery so far. He's back out on turnout and is starting light work. He's not in pain, but we want to make sure that he heals fully."

They both stared at me while I tried to rein in my disappointment. It had never occurred to me that there might be something wrong with Chilly. He seemed healthy. I hadn't thought to look at his legs.

I didn't even know why I cared so much but the fact that I wouldn't be able to work with him filled me with unexplainable sadness that was hard to shake off.

"You know, I think you could work with him if you wanted to," Lorne said finally. "I'm sure Bree wouldn't mind. It wouldn't take much time out of your day and I'm sure he'd like the attention. You just couldn't expect too much of him … he might be a waste of all your talent."

I hesitated.

"You should work with him," Jeremy said encouragingly. "Rehab is interesting and rewarding. And it's good experience if you haven't done it before. Bree has his schedule in the barn and I'm sure she'd be happy to help you out."

"All right," I said, buoyed a little by his encouragement. "As long as it's really okay with everyone, I'd like to give it a shot. I can do my work and ride whatever other horses you need me to as well. I'll stay late if I need to."

Lorne broke out into a wide grin. "Now that's the type of attitude we'd love to have on our team. Welcome aboard, Maisy. Let's have tea."

We had tea and some sugar-coated biscuits, and I half-listened as Lorne filled me in on all the horses they had there and which ones I might be called on to ride.

I nodded in all the right places, but my thoughts had already drifted back to Chilly. I would have to read up on bowed tendon rehab once I was back at home. I'd never dealt with a big injury like that before. It sounded career-ending, but maybe it was just one of those many horse injuries that could be managed.

Maybe I could make a call to Dr. Patel too and see if she had any suggestions. Possibly there were some new sports therapy innovations out there that could be tried.

"Well, I guess we'd better call it a night," Lorne said finally. "Chores start at six, then we have breakfast, and then we ride."

They both looked at me like they were expecting me to argue about the early hour. But, despite what the rumours might say, I was no princess. I was used to getting up before sunrise to do chores.

"Absolutely, I'll be there."

I said goodbye to both of them and reluctantly drove home, already missing the warmth and activity at October Horses.

My headlights cut through the darkness, and a startled family of rabbits shot across the road, scattering in all directions.

I really need a dog, I thought as I stepped into my dark and empty house. I flicked the hall lights on and then the kitchen. Chasing away the shadows as I moved from room to room.

I made a big pot of tea, shook some cookies out onto a plate, and carried everything on a tray to the living room. I turned on the television for company and then pulled out my tablet and settled down on the couch with a blanket. I had a long night of research ahead of me.

It was an hour later that the first phone call came.

I picked it up automatically, even though I didn't recognize the number.

"Hello?" I said, my gaze still fixed on my computer screen.

"We know what you did," the voice hissed in my ear.

I froze and then swallowed hard. I didn't answer. I just waited.

"We know what you did," the voice said again. "And we're going to make you pay."

Then the line went dead.

I sat there for a long time, my heart beating hard. And then I jumped up and did a circuit of the house, making sure all the doors and windows were shut and locked. I turned on all the lights and turned the television volume up, needing to feel that I wasn't alone. Even though I was.

It was going to be a long night.

CHAPTER 21

MAISY

*T*he next morning, the alarm went off at five o clock and I groaned and rolled over, rubbing my tired eyes.

I'd fallen asleep on the couch and there was a crick in my neck.

The night hadn't been all bad. Gradually, my fear had eased, and I'd been able to convince myself that it was just stupid kids playing a prank. They might make some calls and try to bully online, but they weren't going to actually hurt me.

To distract myself, I'd played around on the October Horses' website and then had been sucked down the rabbit hole of reading all of Bree's blogs.

They were actually really good. She'd definitely missed her calling of being a writer. And the pictures she'd included were great, too. I could see exactly why she had so many followers. And I appreciated the work they did with the thoroughbreds a whole lot more.

After all that, I'd done some exhaustive research on bowed tendons. The information had quite honestly been a bit of a mixed bag. Some articles seemed to say that a bowed tendon could be healed in a few months and then never bother a horse again. While others said that recovery could take over a year and the affected leg could never be trusted under hard work no matter how good it felt. I planned to call Dr. Patel as soon as I had a chance and get her thoughts on it. She was a bit of a lameness expert and had a great reputation for fixing things that seemed impossible. I wasn't sure why the October Horses people didn't use her, honestly.

I was still half-asleep when I reached the barn first thing in the morning, oversized travel mug of coffee clutched like a lifeline in my hand.

Julie and Bree were already in the barn feeding and I paused for a moment in the feed room doorway, looking at the grain chart to get an idea of who got what.

"It's a simple system," Julie said, smiling as she swept in behind me carrying three buckets. "Everyone gets soaked alfalfa cubes as a base and then quality minerals and supplements. Is that similar to what Titan ate?"

"Um, he gets … I mean he got… beet pulp and a mix for performance horses. Plus, some joint supplements and his omegas and his ulcer guard."

"Oh, did he have ulcers? He seemed like a pretty laid-back guy."

"Yes, when he showed full-time, the stress of travelling sometimes got to him. He loved being in the ring no matter what. But strange barns and strange horses made him nervous. Sometimes I had to hand feed to get him to eat for the first couple of days."

"Aw, poor guy. They're all so different, aren't they?"

I nodded, thinking again about how much Titan had done for me even when he hadn't always felt like it. Even when he was going through stressful times, he still gave me his all every time he stepped into that arena. He'd been a born performer.

"Here," Julie said, shoving some buckets into my hands. "You can give Ace, Bear, and Chilly their food. Their names are on their doors and their buckets, so just match them up."

"Okay," I went out into the aisle where a sea of eager faces stared back at me expectantly.

I fed Chilly first, smiling when he plunged his nose so deep into the bucket that his nostrils were covered like a hippopotamus. And then I went to figure out who Bear and Ace were.

It was much easier now that I'd read Bree's blogs. I could match some of her stories to their faces and I looked at the plain bay, Ace, with a little more appreciation.

I ferried buckets of food around while Julie mixed them up and Bree went around filling waters.

The horses had already eaten most of their breakfast hay so by the time they were finished their grain it was time to put most of them out on pasture.

"All the seniors can go out in that field behind the barn," Bree said, pointing to the pasture she'd taken me to previously. "And then we'll look at the white board and figure out who will be worked this morning and who this afternoon. Everyone being worked this afternoon will get turned out, too. The morning ones can stay in and eat a little longer. And we always leave someone inside to keep Rory company."

I was surprised at how nice it was doing chores with other people around. I wasn't used to all the laughter and the chatter, but it seemed like the stalls were done in no time, the aisle swept, and the feed room returned to order.

Soon we were all trooping up the hill to the big house at the top.

"No promises on the quality of the breakfast," Julie said, laughing. "I left Chloe in charge and I'm not sure of how reliable she is in the kitchen."

Oh right, I'd forgotten about Chloe. The one person who wasn't thrilled that I was here. I wondered how awkward this was going to be.

But when we stepped inside the cluttered living room and smelled the good, homey scents of coffee, bacon, and eggs, my anxiety melted a little. My stomach rumbled and I put a hand over it to shush it.

"Smells nice," Julie called out and I trailed after them into the kitchen.

"Almost ready." Chloe stood at the counter, her face flushed from the heat of the stove. "I'll just need help carrying it all to the table.

"Maisy, the bathroom is just down the hall there if you want to wash your hands. And then take a seat wherever you like and help yourself. I think Jeremy and Lorne will be joining us soon."

Sure enough, when I came back from scrubbing the dirt out from under my nails, the kitchen table was full. I poured myself a cup of coffee and then slowly went to join them, feeling a little out of place.

Jeremy looked up and pushed out the chair beside him so I could sit down.

"How did you enjoy your first morning? Not too early for you?"

"Nope, I always get up early."

My stomach rumbled again and I fell to filling my plate. The conversation around me swelled as they discussed some horse or another, but I didn't bother to listen until I'd polished off the makeshift egg and bacon sandwich I'd assembled and refilled my coffee cup.

This is two normal meals in a row, I thought, *my stomach could get used to eating like this.*

Finally, the conversation wound around to the morning's chores and the horses that were going to be ridden.

"We'll do Dragon first thing this morning," Julie said and I glanced over at Chloe to see how she was taking it.

She kept her gaze fixed on her plate and plowed determinedly through her food without saying a word. I guessed that I was the lesser of two evils for her.

"And then that will give us an idea of how the rest of the day will go. The rest of the horses will get ridden this morning and then this afternoon will be groundwork for Poppy, Follow, and Jet. Then Bree can go over Chilly's schedule with Maisy."

I looked up in surprise and found Bree grinning at me. She obviously didn't mind that I wanted to help with him.

"He can be ridden at the walk already, right?" I asked.

"Yep, we just started with that. He's allowed to do straight lines only, no sharp turns. He can even do light trail rides. The lower trails around here are all flat so they're perfect for him."

"I still think it's a bit of a waste of your talents." Julie pushed her chair back and went to the coffee maker to refill her mug. "But you're doing us a favour by stepping in to work here so if you want to spend time with him too, then you're welcome to it."

"Thanks," I said, smiling.

Then breakfast was over. We all carried our things to the counter for Chloe to take care of and filed back outside to the barn again.

"Are you excited to ride Dragon?' Bree asked, falling into step with me. "She's a pretty amazing horse. Super powerful and she loves to jump. But the dressage is a different story. Hopefully you can help her with that."

Jeremy turned his head a little, listening in.

"She hates dressage?" I asked slowly. "Why don't you just let her be a jumper then if that's what she likes?"

"Because she's going to be an amazing Eventer," Bree said, "but dressage is part of that so she'll have to come around eventually. Chloe has done a ton of work with her and her attitude has improved a lot."

"Really?" I asked, trying not to sound as skeptical as I felt. How bad had she been in the past if her current attitude was an *improvement?* I hadn't really spent a lot of time with her but every time I looked her way, her ears were pinned or she was pawing or shaking her head or causing some sort of disturbance. She kind of seemed like a bit of a cow, honestly.

"Come on, I'll help you tack up," Jeremy said, "she's a little particular on how her equipment goes on."

Oh great, I thought. *Remind me, why am I getting involved with this horse again?*

I'd thought that everyone was going to tack up their own horses and we'd all school in the ring together but apparently, I was the main event around here and the whole farm was going to come watch me.

Everyone except Chloe, that was. For someone so vocal about who rode her precious darling, she was noticeably absent.

I didn't even get to tack the mare up myself. Bree and Julie had her brushed and her hooves picked in no time. And Jeremy saddled her up, making me pay attention to which hole she liked her girth done to and how tight she liked her noseband.

Everyone talked over each other, showering me with endless advice on how the precious creature liked to be handled. I really couldn't understand why there was so much fuss going on around this horse.

To her credit, Dragon was well behaved during all this. She only made grinchy faces a couple of times, but for the most part she stood still, looking down on her servants like a tolerant queen.

I was sort of impressed by her aloof confidence. She had the air of someone who expected to be treated like royalty and wouldn't tolerate anything less.

"I know it seems like a lot of fuss," Julie said. "But we've come up with some really good tools for managing her. She's not the type of horse you can just use muscle with and hope she'll submit eventually. She can be quite dangerous in the wrong hands."

"Dangerous?" I asked, gulping a little.

"She's big and powerful. She's quick and she can be explosive. But she's not malicious. If you treat her right then she'll do the same for you. Chloe has no problems with her; I'm sure you'll be fine."

"Well, Chloe lets the mare do whatever she wants," Jeremy said, coming up beside me. "That's why Dragon is stuck in her dressage. Sure, she'll jump anything Chloe points her at because she's brave and she loves to jump. But, ask her to do something that she doesn't want and she just says no. It's not doing the mare any favours to let her go along like that."

"Now is not exactly the time for this discussion," Julie said, sending Jeremy a dark glance. "Maisy does not want to pick a fight with this mare today. This is just a trial ride to see how they get along."

You could cut the tension in the air.

"Um, I'm going to go put my boots on," I said, ducking away before things could get any more awkward.

I sat in my car to zip my boots on and took a deep breath, trying to find my inner calm. I was a good rider; I'd been riding my whole life. But I still didn't want to get on a rogue horse who would try to kill me. Everyone was making such a big deal over this that I really didn't want to do it anymore.

I wanted Titan. I wanted him back so badly. I didn't want to be sitting here with these strangers, riding their bad-mannered horses. I was meant to be heading to Europe, my career was supposed to be taking off. I wasn't supposed to be doing ... this.

My eyes stung and I wiped them impatiently and stood up, putting on my helmet and gloves. I took a deep breath and strode toward the ring, steeling myself to get through this next hour. Maybe I'd end up loving the mare. How bad could it be?

All four of them seemed to be having a heated discussion next to the mounting block as I approached but it broke off and everyone turned to me with plastered-on smiles.

"All ready?" Julie beamed at me.

"Yep." I said, pushing back all my conflicted feelings to the darkest corner of my mind. "I'm ready."

CHAPTER 22

MAISY

I strode up to Dragon and ran a firm hand down her shoulder, giving her a reassuring pat. If nobody but Chloe had been riding her all this time then she must feel a bit unsure about having a stranger hop on her.

Titan had never liked when I let other people ride him. It hadn't happened often but once in a while a coach or a clinician would ask to hop on him so they could show me something. And, while I always learned from the experience, it had usually felt kind of wrong, too. Titan would always be tense and worried afterward.

"Good girl," I murmured, tightening the girth a couple of holes, and adjusting the stirrups. If I rode the mare again, I'd use my own saddle as long as it would fit her, but for now this one would do.

Julie was at Dragon's head, holding the cheek piece of the mare's bridle. Lorne was on one side of the mare's shoulder and

Jeremy was on the other. Everyone looked tense and I wondered again why I was doing this. I was no cowgirl.

"When she's working with you, she's a forward and fun ride," Jeremy said, putting a reassuring hand on my boot and giving my ankle a squeeze. "You have nothing to worry about up there. Just ride her like you would a regular horse. You're just up there to assess her, that's all. And if you don't like her, you can hop off."

He kept his face neutral as he said this, but I saw his jaw clench for just a second.

He likes her, I thought, *he wants this ride. He's not afraid of her. She's not a monster.*

That was enough for me to pull myself together. I gathered the reins and mounted up without giving myself a chance to think about it, nosing my feet into the stirrups.

I had about a millisecond to settle myself and then Dragon was off, pushing roughly past Julie and striding forward in a huge rolling walk that actually impressed the heck out of me.

She was a big mare, especially for a thoroughbred, but she felt even bigger from the saddle. It was also like riding on a keg of dynamite; even at the walk I could feel that there was a lot of horse underneath me.

Titan had been powerful but he could be pretty lazy. You had to spend some time waking him up at the start of each ride. This horse was definitely already wide awake and raring to go.

I spent a few minutes walking her around the ring, doing spirals and serpentines.

"That's right," Jeremy said quietly from the rail when I passed him. "Keep her occupied and thinking."

She was surprisingly well-schooled, responding lightly and quickly to my leg. Despite Jeremy's remarks about Chloe spoiling this horse, I had to disagree. Dragon felt like she'd been schooled with a light and educated hand so far.

I asked her for a few short leg yields and a few steps of shoulder-in, encouraging her to bend and supple through the back and shoulders and engage her hocks.

"All right girl, let's see your next gear," I said.

Even though I had worked hard over the years to develop a solid seat, I was still rocked in the saddle when the mare propelled herself forward like a jet engine. Bam, right into an extended trot that nearly launched me upward with each stride.

"Easy," I said out loud, forgetting that I had an audience, "let's just circle here."

I adjusted my seat to glide Dragon into a big, sweeping circle but immediately she pinned her ears and set herself against me. Gone was the light, supple horse of a few minutes ago. Instead, it was like riding a block of unresponsive wood. Rage and irritation marked her every step and she made little muttering noises under her breath, like she was swearing at me in horse language.

"Hey, mare, just relax," I crooned, trying a serpentine instead. She flattened her ears and refused to bend, taking all the curves at sharp angles and curling her neck in to her chest to avoid my light contact. When I shifted my leg ever so slightly to move her hindquarters in, she kicked out with an angry squeal.

"Easy, friend," I said, squashing down the nerves that were threatening to take over. I knew I just needed to be patient with her but the fact that I had minimal control over this powerful, and angry, animal was starting to unnerve me.

"Good, just stay with her and keep gently asking," Julie called, "you're doing everything right, Maisy. She's just testing you. Easy on the reins though, let her stretch down. She curls up like that to avoid the bit."

Letting the reins out just a smidge, I delicately worked my fingers, asking as tactfully as I could for the smallest bit of flex-ion. She flicked her ears back at me and I heard her tail swish rapidly through the air a few times.

But her trot slowed and I felt her energy shift backward, powering through from her hocks.

"Good girl," I said quietly. I let her flow off the circle so we could switch directions, but as soon as she was moving back along the rail, she shot her head up into the air and she slammed her body sideways, nearly mashing my leg against the fence.

"Hey!" I said, giving her a light thump on the side to get her from plowing through my leg aid. It was just a tiny kick, nothing that could have hurt any horse; I'd used way more leg on Titan whenever he was feeling sluggish. But I'd forgotten that I was wearing spurs and it was enough to send that angry mare rocketing forward across the ring, plunging and bucking the whole way.

The noises that were coming out of her would have been enough to terrify anyone. She let out a series of demented grunts and squeals. Then let out two solid bronco bucks before plunging toward the arena fence.

Her bucks were big and mean and had been meant to send me flying. Only the fact that I had a rock-solid core and good balance kept me in the saddle. Barely.

"Whoa," I said firmly as she galloped toward the end of the ring. It was coming up too fast and I had no way to stop her. In a last-ditch effort to save myself I hauled on the left rein with both hands in an effort to slow her down. But it was like pulling on a cement post. There was zero response or any acknowledgement that I was even there. It was like being a passenger on a possessed wooden carousel horse.

I had a split second to decide how I wanted to end this. I could bail off right then, before we hit the fence that I was certain she would try to jump. Maybe I'd hurt myself or break something but at least I would still be alive. The second option was to just stay on board and hope she'd slow down eventually.

Summoning up whatever distant memories of jumping I had from my few years in pony club, I leaned forward and tried to stay out of her way as her hindquarters bunched and she shot forward and upward through the air.

There was a moment where time slowed down and we hung suspended over the fence, my heart soaring with the exhilaration of it all. It was like truly flying.

And then we'd hit the ground with an earth-shattering thud. My feet slipped out of the stirrups and I was knocked against her mane. And Dragon took that opportunity to launch one more rodeo-horse buck. This time I didn't stay on.

The ground came up to meet me way too fast and I hit with a crushing whump that shook every bone in my body and knocked the wind right out of me.

I lay there, flat on my back gasping like a fish, desperate to get air. Dragon's hoof beats pounded away into the distance.

Anxious faces peered down at me, watching me struggle. They were saying things but I couldn't hear. And then Jeremy was there, calmly putting a hand on my shoulder.

"Breathe," he said clearly. And then the air whooshed painfully back into my lungs and I sucked it in greedily, not even embarrassed by the gasping, grunting noises I was making as long as it meant I was breathing again.

"The wind was knocked out of you. That's the worst of it over now," Jeremy said, "Don't move yet, Maisy. Are you hurt anywhere else?"

Everywhere hurt. I was one big ache. But I did a mental check of my body and shook my head in relief. Nothing broken.

"No," I said, sitting up with a groan and letting Jeremy help me to my feet.

"I'm so glad you're okay," Bree said, grabbing my other arm to steady me when I wobbled. "That was a scary fall. I can't believe she did that."

"You had your spurs on," Julie said, not looking pleased. "I told you not to wear them."

Had she said that? I couldn't remember her saying anything like that but they'd all been talking over each other giving me advice. I'd just sort of tuned most of it out.

"Sorry," I said in a quiet voice. "I didn't hear you say that."

Julie made a face and looked away, clearly disappointed in me.

"It looked great at the beginning," Bree said encouragingly, "she was moving so nicely before things went wrong."

"Nicely?" I said incredulously, "she was challenging me every step of the way."

"Well, it didn't look that way to us," Bree said, "you guys looked great. Look, I took a video."

She pulled out her phone and I squinted down at the video of me and Dragon. It did look way better than it had felt. She sure was a nice-looking horse when you weren't on top of her.

I winced as the video ended just as Dragon landed on the other side of the fence, a second before I fell off.

"You jump really well for a dressage rider," Jeremy said, winking at me, "your seat is solid."

"Obviously not solid enough," I said, rubbing my lower back.

"Well, it would have been hard for anyone to ride that last buck. Especially after a jump."

"I suppose you'll want to be done for today," Julie said, sighing. "I guess I'll go find Dragon then while you guys go back to the barn. I hope she didn't break her reins."

I looked at her in surprise, a little resentful of her unsympathetic tone. Her bronc horse had just tried to kill me.

"We shouldn't stand around here anyway," Jeremy said, "you'll just stiffen up if you don't keep moving. And it will be that much worse later."

"Right," I said, wincing a little as I took a few, careful steps. I had the feeling that I would be one big bruise by tomorrow.

Julie gave me a measured look and turned away abruptly, headed in the direction that Dragon had gone.

I watched her retreating back, feeling an angry flush sting my cheeks. She didn't even care that her demented horse had tried to kill me. Somehow the horse's lack of training was my fault.

Jeremy's hand tightened on my arm.

"Don't worry about her. You rode Dragon just fine. She's a particular horse."

"Did you know that was going to happen?" I asked, suddenly suspicious. "You get to ride on her now that I messed it up. It worked out pretty well for you."

He stared down at me in surprise, a look of hurt flashing briefly in his eyes.

"You didn't mess up. And, no, of course not. She's never done anything like that. But I will admit that I knew you wouldn't want to keep riding her, no matter how the ride went today. She's at her worst for flat work. Out on the trails or when she's jumping, she is a totally different horse. It's the memories of how good she *can* be that makes schooling dressage with her more bearable. You would have only gotten to work with her at her most difficult. Not worth it in my opinion."

We walked back to the barn in silence after that, each thinking our own thoughts. Bree had dropped back to match Lorne's slower pace.

And, thankfully, the more I walked the less sore I was. There weren't any sharp pains; just a dull, overall ache that would be fine once I had some aspirin on board.

"Hey, if you're not too sore, we can go on a really short trail ride," Bree said the second we got back to the barn. "I know you wanted to do something with Chilly today. He's so laid back and sensible and he loves the trail. I can take Ace out, too. It will be like a treat for you after that ride on Dragon."

I suppressed a groan. The thought of heaving my aching body into a saddle again sounded like a terrible idea. Still, I *did* want to work with Chilly. And, now that Dragon and I were definitely not a match, Julie might not want to keep me on at the farm. This might be my only chance to try the strange gelding out.

Why do you even want to ride a half-lame horse? I asked myself, but there were no bright answers. All I knew was that I was drawn to him. Just like I'd been drawn to Titan from the second I'd met him.

Chilly was the opposite of everything I'd normally look for in a horse. But it wasn't like I was planning to buy him or anything. I just wanted to see what he was like under saddle because I was curious.

"All right," I said, "let's do it."

CHAPTER 23

MAISY

"Hang on, I'll grab Jet then and come along," Jeremy said. "I've worked with him a couple of times in the ring but he could use some trail exposure."

"I think Bear would like to get out to stretch his legs, too," Lorne said and suddenly we were all smiling at each other.

"I know she tried to kill me, but I do hope Dragon didn't hurt herself." I bit my lip anxiously. "Do you think Julie needs any help finding her?'

"Oh no, don't worry about Dragon." Lorne laughed. "She's near indestructible. I trust her to look out for herself. Julie will find her all right. I think she wanted the walk to clear her head."

To get over her disappointment that I am a dud as a bronc rider, I thought glumly.

"Besides, it isn't the first time she's jumped out of the ring. Sometimes she just takes it into her head to do whatever she likes. Poor Chloe has been dragged out of dozens of dressage tests by now. But Dragon hasn't done much bucking before."

"It was the spurs, wasn't it?" I asked quietly.

Lorne shrugged. "Maybe, or maybe she was just having an off day. You didn't do anything drastically wrong, Maisy. It's just one of those things."

I gulped down a couple of aspirins from the medicine cabinet in the tack room, hoping they would kick in sooner rather than later. There was a spot on my lower back that throbbed painfully and my elbows were missing some skin from where I'd skidded across the ground. The bleeding had already stopped though, so I just cleaned them up and didn't bother with band-aids.

Luckily the horses weren't too far away. Bree and I found them grazing halfway down the hillside, their coats shiny in the morning sun.

"Hey, buddy," I said to Chilly. Despite my half-injured state, I was happy to be able to spend some time getting to know this funny horse.

He reached out and nuzzled me gently, staying very still as I buckled on his halter and gingerly led him up the hill. He followed beside me extra-gently, keeping his nose next to my elbow. Every so often he reached out and softly ran his whiskers over my arm.

"Chilly is so well-mannered." I looked over my shoulder to where Bree was following with the ancient looking Bear. "Are all the thoroughbreds like this? Besides Dragon, I mean."

"Most of them have been handled a lot in training and at the track so they have decent ground manners. Sometimes they're pushy when they get here, but most of them are good. Chilly is being extra well-behaved for you, though. I think he likes you."

Smiling, I reached out and ran my hand down the horse's shiny neck. Suddenly the pain in my body didn't seem quite so bad.

"Are you okay brushing him in his stall?" Bree asked when we got back to the barn. "It's easier for Lorne to groom and tack up if Bear is in the cross-ties."

"Of course," I said quickly, leading Chilly to the stall that had his name scrawled on a paper card attached to the door.

He stood there quietly, half-closing his eyes as I carefully brushed him and combed out his mane and tail.

"We need to tidy you up, handsome," I crooned to him, wondering if they'd let me clip his bridle path properly and pull his mane. He would look so much nicer once he wasn't looking so scruffy.

"I've been using this on him because he's built so wide," Jeremy said, putting a flat, forward cut saddle over the stall door. "It's old, though. Are you okay with that?"

"Yep, thanks,' I said, trying not to wrinkle my nose at the brown leather that looked as stiff as a board. If I was invited back to ride again tomorrow, I would definitely be bringing one of my own saddles.

I looked over at Chilly's broad back, considering. Despite being a much smaller horse than Titan in height, he had the same broad back and withers. Titan's saddle might actually fit him really well.

I picked out his feet one by one, leaving the injured leg until last. Then I knelt down beside him to have my first good look at it.

"That looks painful, buddy," I said, running my hands over the slight bulge on the back of his leg. It didn't look as bad as I'd expected but it was still noticeable. I traced my fingers over the tendons, searching for heat or tender areas. The leg was cold to the touch though, and he didn't flinch, even when I prodded it.

Still, if I'd been shopping for horses, I would have never even considered getting on an animal with a leg like that. Luckily, I was just borrowing him.

"Let's see how you feel under saddle, kid," I said, standing up and giving him a pat.

Chilly stood nicely while I tacked him up and adjusted the

stiffened stirrup leathers until they were roughly the right length for me. I hadn't ridden in a close contact saddle for a long time so I was pretty much guessing as to where they were supposed to be.

I waited for Bree and Lorne to get on their horses and then led Chilly to the block and climbed aboard. He turned his head around curiously and sniffed my boot. Then he reached out and grabbed my toe ever so gently between his teeth. It wasn't a bite exactly. More like he was a toddler holding onto my hand … er, boot.

"Hey, Bree," I said, fishing out my phone so I could take a few photos of him being weird. "What is happening here?"

She swivelled around in the saddle and burst out laughing when she saw him.

"I have no idea, he's such a strange character. Adorable, though."

I dislodged my boot gently from between his teeth and I guided him over to stand beside Bree.

The colt let out a snort behind me and I turned to see Jeremy standing on the mounting block, the horse circling around and around him at a quick, excited prance.

"He can't stay still for even a second," I said, laughing.

"He's probably never used a mounting block before or been asked to stand still when his rider gets on." Jeremy said, waiting patiently for the colt to slow down. "They usually just throw the jockeys on board while the horse is on the move. From his perspective he's not doing anything wrong. He'll settle in a second."

He was right, there was a moment there where the colt paused his circling and Jeremy used the gap to spring lightly on board.

"Good lad," Jeremy said, tucking the colt at the back of the line as we headed out.

I inhaled the good country air deeply. All my nerves of the morning vanished. My riding career with Dragon was over. I was off the hook for doing anything else scary. Julie thought I was incompetent so, if they kept me on to ride at all, then I'd get to ride Chilly and the less lethal horses. Boring but at least I'd be alive.

Despite my bruises, a feeling of happiness settled over me.

I reached down and scratched Chilly's neck, surprised at how good I felt up there, even in the painfully stiff saddle. Despite his small size, he had a nice, free-moving stride and he felt pretty balanced. It was funny looking down at his black and white mane. Like he was two horses mixed into one.

Lorne and Bear moved at glacial speed so pretty soon they fell behind us and then so did Bree on Ace who had a much shorter stride than either Chilly or Jeremy's horse, Jet.

Jet moved up ahead, his ears pricked and his eyes bugging out like he'd never been out in nature in all his life. Maybe he hadn't.

Chilly was excited but he never even tried to break from a walk. I hoped that was just because of his good temperament and not because he was too sore to do anything else.

Birds sang in the air, leather creaked, and the thudding footfalls of the horses sort of settled into my soul. I couldn't remember the last time I'd even been on a trail ride. Titan hadn't loved being in the woods. He had been much happier working in an arena. So, I hadn't had too many opportunities to do this.

Ahead of me, Jet ran out of steam abruptly and Jeremy dropped back to ride beside us, his knee nearly touching mine on the narrow trail.

"How are you feeling?" he asked.

"Sore but I'll live. I think Julie's going to fire me on my first day, though. I hope she's found Dragon. I know the mare tried to kill me, but I don't want her to get hurt."

"She won't," he said confidently. "And even if you're not a match for Dragon, there are lots of other horses to ride. Julie's not likely to fire you when there is so much work to do here. I have outside clients too, so we're pretty short-staffed."

"These guys are okay with you taking outside clients when there's so much work to do here?"

"Sure, my last project horse here sold, and Chloe refused to give up her ride on Dragon. So, Lorne said it was fine as long as all my work was done here first. I'd hate to abandon my clients just because Chloe is off for a few months. They're good horses and I came here to ride full time after all."

"Why did you come all the way to Canada, Jeremy? Aren't there any horses in Scotland?"

I grinned at him to show I was teasing.

"Oh, lots. But I like to travel and see the world."

"Fair enough. I was supposed to go to Europe this fall."

"I heard that. I'm sorry for your loss. All of it."

"Thanks," I said quickly, not wanting to linger on sad topics on such a nice day.

"You could still go overseas without a horse, though. Be a tourist. Or be a working student at some stable, like I'm doing here. It's hard work but it's a good way to see new countries and get experience."

"Maybe," I said with a sigh. What I didn't say was that the idea of starting out on the bottom again made me ill. I'd been at the top of my game here; Titan and I had been poised to take the world by storm. I didn't want to start over as a nobody. Being yelled at in foreign languages and breaking in the horses that nobody else wanted to touch.

"I guess it would be better than sticking around here," I admitted suddenly. "At least nobody would know me on the other side of the world. Small towns are the worst when everyone hates you."

He turned to look at me in surprise and I felt my cheeks burning.

Now why on earth had I said something like that?

"Well, I don't think anyone could hate you, Maisy. But I know all about small towns. I grew up in one of those, too. Maybe that's one reason I travelled halfway around the world to ride horses, too. It's hard to shake off people's opinions sometimes."

We rode in silence after that, caught up in our own thoughts, until Bree called up to us that it was time to turn around.

Chilly was only allowed to walk under saddle for a half an hour at a time and Lorne's ancient horse, Bear, really wasn't up to much, either.

"Wait until you see the rest of the trails," Bree said, once we'd turned around and were all bunched together again. "I love exploring the woods around here. It passes right by your house too, you know. We've seen you riding in the ring before."

"That's right," I said, remembering seeing people on horseback trek by from time to time. "I used to go on them all the time when I was a kid. I haven't done much trail riding in the last few years, though. I wish I'd done more while I had the chance."

"Well, you can do lots of it with us," Bree said, "and, maybe one day you'll decide to have another horse at home."

She gave me a quick glance, probably wondering if she'd set me off and I'd start crying again.

"I might," I said slowly, "but it will have to be a different home. My parents are selling."

"What?" They all turned to look at me at once.

"It's no big deal," I lied. "They've done a lot for me over the years, so I can't complain. They invested in Titan and supported me when I was showing and training full time. I owe them a lot."

I spoke as casually as I could but I'm sure nobody missed the slight tremor in my voice.

"But that farm is beautiful," Bree said. "How could they want to leave it?"

"I know. I feel exactly the same way. But they say they want to live in a condo in the city. If you can believe it."

They all shook their heads like living in the city was the worst fate they could imagine. I guessed that country-people were the same all over. The idea of being surrounded by concrete and high rises was horrifying.

When we got back, I was relieved to see Julie in the barn and a completely unrepentant Dragon in her stall eating hay. But I was less happy to see Chloe there beside her. She was propped up on crutches, glowering at me as she brushed her precious mare.

"Is she all right?" Bree asked.

"No damage as far as I can see." Chloe shot me a pointed glare which I ignored. "She's lucky."

She could blame me all she liked for that horse's bad behavior. As long as I didn't have to get on that creature again then that was fine with me. Chloe seemed just as spoiled as Dragon did honestly. They deserved each other as far as I was concerned.

"I've talked to Chloe about what we're going to do next," Julie said, appearing from out of the tack room with a solemn look on her face. "I don't suppose you'd like to give Dragon another shot, would you, Maisy?"

I stared at her in surprise, slightly flattered that she'd even consider asking me to try again. Or that that's what Chloe wanted. Then I shook my head.

"Sorry, no," I said, "she's not the horse for me."

I wasn't a quitter but there had to be something more in it for me to risk my neck on a daily basis. Maybe if she was a Grand Prix dressage horse who had dropped into my lap but not some homicidal rescue horse with a chip on her shoulder. Even though … I thought about those few powerful steps I'd sat on her, that fleeting moment where everything had clicked, and it had felt like I was floating on air. Still, no. Not worth it.

Julie sighed and nodded like she'd expected me to say that. "Fair enough. Jeremy will ride Dragon then; the mare needs to be in steady work. That will leave him Timely, Jet, and Poppy. Plus, his outside clients. So…" Here she sighed again. "He's not going to have time for many barn chores right now. Maisy, it would be incredibly helpful if you could take over his stall cleaning duties and some of the feeding. Bree and I will be there to help you, of course."

"Sure," I said, trying not to sound too unenthusiastic. I was there to work, after all. And it was still better than sitting home alone and moping.

"Since you like Chilly, you can take over his rehab rides for now, although Adie might like to split that chore with you once she gets home. She really likes him. You'll take over all the rides on Nugget until he sells, and maybe you can put some rides on Poppy and Jet too once they've had a few more miles on them. Does this all work for you?"

"Yes, I can do that," I said, a smile taking over when she mentioned Chilly. I didn't even remember who the other three were but, as long as they weren't Dragon then I was okay with that.

"What about Follow?" Bree asked.

Julie shrugged and shook her head. "She needs slow and steady ground work right now. I think you just keep doing what you're doing until Jeremy has more time to work with her."

"Why can't *you* work with her?" Bree asked, fixing her gaze on Julie.

"Bree, you know I don't work with the horses anymore. I gave all that up," Julie said firmly.

"Well, you give lessons, don't you? You train us so why not the horses?"

"Bree …." Julie's voice held a note of warning.

"Or, how about you give one of us lessons on how to do proper ground work. You can teach us how to do it. I'd do that. I want to help Follow."

Julie stared at her, considering.

"Maybe," she said finally. "Let me think about it."

Then she turned to me.

"Well, Maisy, if you're not too battered and sore after your fall then I think we should take Nugget out right now before lunch. The more light work you do today the better your body will feel tomorrow."

"Um, Sure," I said, giving in to the inevitable. I had the feeling I was about to earn my keep.

CHAPTER 24

MAISY

"Have you heard from the lady who wants to adopt Rory?"
I jumped guiltily and spun around to face Bree,
my lack of sleep making me twitchy with nerves.

"Um, not yet." I rubbed a hand across my eyes and stifled a
yawn. "I'll try her again tonight."

I probably *would* have heard from Abigail if I hadn't turned
my phone off. But there were only so many creepy prank calls in
a row I could take.

After the second night of whispered threats and heavy breathing, I'd just shut the thing off and not turned it on again. They
never left messages. If I didn't actually get the calls then I could
almost forget it was happening.

Hopefully Abigail didn't think I'd changed my mind about
Rory and had found a replacement for him or something.

"Oh, she's probably been busy. Everyone gets busy in the
summer," Bree said, looking at me kindly. "I wouldn't worry too

much about it. He can stay until you find something perfect for him."

"Thanks," I said, smiling at her. "That really means a lot. You've been more generous than you needed to be to me. I appreciate how nice you've all been."

Her eyes widened and then she frowned. "You know we're nice to you because we *like* you, right, Maisy? Because you're a good person."

I froze, the breath whooshing out of me. I never knew how to handle compliments like that. Especially when it came from someone who didn't know the real me.

"Um, okay, thanks." I fumbled out the words and then did my usual abrupt change of subject.

The week had flown by. Rory's cut healed steadily and soon, we were able to leave the bandage off for part of the day to let it air out, only putting the dressing back on at night. The wound had granulated in from underneath, and although there was a deep groove into his flesh, the skin was pink and healthy looking with no sign of infection.

He'd even started going out in one of the small front paddocks for a few hours a day, which was a relief to everyone since confinement made him extra bitey.

Bree had taken to slipping him treats and she'd resurrected some of his old tricks when I'd told her what he was capable of.

He could bow again, and say yes and no. She'd even brought home a ball for him to play with.

Rory had fallen completely in love with her. He didn't try and bite her quite as often as he did the rest of us. And for him that was a big compliment.

"You're good with him," I told her. "He's always up to something bratty."

"Nipper was a bit like that when I started riding him," she said, breaking into a smile. "He really lived up to his name and he was always so busy. Now that he's in full work, he's chilled out a lot."

"Makes sense." I smiled back at her, surprised not only that I liked her, but that I was enjoying this conversation. A week ago, I'd felt like I would never smile again and now, here I was, feeling halfway normal.

"I bet you'll miss him when he goes," Bree said.

"Yeah." I looked at Rory's greedy little expression and gulped. "I will miss him. He's been a big part of my life."

"So, do you know what your plans are after the farm is sold?"

"I actually don't have a clue. I have some money in savings but I guess I'll have to get a job eventually."

"You could keep working here," she said eagerly.

"Maybe. I don't really know what I want yet."

Nugget was another thing that was going well in my life.

Despite being somewhat green, he was a kind and predictable sort of horse. There were no secret wells of hidden power in him waiting to be untapped, but there also weren't any homicidal tendencies. He was exactly as advertised: calm, steady, and a bit of a caretaker.

"Somebody will be lucky to have you, kid," I told him as I cooled him out after our ride one morning. "We'll make sure we find the best home for you."

Word that he was for sale had gone up on the website that morning, and Bree had already had a few enquiries about him. I was excited and nervous at the same time. He wasn't my horse, but I'd grown attached to him in the short time I'd been riding him. I definitely cared where he ended up.

I led him outside into the late morning sunshine, sighing happily at how nice and peaceful the day was.

I unclipped him just inside the gate and then, instead of going back to the barn, I followed Nugget down the hill as he wandered off to find his friends, his halter slung over my shoulder. I had Chilly to ride next and normally, I would have left him inside, so I had easy access to him. But the morning had been so nice that I hadn't been able to bring myself to leave him locked inside. It didn't hurt me to do a bit of walking anyway.

"Hey, wait up."

I turned to see Jeremy jogging easily up behind me, holding a halter of his own.

"Mind if I ride with you today?" he asked, grinning at me as he came close.

I hadn't seen much of him during the week. While I was busy doing manual labour, he'd usually done all his rides in the morning here and then headed over to Lauren's in the afternoons.

I'd managed to watch him schooling Dragon a few times, but he mostly took her out on the hills and worked with her out there.

Despite Chloe's dire predictions, Jeremy and the mare seemed to get along fine, although I noticed that he rarely worked her in the ring. The few times I had seen him with her in there, Dragon had looked tense and anxious, her eyes always roving outside the ring as if searching for something. Or someone.

Chloe had kept her distance from both of us, resigning herself to just sending us brooding, resentful glares whenever either of us crossed her path. She'd hobble around doing her chores and then make herself scarce for the rest of the day.

Bree had confided to me that Chloe liked to go down to the barn late at night, after the rest of us had left, and spend an hour or so just hanging out with Dragon in her stall.

"Did you want to ride on your own today?" Jeremy asked.

I shook my head to clear it, realizing that he'd asked me a question.

My head was still foggy from lack of sleep. I'd gotten another phone call around midnight. This time it had just been the sound of heavy breathing and I'd hung up right away. But it had still spooked me. I'd stayed up late, huddled on the couch, too anxious to sleep much while the house creaked around me.

"Sorry, yes, of course. I'd love company. I'm just tired."

The sunlight dappled across his face as he studied me. My stomach gave a little lurch.

He's ... kind of beautiful, I thought and then flushed as if I'd said the words out loud.

"Are you doing okay?" he asked.

"Um, yeah, of course," I said. "Who are you planning to ride?"

"Poppy. This will be her first time out on the trails. I'm hoping that you'll be so taken with her that you'll want to steal the ride from me."

"Me, why?" I laughed at the expression on his face.

"Because I could use one less. And the rest of them are a handful."

"Timeley's not a handful," I said innocently, sending him a sidelong glance.

"Yeah, he's not available," Jeremy said shortly, giving me a look when I started laughing.

"I know that. Just wanted to ruffle your feathers."

"Brat."

"Guilty. Okay, so what is this Poppy like under saddle?"

I'd seen him riding the fine grey mare a few times, but I'd always been too busy to pay attention. I'd never seen her do anything dangerous or dramatic anyway.

"Small. Sensitive. A bit of a princess. But she's a real sweetheart and she learns fast. You can't muscle her around, of course. But you have light hands and a good seat. You'll be fine."

"Julie wasn't exactly thrilled with my hands or my seat," I reminded him, making a face. Last week's disastrous ride on Dragon still smarted.

"Ah, it wasn't that bad. You stayed on for at least ten minutes."

"Thanks for reminding me," I said, laughing a little.

His arm brushed against mine and there was a tiny fizzle of energy between us, just a spark. I had a sudden memory of him carrying me inside my parent's house that drunken night and how I'd cried against his shirt.

I felt my cheeks flush and I cleared my throat, trying to think of something to say.

"You've taken a shine to Chilly, haven't you?" he asked, breaking the silence.

"I have. He's a great horse. It's too bad that we don't know how long his leg will hold up."

"I've seen worse injuries, Maisy. He might stay sound forever."

"For upper-level dressage, though? It can be hard on them."

"Well, no need for him to get that much of an education. He'll suit some nice amateur or be a steady trail horse for someone."

I felt a possessive growl rise up in my throat but managed to suppress it. I had never shared with anyone how much I really liked Chilly. How the horse just did something to my soul. The idea of him going off to live with a stranger made me feel all sorts of angry.

And yet, it would be irresponsible for me to get too attached to him when I wanted so much more in a horse, so much more than his body might be able to do.

I want Titan back, I thought, my insides twisting. *I want my life back.*

I looked up to find Jeremy watching me calmly.

"What?"

He shook his head.

"Not everything has to be so life and death, so black and white, Maisy. Why don't you just enjoy the ride and see what happens?"

I stared at him, wondering what exact part of my crumbling life he was talking about.

"That's not what I do," I said finally. "I make long-term plans and I stick to them. No matter what. I don't like going with the flow. I don't like surprises."

"I get that." He nodded and then suddenly reached out and tucked a stray strand of hair behind my ear.

It was such a sweet, simple gesture. And so unexpected. My heart gave a little lurch and I found my eyes filling with tears although I had no idea why. I had been perfectly happy a few minutes ago. What was wrong with me?

"Hey now," Jeremy said and pulled me into a hug.

"You have to stop being so nice to me," I said in frustration. "This is what happens."

He was so warm and solid that it took me a second longer than it should have to pull away.

"I hate being such a mess. I don't like being out of control."

"You're doing fine," he said reassuringly. "Grief is a funny thing. Just when you think you have everything handled, another wave of it reaches out and crashes into you. It does get better over time, though."

"Does it? I know that Titan was a horse and not a human, but it feels like I've lost a part of myself that I can't get back."

He nodded solemnly. "I have lost good horses, too. It's awful every time. And you're right, you can never get that part of yourself back. Nothing can take their exact place."

"No," I said, sighing a little.

"But you do heal, those wounds scar over, and you'll learn to love something else. Not to replace Titan, but to go alongside him, if that makes sense."

"It does, I get that. Thanks."

"Now, come on. Let's get these beasts saddled up."

CHAPTER 25

MAISY

We rode in the ring first, just to make sure Chilly was feeling sound and Poppy was settled, and then we hit the trail.

I relaxed in the saddle, glad that I'd finally brought my own tack over to use. Titan's saddle and bridle had actually fit Chilly quite well, although I knew that might change as the horse gained muscle and his back developed. If I stayed here much longer then I might have a saddle fitter come and adjust it to him for me.

There was something about these rides in the woods that just made me feel so alive and the world full of promise. The exact opposite of what I felt when I was at home all by myself.

My parents were due back in a few weeks and, as soon as they started checking their social media, they were going to know all about the embarrassing online harassment. My mom had been so upset the last time it had happened. I knew she was going to try and involve lawyers and cease and desist orders again. But I just wanted to forget the whole nightmarish thing was happening.

"Everything all right?" Jeremy asked quietly, and I shook my head to clear it.

"Yeah, just thinking," I said, struggling to smile.

"They didn't look like very happy thoughts. Care to share your troubles?"

"I—" I broke off, my cheeks flushing. He'd already seen me at my worst so it was tempting to just tell him everything that was happening. But then he'd want to see the videos and I'd have to relive the whole mortifying thing all over again. I was better off to just try and deal with it myself.

I shook my head.

"My father is a very strict man," Jeremy said unexpectedly. "My siblings and I grew up in a house of iron-clad rules. And if you broke them, then you'd pay for it."

I turned to him in astonishment, my fingers tightening on Chilly's mane.

"He's not a bad man, not really. But the only thing he knows how to show affection for is my mother and the horses."

"Oh," I said, quietly, "that sounds like a terrible way to grow up."

Jeremy shrugged. "We had a barn full of good horses, so there was that," he said, grinning. "And there was a roof over our head and food on the table. It wasn't all bad."

"Hmm."

"Even when I was young, I would do anything I could to piss him off, to show him that I didn't care about his rules. It wasn't a very smart idea, but it was all I had. I skipped school, I tried drugs, I shoplifted, and sometimes I drank to relieve the pain of his constant anger and disappointment in me."

"Oh. What did your siblings do? Did they rebel, too?"

"In their own way, I suppose they did." Jeremy shook his head ruefully. "Only they weren't so obvious about it. And with me as the black sheep of the family, I probably kept him distracted. Until finally, he had enough, and he kicked me out. Permanently."

"What do you mean permanently?"

"Exactly that. I ended up with a bad crowd and there was a break-in that I was part of. I was sent to jail for a few days. My dad bailed me out, but after that he banished me from the family. Said I could never step foot on the farm again. Took away my inheritance and wrote me out of the will. Said I was on my own. He told my mother and my siblings that I was dead to them and they should never speak to me or of me again."

"No way," I said in shock, "that's horrible. You were just a teenager. Did they listen to him?"

"No. I talk to them all the time on the phone and through email. But it's not the same as being able to visit. I've only been back one time, just before I came here actually, and it didn't go well."

"Jeremy, that's awful," I said. "I'm sorry that happened to you."

"Well, I had my own part to play in it. I could have used my anger for less destructive things. I'm not proud of the person I was back then. And I've spent my life after that moment trying to be a better person."

"I think you're a great person," I said firmly. "Why are you telling me all this, though?"

"Because a burden shared is a burden halved," he said. "When you let people in, Maisy, they can help you. You don't have to face the whole world alone."

Heat flushed my face and I looked away.

"Thank you," I said stiffly, "but I'm fine. Really. My problems are nothing as dramatic as yours. I'll figure it all out eventually."

"That's fine," he said, not sounding bothered at all. "You know where to find me if you need me. And Bree, and Lorne and Julie. We're all in your corner, Maisy."

I kept my gaze fixed on the ground, my thoughts churning. That was probably the nicest thing anyone had ever said to me.

"Thank you," I said again, but this time I meant it. "I'll ... I'll keep it in mind."

The rest of our ride was much more peaceful. Something had shifted between us; our friendship had deepened and we rode in comfortable silence.

We meandered through the woods, Chilly on a loose rein with his head bobbing back and forth in a steady rhythm. And Poppy stepping lightly with her ears pricked and her eyes wide.

I had to admit that she was a very pretty horse. She had delicate, refined features and large dark eyes framed by lighter lashes. Her coat was dark silver and her mane and tail were a few shades lighter.

She wasn't exactly a powerhouse; she minced along, giving tree branches, shrubbery and tufts of grass a large berth like she was afraid of them touching her. I could see why Jeremy had called her a princess. She looked like she wanted to avoid getting her shiny coat dirty at all costs.

Still, I liked her quite a bit and I thought it would be fun to ride her now and then when Jeremy was too busy.

When we got back the barn, Julie was waiting for us.

She had her arms crossed over her chest and her head tilted to one side. She was staring at Chilly like she was analyzing all his parts.

"Um, do you think we're in trouble?" I whispered to Jeremy as we came closer to the barn.

"No." He laughed. "That's just her thinking face. You haven't seen her mad face yet. It's quite something."

We both jumped down and I managed to smile at Julie as I tried to lead Chilly past.

"Hold up," she said in a quiet voice. "I'd like to see how he's doing. He holding up okay on the trail rides?"

"Yes, he's doing great," I said in surprise. "He hasn't seemed lame at all yet."

"Good." She knelt down beside his injured leg and ran her hands gently downward. She prodded the back of his leg from his knee to his coronet band, checking carefully for heat, swelling or any painful areas.

"It feels good," she said finally. "I'm glad he's able to get out and enjoy some work. He hated being stuck inside for a month on stall rest.

"I was doing a bit of reading," I said slowly, clearing my throat, "and it said that a month of stall rest really isn't that long when you're dealing with a bowed tendon. Your vet said it was okay to turn him out early?"

"Yep. We were given the green light to go ahead. We started out putting him in one of the small paddocks and then graduated to the pasture. He's not a silly horse so we weren't too worried about him tearing around out there."

But anything could have happened while he was running around unsupervised, I thought, *he could have undone all that healing. I wonder if their vet even knows anything about lameness.*

"Titan pulled a ligament once," I said, treading as carefully as I could. Julie was easily offended. I didn't want to put her off by saying the wrong thing. "We did shock wave therapy on him to help with the healing."

"Really?" She asked. And at least she sounded interested rather than defensive. "Where did you have to take him to do that?"

"My vet, Dr. Patel, has a machine that she brings with her. She can do it right at the barn."

"Oh, well now that's interesting. Any idea how much it is?"

"No, but I can find out," I said quickly, hardly able to believe this conversation was going so well. "I was thinking that it might help Chilly recover better. I can pay for it …"

I broke off as she held up her hand.

"Let's just take it one step at a time. Find out the price for me and we'll go from there."

"All right," I said quickly. "Um, also, we had Titan on some supplements that I think could help. I have some left over. I could bring them for Chilly, if you like."

"Hmm," she said, shooting me a look that I couldn't interpret. "Sure, you can bring them down and I'll take a look. Get the prices on them, too. We'd have to make sure it was something we could sustain long-term once the jar ran out."

"I wouldn't mind paying for them if they helped."

"Why?" She stood up, gave Chilly a pat on the shoulder, and stared at me.

"What do you mean, why? Because it might heal him and make him feel better."

"But why do you care about him specifically?"

"I …" I looked over at him and shrugged. "I don't know. Just because I do. I like him."

"Not the best answer, Maisy."

I huffed out an irritated breath. What did she want me to say? That he was the only thing keeping me together right now? That the stress of losing Titan and being bullied had nearly broken me and it was only Chilly that kept me from going off the deep end?

Maybe that was exactly what she wanted me to say but I wasn't going to do it.

"I guess part of me wants something to take care of," I said, settling for a half-truth. "My whole life revolved around Titan. I'm a little lost without him."

That was the understatement of the year.

"So, this is kind of like a rebound relationship," she said, raising an eyebrow.

No, not like that at all.

"I suppose," I said, struggling to sound like I didn't care too much. Like this didn't mean anything to me. "But I'd like to help him."

"Sure." She shrugged. "Fill your boots. We can use all the help we can get around here. Just … don't get too attached, Maisy."

"Why?" I asked sharply, wondering why on earth she'd say something like that.

"Because he might not heal in the way you think. I'd hate for you set your expectations too high and get hurt. Trust me, I've been there."

I looked at her in surprise. She sounded almost *worried* about me.

"Some hope is better than nothing," I said. "I just want to give him a chance."

"Well, we're on the same page then it sounds like. Better get him untacked and put back out on pasture. Lots more chores to get done."

She turned her back and walked out of the barn without a backward glance.

CHAPTER 26

BREE

I picked up the phone, dialing the number carefully, tapping my finger nervously on my knee.

"You've got Howard," the man's thick accent was barely understandable. "Leave a message."

"Um, hi. I'm calling about a filly we have here at the October Horse's project. Her name is FollowTheMoney. I'm hoping to ask you some questions about her if possible. I'd really appreciate a call back."

I left my number and then hung up, feeling a little let down after I'd geared myself up to make the call.

I went downstairs to make myself some lunch and was so caught up in my thoughts that I nearly tripped on the next step when the phone in my pocket began to ring.

"Hello?" I said, sitting down on the staircase to avoid any more slipping. "Bree here."

"Hi, Bree," a woman's breathless voice said, "this is Roxanne, Howard's daughter. You called about the filly?"

"Oh yes, Follow. Thanks so much for calling me back. I just had some questions about her if that's okay."

"Of course. Did you say she's in Canada now? At some sort of rescue?" Her accent was not nearly as thick as her father's.

"It's more like a retraining center," I said quickly. "We are in Canada, on Vancouver Island."

"Well, that's clear on the other side of the continent. She did some travelling."

"She came up from California this spring with some other young horses."

"Was she injured? Is that why she came there?"

"No, physically, she's fine. But mentally, she's not doing so well. I mean, she's much better than she was when she first arrived, but she's still scared of almost everything. I'm just trying to get creative on how to help her out."

"Aw, that's a real shame. She was a nice filly. I remember her. Quiet and very responsive. She wasn't the most confident youngster we had but she wasn't fearful."

"Did she get started under saddle at your place?"

"No, we held her back a bit longer because she was so small. She went to a sale and that's the last we heard of her."

"Okay, well thank you so much for your time. That gives me a place to start anyway. The guy who had her before she came here said he couldn't do anything at all with her because she was so terrified. He didn't have her long.

"And I couldn't find a phone number for her previous trainer, but I sent him an email. I haven't heard back, though."

"Oh, but that was Benny Sykes who had her, wasn't it?"

"Yes, that's the name."

"Sorry, he's dead. That happened last year. There was a big scandal. He had some sort of illegal lab set up in part of the barn and it blew up. There was a huge explosion and he died in it along with a few grooms. They lost some horses, too."

"You're kidding. Was that when Follow was there?"

"Sorry, honey, I have no idea. I'm going to say it happened about a year ago, though. It was all over the news. You should be able to check out the dates easily enough."

"Oh, thank you," I said, "thank you so much."

"You're welcome. Best of luck with her."

The line went dead and I sat there a minute, thinking hard. Then I ran back upstairs to grab my laptop.

An hour later, Nicholas found me in the kitchen staring at the screen, pages filled with notes scattered around me.

"What are you working on?" he asked, making me jump.

I'd been so fixed on what I was reading that I hadn't even heard him come in.

"Follow," I said, waving at the website on the screen. "She was in an explosion."

"What am I looking at?" he asked, pulling up a chair beside me.

"Her trainer at the time, this sketchy guy named Benny, was secretly cooking meth out of his office at the track. He had this sideline going where he trafficked drugs when he was travelling to different races.

"But something went wrong with his miniature laboratory there and there was a huge explosion that took out a whole section of the barn. Benny was killed and some grooms were badly hurt. And a few horses were killed and injured, too."

"That's terrible. So, Follow was hurt in the explosion?"

"Not hurt, no. But she was trapped. Part of the barn collapsed and she was pinned into this tiny corner of her stall for over two days. It wasn't safe enough to go get her out until they'd cleared away some of the wreckage. They didn't even know if she would be alive by the time they got there. But physically, she was fine."

I paused, thinking of the terror that Follow must have felt as she was stuck in that tight space, not able to move. Hearing the sounds of the other horses that had been injured and the sound of the heavy equipment as they pulled debris out of the barn. She must have been out of her mind with fear.

"They sold her shortly after that," I went on. "And Eddie's group bought her as part of a group sale. But the new trainer said that she was a wreck when she got to him and that they couldn't get her to settle down no matter what. They should have turned her out to have a chance to decompress, but—"

"She was an investment," Nicholas finished, "she had a job to do."

"And when that didn't work, then she came here."

"Luckily for her, she did."

"Yeah, kind of. But I'm still not sure what all this information means to what we do with her next."

"Maybe just compassion to give her all the time she needs," Nicholas said. "She was a good horse once. She raced successfully before the accident. Just have faith in her that she can be that horse again."

I looked up at him in surprise.

"Yeah, I think you're right. We need to trust the process and just give her time and not rush her."

"When are you going to realize that I'm always right?" Nicholas reached over to tug gently on my pony-tail. "I'm brilliant."

"Oh wow, and modest."

"And really good looking," he said, winking at me.

"Well, you have me there …" My gaze drifted back to the screen as I thought about Follow's story.

"Uh oh, I know that look. You're plotting something. That's the look you get when you're about to get lost in writing for the next four hours."

"Her story would make a great entry for my next blog," I said dreamily, words and paragraphs already falling into place in my head. I reached out and pulled my laptop toward me.

"And, that is my cue to leave," Nicholas said, scooting his chair back.

"Oh, you don't have to go. I can do this later. It's your day off and we should do something together. I can write any time."

I couldn't help but send a quick, longing glance at the screen.

Laughing, Nicholas wrapped his arms around me and kissed the top of my head.

"The words are calling, Bree," he whispered in a dramatic voice, "you can't ignore the calling."

"Oh, for heaven's sake," I said, making a face at him, but he was already walking out of the room.

"Hey." He stuck his head back in the door. "You don't mind if I run out this afternoon for a meeting with the other summer interns, do you? Bertie wants us all to get together to go over some things."

"Of course not, go have fun."

He hesitated in the doorway, running a hand across his jaw.

"Right, well, you could come along, if you like. You could meet the team."

"Um." My gaze flicked back to the screen in front of me. I really wanted to work on this. "Could I go next time instead?"

"Sure, this one will probably be boring anyway. Bertie wants to organize a team-building bowling party next time. Or maybe some axe throwing."

I suppressed a groan. I was the most unathletic person on the planet. Letting me loose in a bowling alley or with a sharp axe didn't sound very safe. I didn't know who this Bertie guy was but I already didn't like him.

"Sounds great," I lied. Oh, the things we did to be supportive of our partners.

CHAPTER 27

MAISY

*T*he day Rory left came sooner than I was prepared for.
I'd finally turned on my phone and called Abigail.
And we'd arranged for her to pick him up a few days later.

Rory's wound was nearly healed. He'd still have to take it easy
for a while but at least he didn't need his bandages changed twice
a day.

I liked Abigail. She was a friend of my parents and she'd
always seemed like a nice, down to earth person. But I couldn't
help but feel a little resentful when she'd come to pick up my
pony.

This wasn't supposed to be how it happened. Titan and I were
supposed be in Europe and Rory was just to be a short-term loan
to her. Not permanent. Not that I'd never have him in my life
again.

"It's so good to see you," Abigail said, wrapping me in a tight
hug. "I was devastated to hear about Titan. You were such a good

team. Thank you so much for sending your nice pony to keep my Destiny entertained. I know they'll love each other."

I was disarmed instantly by her genuine expression and her hug.

"You'll take good care of him?" I whispered, even though I knew she would.

"The best. I got your email, so I know all about his feed and his routine."

"Don't forget that he likes to bite."

"Oh, I won't forget that. I've met him before so I'm up on his tricks."

"Yeah, well, he probably has a few hidden ones he's saved for you."

She laughed and hugged me again.

"I don't doubt it. Well, the trailer's all ready. Do you want to load him up?"

"I'll go get him. I just want to say a quick goodbye."

My feet felt like lead as I walked back into the barn where he was waiting.

He stared at me with his ears pricked and his little top lip wiggling in the air like it was waiting to latch onto something.

"You be a good boy for Abigail, okay? Not too much biting."

His ears flattened back when I kissed his forehead and then he nickered when I reached into my pocket for the last piece of carrot I'd hidden there.

"Thanks for always being you, buddy." I told him. And that was the truth. He'd been unapologetically cranky, opinionated, and stubborn his entire life. But he'd always kept me laughing. And he'd been a great friend and partner when I was little. Once he'd stopped trying to kill me, that was. I was honestly going to miss him.

His little feet clopped beside me as we headed down the aisle toward the trailer.

"Thanks for giving him a great home," I told Abigail, handing her the lead rope.

"You bet," she said, "and you know you can come visit him anytime. My door is always open."

"Thanks."

I took a deep breath as she led Rory up the ramp and secured him in place. It was the right decision. He was going to have a great life at Abigail's farm. He'd be spoiled and treated like royalty.

Still, it hurt. Tears stung my eyes as the trailer drove away.

"Bye, Rory," I whispered. "I'll miss you."

He let out one piercing neigh as he drove away and I had to turn back quickly toward the barn before I lost it.

When I went back inside, I found Jeremy tacking up Dragon.

"You fancy a trail ride?" he asked, taking in my glum expression.

I looked over to where Chilly was already inside his stall, working on some hay.

"You brought him in for me," I said in surprise. "How did you know I'd say yes?"

"Just a hunch. That horse is good medicine for you."

"Oh, really?" I didn't think Jeremy had known me long enough to know what was good for me. But, in this case he was actually right. Chilly did something for my soul, that was for sure. I just didn't know what it was.

We took our time grooming and tacking up and then leisurely hit the trail, letting the horses walk on a loose rein.

Dragon looked more relaxed than I'd ever seen her. She seemed almost sleepy.

"What's with her? Did you drug her or something?"

"Of course not. This is what she's like in full work. She doesn't like sitting idle."

I looked at her skeptically. No way would I trust riding her on a loose rein like that. As far as I was concerned, she was completely untrustworthy.

"You like bringing these young horses along, don't you?"

He looked at me, considering.

"I do. There is something special about the youngsters. Life off the track is still brand new for them. It's nice to watch them discover the world."

I nodded and reached down to scratch the top of Chilly's withers in front of the saddle.

"Are you looking forward to the Event this weekend?"

"I am. You're still going to ride Poppy for me and lunge Jet, right?"

"Yep. Are you going to give me any pointers on riding her before you go, though?"

"Better than that. You're going to ride her this afternoon for me. She's not tricky once she trusts you. But she's sensitive."

"Oh, great, not another sensitive mare. Why can't they all be like Chilly or Titan? Nice, sensible boys that don't get upset by stupid things."

"Didn't you say that you couldn't take Titan on the trail because he was afraid of wildlife?"

"Nature. He was afraid of nature. He preferred to stay in the ring. But, good point. He did have his prima-donna moments."

"Well, Poppy is all princess. All you have to do is remember that and treat her according to her station."

I laughed and shook my head.

It was nice to be able to just relax and enjoy myself for an hour, forgetting about the phone calls or the videos. Forgetting about Rory or the dark things that had tinged my life.

We joked and talked all the way back to the barn, avoiding any serious topics.

But when I saw Chloe glaring at us from the open doorway, the nerves in my stomach began to jangle again.

The fact that someone I barely knew could hate me this badly sent alarm bells clanging in my head.

"Don't worry about her," Jeremy said quietly. "She'll get over it."

"Are you sure about that?"

Chloe certainly didn't look like she was going to get over whatever chip she had on her shoulder any time soon. She kept her eyes hungrily fixed on Dragon; her jaw gritted as she watched Jeremy hop lightly to the ground.

No, not the look of someone resigned to losing her horse at all.

CHAPTER 28

MAISY

I was having serious doubts about Poppy by the time I led her to the ring. It turned out that the word *princess* didn't mean that she was mean or bossy. It meant that she had to have *every little thing* her way.

She didn't like the way boots felt on her legs so she had to wear soft polo wraps. She didn't like saddle pads that weren't cotton so she had three special ones set aside for her exclusive use. She got rubs from leather touching her sensitive skin so she had to have special sheepskin protectors wrapped around her nose band and cheek pieces. She didn't like curry combs; only soft goat-hair brushes could be used on her delicate self.

"I know it sounds like overkill," Jeremy said when I rolled my eyes. "But she's genuinely a sensitive-skinned horse. And making her comfortable is the difference between a really good ride or a terrible ride where one, or both, of you gets hurt. The choice is yours."

"Fine," I said, sighing dramatically. "Let's go then, Princess."

I had to admit that she looked beautiful all dressed up in my saddle and her matching pink pad and polos that Bree had picked out for her. And, despite her shocking level of high-maintenance, I was looking forward to riding her.

It turned out that I wasn't the only one looking forward to this ride. The ring was full of people who apparently had nothing better to do than watch me work.

Julie and Lorne were standing by the mounting block and Bree was pretending to school Ace at the far end, but it was obvious that she was there to watch my ride, too.

"Easy girl, you're okay," I said as the grey mare pranced excitedly beside me. Her little ears swiveled around in all directions and her breath came out in excited snorts. "We don't have to impress anyone."

"That's right," Jeremy said. "This is no big deal."

"Are you sure this is a good idea?" Julie asked skeptically as soon as we drew close.

I gritted my teeth, annoyed that she thought I couldn't handle this mare as well as Jeremy could. Why was she forever doubting me?

"She's fine," Lorne said, waving his arm in the air, making the filly skitter sideways a few steps.

Taking a deep breath and keeping my body as free of tension as I could, I tightened the filly's girth one last hole and ran down my stirrups. Then I gently put the reins over her head, mindful of not touching her ears which was yet another thing she hated, and stroked her neck gently.

"We've got this, mare," I said to her quietly, and was rewarded by her heaving out a deep breath and dropping her head to sniff at my boot. Both good signs that she was relaxing a little.

I led her to the block and took my time, waiting for her to settle before I climbed lightly on board.

She stood nicely while I nosed my feet into the stirrups and let her walk out on a loose rein.

She wasn't Dragon. She wasn't going to take advantage of a loose rein by pitching me off.

From the direction of the barn, something loud rattled, like a bucket dropping on the floor.

"That's just Chloe cleaning out the feed room," I told the mare soothingly when her head shot up and she took a few anxious trot steps. "She's loud, isn't she?"

Poppy huffed out a breath, her eyes fixed anxiously on the barn and then turned to look at Ace who was ambling around in a circle at the top of the ring.

"See, he's not worried."

"Maisy, come let her trot down at this end for now. She'll settle faster if she can move out a bit and get rid of some of that adrenaline," Lorne called.

Breathing deep, I let the mare flow forward. For a second her nose was up in the air, her back hollow, her hind legs trailing out behind. And then she found her balance and her nose dropped. I could feel her hind legs propelling us along at a ridiculous speed, her hocks snapping like pistons.

I couldn't help grinning at the feel of her underneath me. She was way more powerful than she looked. Her stride wasn't short and choppy like I'd expected, instead, it was long and, despite her low head carriage, she moved uphill in a way that was exhilarating.

"That's her sweet spot," Jeremy called, "let her stay there."

Which was easier said than done. The mare looked up, lost the rhythm and her legs flailed in all directions, nose stuck in the air again.

"Balance her with your seat," Lorne said.

"I know," I growled at him, "give me a second." But my slight loss of temper caused the mare to brace and toss her head. I snapped my focus back on her, making sure to breathe deep and relax my seat, stabilizing her from my core.

She found the flow again, stretching her neck down until I

could just see her ears. I grinned, easing the reins out so she could fully stretch down.

"Good girl," I crooned, loving every step of this ride. By then, I was holding the rein nearly at the buckle. So, when a loud crashing sound came from the direction of the barn, I was completely unprepared. I had zero warning before the filly bolted.

There wasn't even time to react. I was there one second and the next, the reins had been ripped from my fingers and we were flying around the ring so fast that the wind blurred my vision until I could hardly see.

Out of the corner of my eye, I saw Julie slip Bree and Ace out of the ring and shut the gate firmly behind them.

There was no time to even think about being terrified. I sank my weight deep into the saddle, centering myself, locking my core so that I was as rock-solid as I could be under the circumstances.

It was like time slowed down. Dimly, I could hear Lorne and Jeremy yelling something, but I couldn't make out the words. There was nothing I could do but wait this out anyway. The filly would stop. Or she wouldn't.

I would survive this. Or I wouldn't. A feeling of calm settled over me, even when the filly banked so hard around the corner that I swear my shoulder nearly brushed the sand.

"You're doing good Maisy, just keep it chilly. She's almost done." Lorne's voice broke through my fog.

Keep Chilly? What on earth is he talking about?

I had the sudden, irrational, thought that maybe I should buy Chilly before someone else did. His calm, tranquil presence was exactly what I needed in my life.

The mare beneath me surged around another corner and the cocoon that had surrounded me dissolved and suddenly I could feel my legs shaking, my breath shuddering in and out. I wasn't sure how much strength I had left in me.

"Easy, girl," I said, snapping to my senses. "Such a good girl, such a good filly. Good, Poppy. You had a scare but you're all right now, sweet pea."

Nonsense words poured out of my mouth, but it was working. The filly's ears flicked back to me and then she dropped into a canter, and then a lumpy trot. When she dropped down to a walk again, Lorne and Jeremy were there talking to her in soothing voices. Lorne held the mare's bridle and Jeremy reached up and pulled my trembling body right out of the saddle.

"That was amazing," he said, gripping my arms and peering into my face. His expression was half fear and half admiration.

My hands were shaking so hard that I was afraid if he let go of me, I'd crumple onto the arena floor and never get up again.

"Good job, Maisy," Lorne said, patting my shoulder hard enough to make me sway. "That was some fine riding. You were like ice up there."

"Like ice?" I asked in confusion.

"You know. Stone cold. Ice. You kept it chilly."

I looked at him blankly and he sighed.

"What do they teach kids in school these days? It means that you kept calm, stayed centered, and didn't interfere with your horse. You became a part of her. Many a jockey has survived a wreck by doing that."

"Oh," I said. "Keeping chilly. That's what you were bellowing at me?'

Not to buy Chilly then, I thought, strangely disappointed.

"Well, I resent the word *bellowing* but yes. I was telling you to stay cool. Not that you needed my advice. You did all right up there."

"Why did she bolt, though? She was doing so good." Still using Jeremy's arm for support, I reached over to stroke the filly's steaming neck. She looked exhausted.

"Some noise in the barn scared her," Jeremy said, his eyes

narrowing. "Let's get her cooled out. I'm sorry that was your first ride on her, though. She's actually a good horse."

"No, it wasn't her fault. I let the reins go so that's on me. And, yes, she bolted, but that was it. I was completely at her mercy and she didn't buck or try and launch me off in some nasty way. I'd like to ride her again if you're okay with that. I trust her."

"Well, you can ride anything here you like, Maisy," Lorne said, giving me another forceful pat on the back that made me stumble. "We need to keep you around."

"Good riding," Julie said as we headed out of the ring. Her face was pale and she had one hand clasped tightly around Ace's reins as if he might bolt, too.

"Oh my gosh, Maisy, are you okay?" Bree asked worriedly. "That was so scary."

I nodded at her, too exhausted to say anything else.

We all walked slowly back to the barn together. The mare's breathing steadied and she reached over to itch her sweaty head roughly on Jeremy's arm.

"That's enough out of you, miss," he said, pushing her gently away. "I'll give you a bath in a minute."

In the doorway to the barn, I slid to a stop.

"What in the world?" Lorne said, surveying the mess. Feed buckets lay everywhere, scattered in all directions and there were shovels on the floor and the wheel barrow was tipped over.

Chloe stood in the middle of it all, a small stack of buckets beside her while she vainly tried to scoop up the others while balancing on her crutches.

"I'm so sorry," she said, her face pale and anxious. "I was trying to take them all to be scrubbed out. I dropped them and it made a mess. I'm cleaning it all up right now."

There was a long silence while all of us surveyed the littered aisle in shock.

It was obvious that way more had happened here than a few

dropped buckets. This looked like things had been thrown around in a tantrum. On purpose.

Jeremy must have been thinking something along the same lines because he handed me Poppy's reins and stepped forward with his hands balled into fists at his sides.

"Maisy could have been killed," he said in a low voice. "Poppy was terrified."

"I know." Chloe's face flushed beet red. "It was an accident. I'm really sorry."

She gulped when she turned to face Lorne.

"Chloe." There was such a note of disappointment in his voice that she visibly wilted and her lower lip trembled.

Behind us, Bree and Julie stood silently.

"Okay, okay, well, let's get this cleaned up," I said finally, to break the tension. "Chloe, can you find Poppy's cooler for me? She needs to be walked out. We can clean up this mess."

Chloe sniffed loudly as if she was holding back tears and, with one last look at Lorne, she got her crutches in place and propelled herself into the tack room.

"Maisy, she won't get away with this," Jeremy began but I shook my head.

"We'll deal with this ... whatever this is, later," I said tiredly. "We'll clean this up while you take care of Poppy. I need to get some food into me before I deal with any more drama. I'm going to pass out if I don't eat something soon."

Jeremy huffed out a breath then took Poppy's reins from me and led the mare down to the cross-ties to untack her. She would get a bath and be cooled out properly so she wouldn't be stiff later. Hopefully, she hadn't injured anything with all that galloping.

"I'll go up to the house and make some lunch," Julie said quietly. "Bree, why don't you help me?"

Wordlessly, Lorne and I stacked all the buckets, righted the wheelbarrow, and picked up the shovels. I didn't even know how they'd gotten in here. We always used the plastic pitch forks to clean the stalls, never metal shovels.

At one point, Chloe slipped past us silently, put a cooler near the spot where Poppy was stationed, and then fled outside as fast as a person could on crutches.

"She's a good kid," Lorne said glumly. "She's going through a rough patch."

"I know," I said. "I'm going to talk to her."

He sighed and I glanced over to see him standing there looking lost and disappointed, his shoulders drooping.

"I'm okay, Lorne," I said quietly. "Poppy's okay and nobody got hurt. Chloe already knows what she did was wrong. She'll probably beat herself up over it harder than any of us would."

"I suppose," he said sadly. "I just thought I knew her better than that. She hasn't been right since she left home really. I think that getting kicked out of her house was a shock. But that still doesn't excuse her behaviour."

"I'll talk to her," I said again. "Nicely, I promise."

He smiled and patted my hand.

"You're a good girl, Maisy. We're lucky to have you here."

Then he turned and walked slowly in the direction of the house.

Poppy was none the worse for wear after her bath and a rub-down with liniment. She didn't even seem upset at all. And she was happy to take cookies from my hand and let me lead her out to pasture.

"You were a good girl out there," I told her fondly. "We'll try that again tomorrow, but this time with less drama. Okay?"

I watched carefully as she trotted off to find her friends, but there was no hesitation or shortness in her stride. Tomorrow we would do a nice, easy workout and get to know each other properly.

I was excited to be taking her on as one of my rides now. All three of my projects had completely different personalities and

I was surprised at how fun it was to discover their hidden talents.

We had a good lunch of sandwiches and a cheese, meat, and cracker platter, and divided up some leftover cake between us.

Only Chloe was missing and it wasn't until much later in the day, until it was nearly time to go home, that I caught up with her.

When I went to my truck, Chloe was waiting there for me. She'd parked her car beside me and was sitting in the passenger seat, her leg propped up against the open door.

"Hey," I said casually, taking in her pinched expression and puffy eyes.

"Hey," she said woodenly but then was silent.

I waited for a second and then climbed into my truck. It was up to her to make the first move.

"Maisy, I'm sorry. I never meant for that to happen," she said, her words tumbling over each other. "I was just mad when I saw *him* riding Dragon. But I would never hurt you or Poppy on purpose."

"Are you sure?" I asked quietly. "That wasn't an accident."

She hesitated and tilted her head to one side, thinking.

"Yes," she said finally. "It was Jeremy I was really mad at."

"And Poppy and I were just collateral damage, I guess."

She cringed back and fixed her gaze on the ground. "I was dumb. This rage just fell over me and I wasn't thinking properly anymore. It was a horrible mistake and I'm glad neither of you were hurt."

"Okay." I waited until she looked up to continue. "Apology accepted. Can I ask one thing, though?"

"Sure," she said in relief, "anything."

"Why do you hate me so much?"

"Oh, I don't …" she broke off. "It's just … I don't hate you, exactly. I am, I mean, I am just … angry at life, I guess. It's so unfair."

"In what way?"

"You have no idea how much I wanted to buy Titan," she said in a rush. "I knew him when he was a baby. I rode at that barn and I visited him every damn day. I was sure my parents were going to buy him for me. They talked to the owner about a price and everything. And then you came along."

"Oh, Chloe. I had no idea."

"I know," she sniffled and wiped her eyes. "And honestly, my parents probably wouldn't have bought him for me anyway. You just swooped in and bought him so fast. I never even got to say goodbye. He was just gone one day. And, well, all my dreams sort of went with him. I just wanted my own horse so badly. And he was special. It took me a long time to get over that. Maybe I never did."

"I'm sorry," I said quietly.

"I can see now that it wasn't your fault, Maisy. I know it's ridiculous to feel this way, believe me. But it was just easy to resent you. And then that thing with your coach happened, and then those videos. It was just easier to hate you for everything going on with my life, I guess."

"You saw the videos?" I asked quietly.

"Maisy, everyone saw the videos. They were everywhere."

Of course, they were.

"Do you know who made them?"

Her eyes went wide and then she looked away.

"No, not really. It was a bunch of girls, I think. They were older than me so I didn't know them."

"You know the videos have started up again, right? Did you have anything to do with that?"

It was just a hunch that I asked her, I'd never actually

suspected her of anything to do with the videos before, but something in her face made me wonder.

"No!" she said. "Absolutely not. I had nothing to do with making them."

"But you know something about them."

"Okay, I do. But it won't help you find out who did it. Back when the videos first started last year, this email went out to a lot of horse people. It asked that anyone with old pictures and videos of you from any horse shows should send them in. It said they were putting together a surprise for you."

"Some surprise," I said bitterly.

"I know. I'm sorry. I didn't know you at the time. I sent a few pictures in. They were just boring shots you happened to be in. It wasn't like I was stalking you to get paparazzi shots or anything."

"But you knew what they'd be used for."

"Yeah." She nodded. "I did. But other people were sending them in so I ... I did, too."

I took a deep breath to control my rising anger. She was telling me what I needed to know. There was no point taking it all out on her now.

"That was last year. Did a new email go out asking for more pictures and videos?"

"No, not that I saw anyway. I did see the new videos. But I had nothing to do with them. I swear."

"Well, thank you for telling me," I said finally. "I wish I'd known how you'd felt about Titan sooner. I would have let you visit him."

"You would have?" she asked incredulously.

"Of course. I loved Titan, Chloe. I tried to take the best care of him. I would have done anything to make him happy. So, if you were his friend then I would have made sure that you had some time to hang out."

"I'm an idiot," she said. "And I'm genuinely sorry you lost

Titan. I know you really loved him. And, for what it's worth, I always thought you rode him beautifully."

"Really?" I said in surprise.

"Really. You deserved to be on that development team. They should have let you go to Europe despite the stupid videos. And ... if there's anything I can do to stop those videos then I will. Promise."

"Thank you."

"I'd better go," she said finally. "My leg is killing me."

She hobbled around to the driver's side and slipped inside before I could say anything else.

I stared after her retreating car thoughtfully. The apology had been nice, and her confession about loving Titan had been really heartfelt. So, why did I feel like there was still something she was hiding?

CHAPTER 29

MAISY

*J*eremy, Lorne, and Julie left for the mainland two days later with Timely and Dragon, leaving the rest of us in charge.

I would have loved to have gone with them to see Jeremy compete, but someone had to stay home to help take care of the barn; and this time it was me, Bree, and Chloe.

My last two rides on Poppy had been completely uneventful and Julie had started talking about me taking her to a schooling show at the end of the month to see how she'd handle the atmosphere.

I'd also gotten the go ahead from Julie to have Monica, Dr. Patel, come out and give a second opinion on Chilly's leg. I'd wasted no time making the appointment.

I was both excited and terrified to see what she thought. Monica was known as one of a handful of lameness experts on the island, but she was also not shy about telling it like it was. If she felt that Chilly didn't have a future as anything more than a trail horse, then she was going to be blunt about it.

I groomed Chilly within an inch of his life in preparation for her visit, trimming his mane and bridle path, wanting him to look his very best.

Luckily, Bree and Chloe had gone to town to do some shopping. I was crossing my fingers they'd be gone all afternoon. As silly as it was, I didn't want anyone around to witness my disappointment if Dr. Patel was going to deliver bad news.

My heart jumped with anticipation when I finally heard her familiar truck crunching up the driveway.

"All right, buddy. Let's be on your best behaviour now. We want to make a good impression."

I needn't have worried though, Monica fell in love with him the second she saw him. That's part of the reason she was a great vet; she genuinely cared for all her patients. Whether they cost a half million dollars or were a backyard pony. She loved them all.

"Look at you, handsome boy," she said to him, putting down the plastic case she'd been carrying and coming over to meet him. "Aren't you a picture. What is he, Maisy?"

"He's all thoroughbred, actually. They said he had some sort of gene mutation that made him a pinto in colour."

"Well, he's adorable, look at those eyes. And he has nice feet. Some thoroughbreds have these tiny, crumbling hooves but this guy looks solid."

She walked around him, running her hands over his shoulders and his back, feeling down each leg. She took more time over his injured leg, frowning as she gently prodded the scar tissue over his tendon. Then she stood back and surveyed him from head to toe.

"Is this one you want to buy?" she asked, switching her gaze to me.

"Oh, ah," I stammered, finding myself blushing for no reason.

"I'm not ready for anything like that. I just ... I like him and I want to help him. I want to give him the best chance to heal."

"Okay, fair enough. Well, so far, I really like him. He's well-built and his temperament is perfect. Are you riding him already?"

"At a walk mostly, and a bit of trotting."

"How long was he on stall rest?"

"I think they only kept him in a month." I looked at her worriedly.

"Not a very long time." She frowned. "But light exercise can be beneficial in some cases. If they are on stall rest for too long it can cause the scar tissue to heal in a big clump rather than with the fibers lying smooth. The injury looks better than I'd expected, though. From what you told me, I thought there would have been a lot more thickening over that tendon."

I looked over at her hopefully. "I saw pictures of it from when he first arrived and it looked really bad compared to now."

"Okay, get the records sent over to me so I can have some comparison. Do you know if they had an ultrasound done?"

I shook my head. "Sorry, I'm not sure. I know that Bree said it was a partial tendon tear. And that they were wrapping and cold hosing it when he was on stall rest."

"Hmm, well, let's do an ultrasound now. We might be able to get some more clues on how he's healing. Then we'll do some shockwave therapy on him today. Later, we can add in laser treatment if we need to. It's too bad I didn't see it right when it happened because they are doing great things with stem cell therapy to treat tendon injuries now. Is he on any supplements?"

"No, not really. He gets minerals and flax with his food. He was on pain control at first but he hasn't needed it lately."

"Well, let's set him up with something. I often recommend a rehab blend that has collagen in it to help with recovery. I brought some with me just in case you wanted to try it."

"Yes, absolutely. Whatever he needs."

She smiled at me warmly.

"Right, well, I'm short an assistant today so if you can help me haul my gear in, then we can get started."

Together, we rolled the ultrasound and the shockwave machines into the barn since they were both packed into compact folding carts on wheels.

Chilly watched us with interest, not alarmed at all by the commotion.

Dr. Patel fired up the ultrasound machine, filled a bucket with warm water and washed Chilly's leg first. Then she gooped one of the flat attachments with gel and carefully ran it up and down his leg. She watched the screen carefully, pausing every now and then to tap the button that saved a picture of any area that concerned her.

I watched the screen anxiously. It all looked like grey, wobbly blobs to me. I didn't know how the vet even knew what she was looking at.

After a few minutes, she toweled off Chilly's leg and flicked a few buttons on the machine.

"So, there are still a few mild lesions on his leg, that's areas that haven't healed yet, but most of what we're looking at is scar tissue that's has built up over and around the tendon."

"That's bad?" I asked, feeling my heart flutter.

"No, actually. It's better than I expected. I'd like to look at whatever diagnostics were done for him earlier so I can see how fast and how cleanly the injury has healed so far. But, Maisy, I am cautiously optimistic that this will heal and he'll be able to go back into work."

"Seriously?" The rush of relief that washed over me nearly knocked me over.

"Now, with that being said, I wouldn't want him to go back to being a race horse or into high-level eventing. What would be your plans for him going forward?"

"I'd like to see how far along he could go in dressage," I said, without thinking. "I know he's not destined for the Olympics or anything, but it would be fun to see how he develops."

"I see." She pushed back a smile. "But of course, that's in theory, right? You're not interested in him for yourself?"

"I … ah." I stopped. Monica had known me since I was a kid. If anyone would understand what I was feeling, it was her. "I know that this horse most-likely can't take me where I want to go, competition-wise. I know he's not like Titan. But there's just something about him. I really like him. I just don't know what I want to happen next in my life. Everything sort of crashed around me and I'm not sure how to find my way out of the rubble. I know that I could start over again. But I'm not sure that I want to."

"Oh, Maisy." She reached over and gave me a tight hug. "You know, when I first walked into the barn and saw you with Chilly, I said to myself that I had not seen you looking that happy since you were a little kid. Not being under pressure suits you, Maisy. Maybe just enjoy that and take it one day at a time."

I stared at her in surprise, not able to think of a response.

She unfolded the next machine and squirted out more goo on Chilly's leg.

"Some horses don't love this. It makes a bit of a popping sound. We'll try him without sedation first but we can always add some if we need to."

It turned out not to be a problem. Chilly stood with his eyes half-closed as she ran the attachment up and down his leg. It looked a little like a lightbulb and made a small snapping noise as she carefully maneuvered it over the back of his leg.

"I think he likes it," I whispered, not wanting to wake him up.

"It has a bit of a pain-dampening effect as well as healing. We'll do this once a week for a few sessions and then see where he's at. Is the rescue covering this, or are you?"

"I will," I said quickly. "I sort of pushed them into it. And I'll take the supplements, too. Whatever he needs."

"He's a very nice horse, Maisy. He seems like a guy you can have a lot of fun with. And, who knows, he might be able to be quite a competitive horse down the road."

After a few minutes she sat back and surveyed him, shutting off the machine with a click.

"Well, let's see how that holds him. Let me know if he's uncomfortable at all. See you next week."

And with that she packed up her gear and was gone, leaving me feeling happier and more hopeful than I had in a month.

CHAPTER 30

MAISY

*C*hilly and I had been given the go ahead to do a very light work session after the treatment, and then I was to turn him out for the rest of the day to loaf around with his friends.

So, as soon as her truck had pulled out of the driveway, we headed up to the ring.

"Let's try something different today, buddy. To celebrate your good news."

I'd slipped his bridle on but hadn't bothered with the saddle. Today was just about playing.

I positioned him at the mounting block and then slid onto his broad warm back. I stayed still for a moment, just patting him and getting used to the feeling of being without a saddle. But he didn't seem bothered at all.

I leaned down and offered him a cookie and he reached his nose around past his shoulder, stretching his neck out and lipping the treat off my hand. Then we did the same on the other side. I'd been incorporating these stretches into his rides lately.

And, when nobody was around, I'd started teaching him to bow in his stall and we'd even played around with learning how to fetch. Just silly, fun stuff.

We walked around for a few minutes. I let my legs swing loosely, amazed at how much more I could feel the subtle movements of his back without a saddle between us.

I let the reins lie on his neck and practiced some walk-halt transitions and turns using just my seat.

Finally, when I was sure he was listening to me, I drew him to a halt and hopped off.

"Ready for something different?" I asked him, scratching the spot he liked behind his ear. Before I could lose my nerve, I undid the buckles on his bridle and carefully pulled it over his head.

He stared at me in surprise but made no move to run away. When I turned away from him, he followed me the last two steps to the mounting block.

"Right, here goes." I swung back on, a shiver of excitement winding through me. I trusted Chilly but this was a whole new level of risk. I couldn't stop him if he wanted to buck me off or run away.

"Good boy, walk on." Without hesitating, he marched forward, acting exactly the same as if he were fully tacked up.

My confidence rose with every step. We cruised around the ring at a walk, changing direction a few times. I didn't ask for more than a walk. We had lots of work to do on the ground first before adding speed into our routine. But right then this was enough. More than enough.

I jumped down and wrapped my arms around his neck, quietly thanking him for being the good horse he was.

"Okay, let's try some other tricks."

I turned away from him and moved briskly across the ring. Then turned around and called his name.

"Chilly, here."

He'd already been heading my way anyway but his march

picked up speed and he made a little nickering sound as he hurried toward me and stopped a foot away.

"Good boy." I let him lip the cookie off my hand and spent a minute rubbing his neck and head. "Let's go for a walk."

I walked away slowly, half-turned to make sure he was following and then made a looping path around the ring, circling and changing directions to keep things interesting.

Chilly stayed glued to my side the whole time, never breaking away to explore on his own like I half-expected.

A warm glow filled my heart and I stopped suddenly and impulsively wrapped my arms around him, squeezing gently into a hug.

"That's enough for today, buddy. You go spend some time with your friends."

Humming under my breath, I led him out to pasture.

Tomorrow, I would teach him how to bow. Somewhere in my house I had a book on trick training and liberty work. I would study it and make a list of all the things I could teach him. It would help make his rehab a little less boring for him.

Hopefully, Julie wouldn't mind that I was turning her race-horse into a circus pony.

The next day I managed to sneak in a session with him when Bree went up to the house to have a shower and Chloe was eating lunch. I wanted to work with him, and figure things out, without an audience.

It wasn't until the third day that I was caught.

"How was your ride?" Bree asked innocently when I came up to the house for lunch.

"Good," I said casually. "He's always good. What?"

They were both staring at me and grinning. I looked down to see the binoculars on the table and groaned inwardly.

"Are you going to tell Julie on me?" I asked with a sigh.

"Julie? Why would she care?" Chloe looked at me in confusion.

"We just want you to teach us some of that stuff," Bree said, clasping her hands together. "I'd love to try riding Ace without a bridle. And were you getting Chilly to bow?"

"Uh, yes," I said, slightly embarrassed. "Titan could do all sorts of tricks, although I hadn't done that stuff in a while. Rory, too. I thought Chilly might like it."

"He looked happy enough," Bree said. "So, will you teach us? Please?"

"Um, sure," I said doubtfully. "But, won't Lorne or Julie mind?"

"No, of course not. You're just having fun. It's not like you're ruining the horses or anything."

And, that's how I started some unofficial, and very amateur, liberty classes at October Horses.

That afternoon, Bree brought Ace and Nugget down to the ring for her and Chloe to play with.

And, despite my earlier misgivings, it was a whole lot of fun. The girls laughed the whole time, but they took my instructions seriously, and Bree was riding Ace around with just a rope around his neck in no time. That horse was so calm I doubted he even noticed the lack of a bridle and saddle at all.

Chloe's pure joy at being able to teach Nugget how to bow was contagious. It felt good to just laugh around with other people and the horses without any pressure or deadlines. I'd been missing that in my life lately. I just hadn't realized how much.

"I want to do this every day," Bree said, beaming down at me from Ace's back. "You'll teach us everything you know, right, Maisy?"

They looked so excited that I didn't have the heart to tell them that I didn't know much more beyond those few tricks anymore. It had been a very long time since I'd played with this stuff.

"Sure, of course. We'll just take it slow. Very slow." That would give me a chance to read some books and watch some videos online so I could refresh my skills.

That night, I was practically humming as I drove home, feeling the strange sensation of being alive and with a purpose again. I hadn't felt that in ages.

CHAPTER 31

BREE

"Hey, Maisy, are you okay?" I asked tentatively.

I wasn't sure what had set her off. But she'd received a phone call just as we'd been finishing morning chores and had been strangely quiet and distracted for the rest of the morning. There seemed to be a cloud of sadness hanging over her.

"Hmm?" she said, barely paying attention to me. She looked glumly off into the woods, her reins at the buckle. Her fingers wrapped around a strand of Chilly's long mane like he was the only thing anchoring her in the saddle.

"Well, I was wondering ... How would you feel about me doing a spotlight on you and Chilly?"

"Spotlight?" She shook her head as if to clear it and looked at me, now fully alert.

"You know, for my blog. I think it's time for me to do an article on Chilly. I want to show all the great work you've done

with him. Both the rehab and the liberty stuff. I think the readers
will love it."

She sighed heavily and looked away, her shoulders drooping
again.

"I don't want to draw any more attention to myself, thanks.
And I think I've had my fill of social media. You should probably
leave me out of it. If the wrong people knew I was riding here, it
could be bad for October Horses. You don't want to get mixed up
in my bad publicity."

"Bad publicity? Do you mean … is this because of the videos?
Is that still going on?"

I'd never mentioned the videos to Maisy. I hadn't watched any
of them except the one Chloe had shown me. I'd assumed that it
was all over with. Chloe had never talked about them again.

"You know about them?" she asked dully.

"Kind of. I saw one and it was stupid. I don't know the whole
story. Something about your coach going to jail for a bit?'

"Yes, Dirk. A bunch of his old students and clients sued him
and brought all sorts of charges against him. He was found guilty
of some of them but not others. He did a few months of jail time.
But his accusers had been hoping he'd get put away for years."

"Okay, what does this have to do with you?"

"I wouldn't testify against him. And this group of people
thought I was trying to protect him. Which wasn't true. I hadn't
witnessed anything they'd accused him of."

"What did they accuse him of?" I asked slowly.

"Um, assault, verbal abuse, physical abuse. Drugging the
horses, abusing the horses. Embezzlement. Just to name a few. He
had a lot of things on the go."

"And you didn't see anything going on when you were there?"

She looked up at me sharply, her expression suddenly wary.
Like I might be trying to trick her.

"No, nothing out of the ordinary. He yelled at us at every

single lesson. Everyone knew that. It's what we paid him for because he made us winners. He wasn't there to hold our hands."

"And the other stuff?"

"No, I mean he was rough on the horses sometimes. And it was obvious that his working students hated him. But he never beat anyone up in front of me or anything."

"But this group of people thought you knew more than you did."

"Yes," she nodded. "They thought I was lying. One of the accusers tried to kill herself when he was let off on a lot of the charges. She'd been one of his working students."

I inhaled sharply. "That's awful."

"It was. I actually knew her pretty well. She was a nice girl."

"Was? Do you mean she—"

"No, no, last I heard she was alive. She gave up riding, though. And I heard she had some struggles with mental health, but I'm not sure how much of that is true. You know the horse world, most of the gossip is made up."

We were quiet for a moment and then she went on.

"The worst thing about these videos is that they took all my worst moments and made them public. Everyone struggles with their riding sometimes, but not everyone gets their mistakes broadcast for the world to see."

"I'm so sorry this happened to you," I said quietly. "Nobody deserves to live like this."

"Thanks," she said and then sighed. "I hate to say it but I think … I think it's getting worse."

I stared at her in shock.

"Wait? You mean the videos are still going on? They're making new ones?"

"Yeah, and now I've been getting these phone calls, too. I try not to let it bother me but …"

She broke off and her mask slipped for just a second,

revealing the agony underneath it. Then she smiled at me and shrugged.

"That's harassment, Maisy. You need to go to the police. Why are they doing this anyway? Are they trying to blackmail you to testify or something?"

"No, it's too late for that. I think they just want to hurt me. To get revenge. I don't know."

"Do you know who it is?"

She shook her head, biting her lip. "I have no idea. Back when it happened the first time, we made a list of everyone involved. My parents wanted to hire a private investigator to find out who was doing it so we could make it stop. But it just went away all on its own one day. I thought it was all over until this happened. Until Titan died."

I was silent for a long time, my thoughts racing. "Maisy … you don't think they had anything to do with—."

"No," she said quickly, guessing my train of thought. "I was worried about that too at first, but the vet ruled out anything suspicious. Titan had a genetic defect that just gave out. It wasn't anyone's fault."

"Good." I breathed out a deep breath, relieved that nobody had purposefully hurt Titan. That would have been beyond awful. "But they still took the video of him falling and sent it to you. They posted it online for everyone to see."

She looked down at Chilly's neck and sighed. "They're still sick. But at least they're not murderers."

"Maisy, you shouldn't have to handle it on your own. You seriously need to tell the police."

"I don't think the police can do anything," she said, "and I don't want to cause anymore waves. It will probably go away on its own."

"I don't think that's how bullying works," I said but she'd nudged Chilly and moved him up ahead of me.

"Don't tell anyone, okay." She turned to look at me over her shoulder.

"If that's what you want then I won't. But I think you should tell Lorne and Julie, and Jeremy. They could help. And you could move in with us. There is lots of room upstairs. You shouldn't be staying in that house alone."

She hesitated, and for a second, I thought she'd take me up on the offer.

"No, I'm all right, but thank you."

We rode in silence for a few minutes.

"I won't write about you and Chilly in the blog if you really don't want me to," I said finally. "But I think the rest of the world should know you like we do. Know the kind, smart, and funny person who is crazy-talented with horses. I think that maybe it would be a way to sort of gain control of what people said about you. Sort of a good publicity campaign. To, you know, fix things."

I paused, waiting to see if I'd offended her but she just shook her head.

"I don't think I have a reputation left to fix, Bree. Those videos have finished me. I think you're the only people who'd let me ride their horses now."

"No," I said firmly, "that's not true at all. You have way more people on your side than you think. When we were at that show, when ... when Titan died there was this girl standing near me in the audience who was saying all sorts of stupid stuff."

Maisy looked back at me quickly, narrowing her eyes.

"But she was only one person," I went on hurriedly. "The other people standing around us defended you. It's just because your critics are loud and mean that they seem to be everywhere. But, in reality, there are a lot of people on your side."

"You think so?" She said doubtfully. But at least she looked like she was considering it.

"I do. I know so. We'll help you if you'll let us, Maisy. Those people shouldn't get away with treating you like that."

"And you think doing a spotlight on me would help somehow?"

"Yes, I'll highlight all the good you do here and your brilliance with Chilly. When I'm done with you, you'll look like a saint."

"Well, I'm definitely not that," she said dryly. "But okay, fine. Do your blog. But I get to read it first. And only good pictures of Chilly. I want him looking regal."

She smiled a little as she said that and dropped back to ride beside me again. I reached out and squeezed her arm.

"It's going to be okay," I said. "I promise."

She looked at me in surprise, her mouth open and her sad eyes filled with something like hope.

"You think so?" she said doubtfully.

"I do, I really do. You were dragged through the mud, Maisy. Let your friends help you."

"All right," she said slowly. "It's worth a shot."

CHAPTER 32

MAISY

*O*f course, when Jeremy and the crew had their triumphant return late in the night, it had apparently taken less than an hour for Bree and Chloe to rat me out about the liberty stuff.

Which was why I found myself down at the ring putting on an impromptu demonstration for Jeremy the next morning.

Lorne and Julie had chosen to sleep in but when I arrived at the barn a half hour earlier than usual so I could start chores, Jeremy met me at the door with a coffee in one hand and a grin on his face.

"Well, if it isn't our circus trainer," he said and I stifled a groan.

"They told you, did they?"

"Yep, they were pretty excited. Something about bowing and galloping around bareback without a saddle or bridle."

"Ah, not quite," I said, looking up at his kind, familiar face with happiness. "I missed you."

The words came out of my mouth unbidden and I nearly choked on my coffee. Why had I said that?

His surprise morphed into a smile and, instead of laughing at me for being stupid, he pulled me into a quick hug.

"Actually, I missed you quite a bit, too. It wasn't the same without you. Are you going to show me those circus tricks now?"

"If you help me feed everyone breakfast. Chilly doesn't perform on an empty stomach."

"Fair enough. I can appreciate that. I'm a big fan of breakfast myself."

We fed in record time and I topped waters while we waited for Chilly to finish at least some of his breakfast before pulling him out of his stall.

"You know we're not pros at this or anything, right?" I warned. "I just play around with this stuff."

"I know. I know. I didn't expect you to put on a tutu and some tights. I just want to see what all the fuss is about."

"Okay, right this way then."

We walked together up to the ring and I took off Chilly's halter and set it on the mounting block.

"Here, Chilly," I called softly and he walked the final five feet toward the block and set himself up beside it, just at the perfect spot for me to get on.

"Good boy," I said, giving him a cookie. Then, I lightly hopped up so my stomach was briefly lying across him, and then swung my leg over his back.

"So, you're just going to ride him like that? Without anything on him?"

"Yep." I sat there for a minute, just scratching Chilly's neck and talking to him softly before we began our routine. Then I reached into my pocket for a cookie and held it by his shoulder. "Here, Chilly."

"Why do you feed him cookies like that when you get on?" Jeremy asked, frowning. He wasn't the type of guy to dole out cookies or praise to the horses unless they'd done something spectacular so I could see how he might be a little confused.

"I'm not rewarding him for standing still or anything," I said. "They are just to stretch his neck and shoulders out. See the way he has to bend sideways like that to take the treat out of my hand? It's a little like us doing warm-up stretches. It helps to loosen up any tight areas. And it has the added bonus that he stands stone-still at the mounting block until I'm ready for us to move out. And it puts him in the right frame of mind for learning."

"Huh," Jeremy said, "that's interesting."

"A massage therapist showed me that a long time ago and it sort of became a habit, I guess. I did it with Titan all the time."

"He didn't get greedy and pushy because of all the treats?"

"Nope. Never." I shook my head. "Although Rory was always a greedy-guts. You had to watch your fingers around him."

Jeremy laughed and took a sip of his coffee.

"Actually, when I first got Titan, I played around with doing liberty stuff all the time before he was started under saddle. He could bow and count, and he could kneel down for me to get on him. He could shake his head yes and no. We used to have so much fun before—"

I broke off, surprised at my own train of thought.

"Before what?" Jeremy asked.

"Well, I guess before things got so serious. I just started training all the time and there wasn't much left for anything else. I didn't stop on purpose, but I guess it just fell by the wayside."

I ran my hand down Chilly's neck, exhaled, and asked him to walk forward.

"It's not always easy to find balance," Jeremy said quietly, turning to walk beside Chilly's shoulder. "That's one thing that my father always did right. The horses at our stud always had days out riding in the hills alongside training in the ring. His program made sure that the horses were never bored or overtrained. Although I doubt he would have considered circus training productive."

I smiled down at him and shook my head. "We're not quite good enough for the circus yet but give us time. Wait, you mean your parents owned a breeding farm? I thought you just had a few horses."

"Yep, Glenbrittle Stud has been in our family for generations. We breed sport horses and have a training program, too."

"Oh," I said quietly. When Jeremy had told me he'd been kicked out of his home, I hadn't realized that he'd had to leave behind an entire horse farm. "Hey, do you want to hand me that lead rope?"

We'd come around back to the mounting block and Jeremy unclipped the lead and handed it to me.

I reached down and looped it around Chilly's neck and tied the ends in a loose knot.

"I'm not brave enough to do faster work yet without something to hang on to for emergencies," I confessed. "We haven't done this part too much so don't laugh."

"Never," he said seriously, stepping back to sit on the edge of the mounting block.

Turning my focus to Chilly, I asked him to shift his weight backward a hair and then we moved up into a flowing trot. He wasn't supposed to do much trotting or tight turns yet so I stuck to straight lines and large, shallow circles. I wanted more than anything to canter him but we had at least another month of rehab left before we were allowed to try it.

After a few minutes I brought him back down to a walk and then a halt. I had to be conscious to use just my seat and not rely on the neck rope to ask him to stop. It was too easy to use it as a crutch.

I jumped down and praised the horse like crazy. And then I stood back and asked him to back away, and then to move his haunches to the left and then to the right in a careful turn on the forehand. And when he was done with all that, I asked him to bow.

"So, what did you think?" I asked, feeling a little nervous. It was hard to read Jeremy's expression.

"Pretty fancy stuff, miss." He winked at me. "Can't wait to see you two on stage."

"Oh, stop teasing me," I said, giving him a little punch on the arm. I slipped Chilly's halter back on and gave him a final cookie.

"Nope, I mean it." Jeremy slung an arm over my shoulders. "You did good with him. I'm impressed. I have to admit that I've never ridden a horse without a bridle or a saddle. You could show me how."

"Oh sure, let's use Dragon," I said innocently and was rewarded by him giving me a little shake that made me laugh.

"You're pretty cheeky, aren't you?"

"Yep. I come by it naturally."

"Good, don't stop. It suits you. Let's go get some breakfast before those girls eat it all."

I leaned into him just a little bit. It was so easy to be natural with Jeremy. He was a bit like Chilly in that way. I didn't feel any pressure from either of them to be more than just myself.

You should tell him about the videos, a little voice in my head said. *And about the phone calls. He could help.*

Maybe another day I would. Just not now.

CHAPTER 33

BREE

*H*umming to myself I hung my jacket up and turned toward the living room, thoughts of a snack and some writing filling my head.

I didn't see Chloe until I was nearly on top of her and I let out a startled yelp.

"Chloe, you scared me. Why are you looking at me like that?"

"Like what?" She blinked at me innocently, a smile fixed on her face.

"Like you want something from me. What's up?"

"Oh, nothing, nothing. I made some cookies for you, though. They're in the kitchen."

"Okay." I narrowed my eyes at her suspiciously and sniffed the air, noticing for the first time that the whole place smelled like baking. "Why?"

"Just because you're my friend and I wanted to show you that I care."

She turned and hobbled toward the kitchen, motioning me to follow.

"Uh huh. Well, thanks."

"And," she went on, setting a plate of cookies on the table and ushering me to have a seat, "because I have a favour to ask of you."

"Thought so." I bit into a cookie and melted a little. They were really good. "Peanut butter chocolate chip. My favourite."

"I know." She pulled out the chair next to me and sat down, staring at me eagerly with her hands clasped under her chin. "It's no big deal, I just need a ride. This stupid cast makes driving so awkward. I'm pretty sure I'm going to run over someone if I keep trying it."

"I'm glad you came to your senses on that one."

"Yeah, well, eventually I do know my limits. And I know that tonight I need a sidekick. Are you in?'

"That depends, where are we going?"

"It's kind of secret. I'm doing research ... on a project. I can buy you dinner too if you like. Anything you want."

She smiled at me, but I could see some uncertainty in her eyes. Whatever it was, she wasn't sure I'd agree to go along with her.

"This isn't about Maisy, is it?" I asked, watching her face carefully. I didn't think Chloe was involved with all that video stuff. But I couldn't be positive.

"What? No, of course not. I already told Maisy I wasn't involved in that. This is something totally different. Please help me?"

I sighed heavily and threw my hands up.

"Okay, fine. Whatever. But if I don't like whatever it is, I will be turning us around and driving us home."

"Deal. Okay, be ready to go tonight at eight. Wear dark clothes."

"Dark clothes? What on earth ..."

But she'd already leapt up and hobbled out of the kitchen, leaving me staring after her in dismay.

Grumbling, I picked up another cookie. Whatever it was had better be worth it.

"So, where exactly is it that you're going?" Nicholas asked a few hours later, looking at me skeptically as I fished around for some appropriately dark clothing. "That's pretty late for dinner."

"Eight o'clock isn't late. And Chloe didn't tell me where she planned to go. Just that I needed to wear something dark."

"Well, that sounds sketchy."

"It definitely does. But she's been acting almost normal lately, a little like her old self. I don't want to miss a chance to hang out with her. Besides, I'll be the one driving. There's only so much trouble we can get into. And aren't you doing your school thing tonight anyway with Bertie and the group? It's not like I'm ditching you for Chloe."

"No, I don't mean that. I just want you to be careful, that's all. I don't want Chloe to drag you into anything shady."

"Okay, well, thank you for worrying. But, number one, I'm an adult and am perfectly capable of getting in and out of shady situations without Chloe's help, and two, I'm supposed to be the worrier in this relationship. You're supposed to be the fun and spontaneous one. You sound a little like my mom right now."

Nicholas quirked a smile and shook his head. "I don't think anyone has ever, ever called me spontaneous. I like to plan."

"Yeah, I know. Like my mom." I leaned down and kissed him softly and then ruffled his hair. "Go on, you're going to be late. Aren't you supposed to meet your group in like half an hour?"

"It's okay, Bertie's always late anyway." He gave me a strange look, opened his mouth like he was about to say something and then shut it again. "But, yeah, I guess I should head out. Unless you'd prefer me to stay home?"

I tilted my head to one side, studying him, trying to figure out what was really bothering him.

"Why would I want you to skip your study group thing? Go, have fun. Learn things. I have my cell phone on me and Chloe said we'd only be a couple of hours. So we should be back a little ahead of you. I'll call you if we're going to be late."

"All right, have fun. Stay out of trouble," he said, sounding doubtful.

"Yes, mom."

Chloe was waiting for me impatiently downstairs, twirling her keys around one finger.

"We have to go," she said, "we still have to get food and we're going to be late."

"Late for what?"

"You'll see. Let's move out."

She tossed the keys to me and tottered outside, heading for her little car.

"All right, where are we grabbing food?" I asked.

"You pick. Somewhere not too far from here. And it has to be takeout."

We settled on burgers and Chloe tapped her fingers on the dashboard the entire time we were waiting for them to bring us our food.

"Should we park here and eat first?" I asked.

"No, no. We can eat when we get there. Here, I already programmed the address into the gps. It will lead you right to it."

"Um, okay," I said, sighing as I glanced over at the fragrant bag of food. My stomach rumbled in protest at having to wait.

I followed the glowing dot on the screen, making three left hand turns before it finally said that we'd reached our destination.

"Park over there," Chloe said in an excited whisper. "This is perfect."

"Why are we whispering?" I hissed back.

"You'll see. Let's eat."

Shaking my head in bewilderment, I fished out my burger and fries.

Chloe popped open the glove compartment, pulling out a black case with straps, a notebook and three pens. She set them all on the dash and pulled out her phone and laid it neatly beside them.

"Chloe? What is all this?"

She reached over suddenly, lunging for the keys that were still in the ignition and put them in her pocket. Then she opened the black case on the dashboard, revealing an oversized pair of dusty binoculars.

"What on earth? Where did you get those?"

"Julie. She thinks I'm taking up bird watching. Now stay low, Bree, we don't want to attract any attention."

"From who?" I asked, dropping my voice into a whisper again.

"From Jeremy, of course."

"Jeremy? Chloe, what are we doing here?"

"A reconnaissance mission, Bree. I know you don't believe that he's up to anything, but I'm going to prove to you that he's shifty. I followed him last week so I know this is where he goes, but I couldn't get my crutches out of the car. And then I nearly hit someone on my way home. That's why I needed you with me this time."

"This is ridiculous. Give me the keys, we're going home."

"No. Not until I've proved to you what he's up to. He's staying in Lorne's house, for heaven's sake. A vulnerable old man. You couldn't live with yourself if something happened to Lorne, could you?"

I glared at her, grumbling under my breath. But there was a small part of me that was listening. I liked Jeremy, and Lorne was hardly a vulnerable type of person, but once in a while things did seem a little off about Jeremy.

He'd come out of his shell quite a bit since he'd arrived. He was much more relaxed and friendly, especially now that Maisy was working at the farm, but sometimes there seemed to be a shadow over him. Like he'd had a dark past.

"We can't spy on him," I said firmly, pushing my doubts away. "He'd be so mad if he found out. And hurt."

"So, we don't let him find out. Finish your food, Bree. He should be here any second."

"This is so wrong, Chloe." I paused, frowning at her. "How do you know when he'll be here?"

She shrugged. "I'm not a hundred percent sure. But he leaves Lorne's at the same time on Wednesdays and he's gone for a couple of hours. This is where he came last week so I'm assuming it's the same place."

She gripped my arm suddenly, finger nails digging in through my sweater.

"There he is. Stay down."

I squished down automatically, my eyes level with the edge of the window.

Chloe whipped out her binoculars, half leaning across me in her effort to see.

"Definitely him," she whispered. "He's going inside that building. Look."

I peered out, barely recognizing Jeremy's leather jacket in the dark. He wasn't alone, either. Three other people followed him, two men and a woman.

"They look like drug dealers," Chloe hissed, shifting so her elbow dug into my side.

"Ow, you're crushing me. They look like regular people to me."

"Nah, they're definitely shifty."

We watched as Jeremy pulled open the door to a building

directly across from our car and disappeared inside. The other people hustled in close behind him.

A few more people showed up, some of them looking around furtively before slipping quickly inside.

"What kind of place is it?" I whispered. "It looks like a community center or something."

"I think it's a school. But I'm not sure why it's open at night."

"Maybe he's upgrading some courses or something."

Chloe snorted and rolled her eyes. "No way. Come on, I'm going to go check it out."

"Chloe no," I hissed as she flung her door open. She held onto the car long enough to pull her crutches out from the back seat and then hobbled across the road as fast as she could.

"Damn it," I swore under my breath. "Why is she so much trouble?"

I slowly got out, looking both ways before I strode across the street to join her. She was standing outside taking pictures of a sign that was propped up on a wooden easel outside the door.

"Look," she said triumphantly, "we got him."

I studied the sign, which just had a list of conference rooms on it and then looked back at her. It was obviously a place where different groups could rent out rooms to hold their meetings.

"I don't get it."

"Right there," she pointed, "Clean For Life. I'm sure it's one of those self-help groups for addicts. That's what Jeremy has been hiding. He has a drug habit."

"That is a pretty big leap, Chloe. He could be in any one of these meetings—"

"Oh, like this parenting group or the knitting club?" Chloe snapped, rolling her eyes.

"No," I said sharply. "But you're leaping to conclusions."

"Fine. Well, I took a picture so I'll do some research and figure out what the rest of them are. I'll narrow it down. But I'm telling you that Jeremy is bad news. This is his big secret."

I sighed unhappily and followed her back to the car.

"All right," I said, "give me the keys, let's go home."

"What, no? We're on a stakeout, Bree. We have to wait for him to come out and then follow him."

"Oh my gosh, Chloe. That's called stalking. We're not doing that."

"Wow, I really thought you'd be more cool about this. You're not really that fun at all."

"Sorry, I'm not." I held out my hand and, after a lot of muttering and dramatic sighing, she slapped the keys down into my palm.

I started the car without a word and headed down the block, past a strip of well-lit restaurants and cafes.

"Um, Bree isn't that Nicholas?"

I looked over to where Chloe was pointing and barely missed running into the car ahead of me.

Two people stood just outside the door of a restaurant. A guy who looked identical to Nicholas and a beautiful girl with long blonde hair and a skin-tight top who had half her body draped all over him.

As we looked, she suddenly reached out and pulled him in for a kiss.

"No," I said, feeling cold prickles all over. "Nicholas is out with his study group. It must be someone who looks like him."

"Bree." Chloe looked at me anxiously, her face pale under the street lights. "I don't know what to say."

"Then drop it," I said sharply. "Let's just go home."

Chloe snorted and then turned to face the window, refusing to say another word the whole way back. When we pulled up to the house, I stayed in the car while she stomped and hobbled her way inside.

When I was sure I was alone I leaned my head against the steering wheel and allowed myself to think about what I'd seen. It had definitely been Nicholas. I'd recognize him anywhere.

But there had to be some logical explanation that I just wasn't seeing. It wasn't like when my last boyfriend, Duncan, had cheated on me. Something like that couldn't happen with two relationships in a row, could it? Was I just that naïve and stupid that I'd missed all the signs?

No, the Nicholas I knew would never do anything like that. He was the most honest person I knew. If he wanted to see someone else then he would just tell me that. He'd never sneak around. Would he?

CHAPTER 34

BREE

I crept up the stairs, going to my own cold, lonely bedroom to curl up in the dark and lie awake, listening for the sound of Nicholas' car returning. My mind kept going back and forth over what I'd seen. Half of me believed that it was just an innocent misunderstanding that he'd easily explain. Or that maybe it hadn't been him at all. The other half was certain that he was seeing someone else and my relationship was dead.

I tensed, clasping my hands together as I heard the familiar rumble of his car crunching up the gravel driveway.

As much as I wanted to focus on anything else but him right then, I couldn't help but track every step he made as he entered the house, went to the kitchen, ran the tap and then made the climb upstairs. It was like my whole body was tuned into him. Whether I liked it or not.

I heard him go to his own room, pause, and then his footsteps came down the hall in my direction.

There was a beat of silence while I lay frozen and then a light knock at the door.

"Bree, are you still awake?"

Part of me wanted to pretend to be asleep. The more mature part of me sat up and flicked on the light beside my bed.

"Yeah," I said quietly. "What's up?"

He stood in the doorway, his leather laptop bag still over his shoulder. His hair was all mussed up and he looked upset.

"Um, can we talk?"

The words turned my belly to ice. This was it. It was happening. He was leaving me for her.

My mind went instantly into protective mode. This was okay. I could handle it. I'd handled much worse in the past. It would hurt, badly, but in the end I'd survive.

"Okay." My voice came out a frightened squeak and Nicholas looked at me in surprise.

"Bree, what's wrong?" he said, coming to sit on my bed and peer at me anxiously. He went to take my hand, but I snatched it back out of his grasp before he could touch me.

"Just say it," I said woodenly. "Whatever you have to say, just get it over with please."

My heart was going to burst if he drew it out any longer. I was two seconds away from losing what little control I had left over my emotions.

"Okay," he said slowly. "Something happened tonight that I want to tell you about."

"Something on your study date with *Bertie*?" I didn't even recognize my anger-filled voice.

"Um, yes actually." He frowned at me, looking very confused. "I met her at the café but none of the other group members showed up. It turned out that she hadn't invited them. I don't know why she thought something was going to happen between us but, um, it was all very awkward. And she kissed me."

He stopped to stare into my face, trying to gauge how I was

taking all this. When I just stayed frozen in place, not saying a word, he went on.

"I didn't see it coming, Bree, but I probably should have. I told her I was switching study groups and that I wouldn't see her again. She works as one of your dad's assistants too, though so I didn't want something getting back to you. I thought I'd better tell you right away. Hey, are you okay?"

Somewhere during his confession, I'd started breathing again. And my mind had sifted through everything he'd told me.

"Why didn't you tell me in the first place that Bertie was a girl?"

"Huh? I thought you already knew. She's worked with your dad for over a year. She said she'd met you and everything."

"Oh, jeesh, you mean Roberta, don't you?" The pieces clicked together. "Dad's never called her Bertie before. Right, I met her briefly." I hadn't liked her then, either. She'd been stuck up and very aware of how pretty she was.

"So, you're okay?" Nicholas looked down at me anxiously.

"Ugh, I will be. I'd feel better if I could punch her or something. I had an awful night because of her."

"What do you ..." He broke off. "You saw us, didn't you? When you were out tonight."

"Yeah, Chloe and I drove past when she was basically feeling you up."

He looked at me in horror.

"You didn't think—"

"Part of me did, honestly. It's happened to me before, Nicholas. So I'm a little jaded. But the other part of me, the part that knows you, trusts you, and loves you ... that part had hope."

"Bree, look at me."

I tilted my head up and met his gaze.

"I promise you, right now, that I will never do anything to betray the trust you put in me. Never."

And then he was crushing me to his chest and I clung to him

like my life depended on it, my eyes overflowing with the tears that I hadn't let myself shed earlier.

I scootched over so he could get into bed beside me and we just lay there, pressed side by side with our arms wrapped tightly around each other, maybe both a little overwhelmed about what we'd come close to losing.

We stayed curled up for hours, just talking about all sorts of things. Life, philosophy, and horses.

"Hey, I never asked you about your mission with Chloe. What was it all about?"

"Ugh, you don't want to know. I think that girl has finally gone off the deep end. Our mission was to stalk Jeremy, of all people."

I told him the whole thing, only making him swear the he wouldn't tell Lorne or Julie about any of Chloe's wild theories about Jeremy.

"No, I wouldn't do that," Nicholas said. "She doesn't have any proof for one thing. And secondly, so what if he's going to some sort of self-help group. Lots of people are messed up in one way or another. As long as they're dealing with it and not a danger to anyone, then that's all that matters, right?"

"Yeah, that's what I was thinking. If he really is an addict, then at least he's getting help for it. It's an illness right, just like mine? I'm always going to have to maintain myself a little better than the average person. I don't know if I'll ever be able to stop the medication from the drug trial. But I'm still able to live a good life."

"You mean a great life." Nicholas pulled me more firmly against his chest.

"Exactly, and I've never seen Jeremy do anything shady. Although, his first week here, he was pretty weird. I remember how strange he acted when we picked him up from the airport."

"True. Sometimes people are not quite themselves when

they're in a new place, meeting new people, maybe he was just awkward."

I nodded thoughtfully. We hadn't exactly been welcoming to him when he'd first arrived, either. We'd thought we were getting a teenager as a working student and nobody had quite known how to act when he'd turned out to be a grown man with a bit of a chip on his shoulder.

"He works hard, he's good with the horses, that's all I care about," I said. "And he's been downright pleasant since Maisy arrived. I think he likes her."

"Oh yeah? Does she like him?"

"I think so. It's hard to tell with her. She's not the best at sharing."

"Bree."

He paused so long that I thought he wasn't going to say anything else.

"Um, yes?"

"I think we should spend the rest of our lives together."

"What?" I tried to turn around to face him, but he tightened his arms, not letting me go.

"You and I are good together. I can't imagine being with anyone else but you. Ever. I'd like us to get married."

As shocked as I was by this casual announcement, I couldn't help the smile tugging at my lips.

"Are you asking me to marry you, Nicholas?"

"Yes, but not yet. When I'm out of school, I'll ask you properly. This is like me pre-asking you to make sure you don't think it's a horrible idea."

"Hmm, well, I think it's a great idea. But if you take too long then I might ask you first."

"Like, you'd drop down on one knee at a restaurant?"

"How about a horse show? Or like in a grocery store line-up. Anywhere you least expect it. No need for us to start being conventional now."

We both started laughing at the same time.

Yes, I thought, *this is exactly who I wanted to spend the rest of my life with. No doubts at all.*

CHAPTER 35

MAISY

This should have been you, this should have been you, this should have been you. The words repeated in my head to the sound of Poppy's rhythmic footfalls as she bounced across the arena dirt.

Light and airy, her neck arched and all her steps seemed to float. Her mane was braided in a perfect row, silvery light strands wound with the dark gray ones so that the hair seemed to take on an inner glow.

She was behaving perfectly, and she was stunning. I could feel people watching us with envy as she trotted by. But right then, I despised every minute of time I had to spend on the mare's back.

I miss you, Titan.

I had thought this horse show would be a breeze. It wasn't like it was the same venue where Titan had died or anything. I shouldn't have been bothered this badly. But I was.

It had started the second we'd driven into the show grounds.

Something about the smells and the sounds and the familiar, and yet oh so different, routine.

And all those people staring. Okay, not *all* of them had been staring. But I'd seen the startled sidelong looks when I'd walked into the show office, heard the whispers behind my back. And all I could think about was that somewhere here, someone hated me enough to film my rides. To film me eating lunch. Anything I did here could be twisted and used in this sick game.

Jeremy and Bree had both asked me a few times if I was okay. But I'd smiled and lied my way through it. Doing my best to keep from having the mother of all meltdowns.

Luckily, Poppy, despite normally being the world's most sensitive princess, didn't seem to care at all what I was feeling up there.

The second she'd sashayed into the ring and saw all those people watching her, she'd puffed right up and put on the training level test of her life. Which was also the first training level test of her life, but she was giving it her all.

We weren't there to win that day. It was just to give her experience and see how she handled the crowds and other horses. But nobody had told her that.

She threw her whole heart into that test while I sat there on autopilot, barely able to give her directions.

A knot had formed in my throat and I could hardly breathe.

Do not cry. Do not cry. Pull yourself together. Titan is not coming back and this horse needs you to be there for her.

My internal pep talk worked and I managed to guide Poppy through the whole test and back to the center line. She slid to an enthusiastic square halt, pricking her ears and probably batting her long lashes at the judge.

Why did you have to leave? We were a team. And you left me behind.

I realized that I'd been standing there about a minute too long and I pulled myself together, gave Poppy a well-deserved pat and let her walk on a loose rein toward the gate. A handful of people outside the ring started clapping for us, and I was relieved to discover that I hadn't completely messed her test up.

"You're such a good girl," I said automatically, trying to add some warmth to my voice. She had been a perfect, brave baby horse on her first outing. Better than I could have hoped, actually. The only one messing up here was me.

"Oh, I should have been watching," Julie beamed up at me as I rode over to our temporary stalls. She had her hat pulled low to cover the burn marks on her face. Not so much to hide them as to protect the more sensitive skin from the sun. "I missed the whole thing. How was she?"

"Perfect," I forced myself to say, swinging down to land on the browned, trampled grass. "She didn't put a foot wrong."

"Well, you could have smiled more," Chloe said, puffing up behind me on her crutches. Her face was red and blotched with the effort of having to move so fast. "You looked like you were in agony the whole time."

I was, I thought, busying myself with the mare's girth.

"Sorry, that's just my game face." I turned away from Chloe's accusing look.

"Well, the test itself looked good," she said grudgingly. She'd been trying hard to be nicer to me lately and we'd become much more friendly toward each other. This show seemed to be making her extra cranky in general.

Julie looked over at me in concern, her smile slipping away.

"Oh, Maisy, are you doing okay? Is this too much for you? Do you want me to get Jeremy?"

"No, no," I said impatiently, waving her away. "I don't need a babysitter. It's just … it's a lot. I'm okay, though. I can handle it."

The last thing I wanted to do right then was talk about how I was *feeling*. The only way I was going to get through the rest of the day was if I just kept moving, working, and riding.

"If you're sure," Julie said doubtfully. I definitely wasn't fooling her.

"I am. Is Nugget ready? He needs to be warmed up now."

"Um, yes. He's clean and braided. He just has to be tacked up."

"Okay, great. I can do that if you guys take care of Poppy."

I handed the reins to Julie and turned away abruptly, heading to Nugget's stall.

I needed to be somewhere alone right then, just to gather my thoughts and pull myself together.

I took a deep breath as I slipped inside, inhaling the good smell of pine shavings and a freshly bathed horse.

Nugget turned to me with a rumbling nicker and I went right to him, running a hand down his neck. I instantly felt calmer.

These were good horses and I was going to do my best by them if it killed me. I'd already half messed up Poppy's ride, but I wasn't going to make the same mistake with Nugget. His future owner might be here somewhere, so I wasn't planning on letting him down.

I tacked him up in record time, waving off Julie and Chloe's efforts to help. Bree was off helping Jeremy with Timely, and Dragon would be up next. I could easily do my own warm up. I'd been showing on my own for years after all.

Nugget was a relaxed type of guy, and he already had a few shows under his belt, so he wasn't worried about the crowds of people and horses. It was a smaller show and it didn't have a carnival next door to it this time. So the atmosphere was pretty chilled and I felt myself relaxing as we headed to the warm up ring.

There were only four or five other horses in there, so I set myself on the rail and let him trot out on a long rein to loosen up. I was so focused on him that I didn't notice the girl standing at the far corner at first. Not until I'd passed her a few times.

She stood alone, her arms crossed over her chest, and she was staring at me with a look of pure hatred. I half-recognized her but, she was blonde, pretty, and dressed in breeches and a show-shirt which meant she looked exactly like half the people here.

Nugget faltered a step as I lost concentration and it took me a second to regroup. When I looked up again, she was gone.

I pushed her out of my mind while I carefully took Nugget through his test. He put in a steady, if not brilliant, performance that I was happy with and I rubbed his neck enthusiastically as we left the ring.

"Good job," Jeremy said, meeting me just outside the entrance. He was mounted on Lauren's horse Sassafras and he reached over to give me a hug. He must have had to jump right on her as soon as Timely's test was done.

"Yes, well done."

I glanced down to see Lauren staring up at us, her eyes slightly narrowed on the hand Jeremy had left casually on my knee.

"Hey, Lauren. Sassafras is looking good."

"Thank you." The smile she sent me didn't quite meet her eyes and I frowned. Lauren had always been pleasant to me in the past. What had changed?

"I'd better get back.," I said quickly. "We'll get Dragon ready for you. Good luck out there. Bye, Lauren."

I nudged Nugget toward the stalls without glancing back, letting him walk on a loose rein as he ambled through the show grounds.

"Can you believe she had the nerve to show up here with everything she's done?" a voice said loudly behind me.

I stiffened and willed myself not to turn around.

"She thinks she can kill one horse and then just show up with another one. Like they're disposable."

That's it.

Without thinking, I leapt off Nugget's back and whipped around to face them.

It was two girls I didn't even recognize. They looked like they were about seventeen years old and they were both staring at me with shocked, panicked expressions.

I took two steps toward them and stopped, my hand bunched tightly around the end of Nugget's reins.

"I loved Titan." I said loudly. "And I didn't kill him. He was my best friend. I don't know why you hate me so much. But this has to stop."

They both just stood frozen, gaping at me in horror like I was about to knife them or something. A few people drifted to a stop around us, watching us curiously.

"Hey, there you are," Bree said, coming up beside me and linking her arm tightly through mine. "Come on, we need you back at the barn. That was a great ride by the way."

She turned her hundred-watt smile on the two girls.

"Hi, I'm Bree," she said. "Are you guys enjoying the show?"

"Um, yes," the one girl said, "we've got to go." She grabbed her friend's hand and they both hurried away.

"Nice to meet you," Bree called after them and then steered me back toward the barn.

"Are you okay?" she whispered, holding my arm tightly. "I was right there. I heard what they said. I can't believe anyone would say that stuff to you. We should report them to the show office."

"No," I said, dully. "It isn't worth it."

"It is. You're worth it, Maisy. You matter. You shouldn't be treated like that. People need to know what's going on."

I shook my head and squeezed her arm tight. "You're a good friend, Bree. I'm so glad you were there.

The adrenaline and anger from my confrontation faded. And I was surprised to find that I actually felt okay. The worst had happened, I'd been confronted in public and I'd survived. There was a kind of strength in that.

After that, I was ready for anything.

CHAPTER 36

MAISY

*W*hen we got back to the farm, all I wanted to do was see Chilly. But we had horses to unload, a trailer to unpack, and a barn to take care of. So it wasn't until nearly evening that I got a chance to work with him.

The sun was well on its way down and the sky had turned dark blue on one side with the last pink stains of the sun on the other. It looked like some beautiful, alien skyscape.

I brought a few brushes with me out to the ring and sat on the mounting block while Chilly wandered around, laughing as he dropped down into the sand for a good roll. Then he stood back up and shook himself from head to tail like a dog, a dust cloud poofing up over his back.

"Chilly, here," I called softly, and he looked up and ambled over to me.

I wrapped his neck in a tight hug and inhaled deeply, taking in his familiar warmth and scent. A smell that now meant home to me.

I stepped back and gave him a cookie. Then I put him through his groundwork routine, working on him backing and stepping sideways in a rhythm, yielding his quarters and then his shoulders in turn.

Then I called him to the mounting block and climbed on board.

Guiding him around the ring with just my seat and legs, I moved him up into a trot, doing a series of wide loopy serpentines, circles and figure eights. We practiced stopping and backing up and some of the easy lateral movements that the vet had okayed.

"Well, would you look at that."

I looked up in surprise to find Lorne and Julie leaning against the arena fence. I'd been so absorbed that I hadn't even seen them come up.

"Are you sure that's safe?" Julie called.

"Of course, it's safe," Lorne said, "look at them. Nothing to be worried about."

I gave Chilly another pat and then jumped to the ground, taking a second to scratch his neck and quietly thank him.

"Bree has been telling us all about this," Lorne said, beaming at me proudly. "She says you've taught him to bow, too?"

"Um, yeah." I moved back to Chilly's shoulder and touched a spot below his elbow. "Bow, Chilly."

He immediately dropped his nose between his knees, sticking his front leg out and dipping down into a bow.

"We've been working on some liberty stuff, too. I can show you if you like?" It came out a question, my voice rising nervously at the top. I was used to people watching me ride, coaches yelling at me, critiquing my every move, but this felt more private and personal somehow. I always waited until I was alone to do this stuff.

"I'd like that," Lorne said, smiling at me.

"Okay," I said, picking up the lunge whip from its spot beside the mounting block. "Chilly, trot on."

He blinked at me in surprise. He'd thought we were done and was already staring at the barn thinking about his hay.

"Go on, just a couple more minutes."

He sighed and moved out toward the rail at a walk and then broke into a trot.

"Good boy, Chilly, switch."

He made a loop and changed direction, one ear twisted inward to fix on me.

"Okay, Chilly, here."

He swiveled around and trotted right up to me, not stopping until his big head was touching my chest.

"Good boy. Now, around."

He backed up a step and then did a circle away from me before returning back to rest his head on me again.

"Such a good, smart boy," I whispered to him. I scratched both sides of his neck and gave him a kiss in the middle of his forehead.

"That's it," I said, turning to Lorne and Julie. "We've just been playing around so he only knows a few things. I didn't want to teach him to rear or paw just in case he started doing it all the time."

"Yeah, rearing would be a bad idea," Julie said quickly. "But that other stuff is great, Maisy. He looks like he's having a lot of fun. How did you learn to do all that?"

"Um, I took a couple of clinics when I was a teenager and read a few books, watched a few videos. It's really just playing around. I haven't done it in years to be honest."

"Well, you seem to be a natural at it. Do you think you could help Bree try that with Follow?"

"Follow?" I said in surprise. I hadn't had much to do with the timid little mare.

"She could use a confidence boost and I think this might be the ticket. Would you be interested?"

"Yes, actually. I'd love that."

"I work with her in the mornings doing lunging and ground-work, so I think you could do some short afternoon or evening sessions with her. Honestly, the more positive handling she gets right now, the better."

"Sure," I said again.

"You're a good addition to the team here, Maisy," Julie said as she turned away.

I stared after her in shock. Then a small smile tugged at my lips.

That was the first compliment that Julie had ever given me.

CHAPTER 37

MAISY

I curled up on the couch, pulling a newly purchased book on liberty work onto my lap, stifling a yawn. I'd had a shower and thrown on a pair of shorts and a tank top, and now I was ready to just relax after my busy day.

A cup of tea sat on the end table beside me and I'd made myself a little plate of assorted cookies to go with it.

Despite being a roller coaster of a day, I actually felt, well, I felt good. Like I'd faced another part of my sorrow over Titan and won. I looked up at his painting on the wall and felt only fondness. No guilt, no horror. Just love of a good friend. It was probably the most comfortable I'd felt since Titan had died. Since before that maybe.

A sigh of contentment rippled through me and I snuggled deeper into my corner of the couch, opening the book to the page I'd left off on.

From somewhere outside I could hear the heavy thump,

thump, thump of a car maxing out its stereo as it headed up the road in my direction.

Gravel skidded and I could hear the sound of people cheering and yelling.

Stupid kids, I thought, not looking up from my book. Every summer since as long as I could remember, teenagers would let off steam at night by burning up and down the gravel roads, popping their e-brakes to send their cars spinning and drifting on the soft surfaces. It wasn't my idea of fun, but it was mostly harmless. Unless they hit an animal or a person, of course.

Our road was a dead-end street with a circular turn-around at the very end so we seemed to get more joyriders than other neighborhoods.

Gravel skidded again and there were more shouts of excitement. They were chanting something, too. An engine revved close by and I sat up suddenly.

Were they in the driveway?

The motion lights outside kicked on and then headlights lit up the front of the house and the air was filled with sound. I got up off the couch and hurried cautiously toward the kitchen where I'd have a better view. Why would they have turned in here?

But, before I could take more than a few steps, there was a violent explosion as the kitchen window shattered in a burst of glass.

Outside, the car revved and spun out, I ran to the front door and flung it open, watching in horror as the car fishtailed sideways and slammed into my truck.

Yells of alarm came from the car and then it shot forward, tires spinning hard. The car was hung up on the fender of the truck somehow and metal groaned as the driver struggled desperately to get away.

I need my phone. I need the police. I turned and ran back toward the living room, snatching my phone off the couch and turned back, camera already fired up and ready.

I got there just as the car detached itself from the truck with a screech of metal and burned up the driveway toward the road. I took photo after photo, hoping desperately that I could lighten the pictures up later and catch a license plate or something.

And then I called the police, telling them what had happened as calmly as I could, my voice shaking the whole time.

"Someone will be right there," a kindly operator said, "you just stay put until they get there. I can wait with you on the phone if you like."

"No, I'm all right," I said, catching sight of the brick that now lay under the kitchen table. "I'll be fine."

I hung up, my heart thumping. The kitchen window was in ruins and dimly, I wondered who you called when you needed a window fixed.

I went back to the open front door and shut it carefully, and then slipped on my barn clogs and went into the kitchen, glass crunching underneath my feet.

The brick was wrapped in paper with a piece of orange twine around it. Binder twine like the type used to hold hay bales together.

My breath caught in my throat and I let out a sob.

Why are they doing this? Who could possibly hate me this much?

Gingerly, I reached forward and grasped the edge of the twine, sliding the brick toward me. Glass shards sprinkled down off of it as I carefully pulled it free from the debris.

I knew I shouldn't touch anything. It was a crime scene after all and there might be fingerprints. But I needed to know what was on that paper.

Stepping backward, I went to the kitchen drawer and fished around until I found the sharp pair of scissors that usually lived there.

They bit easily into the tightly wrapped twine, and I took a deep breath as I pulled the note free. My fingers were shaking as I unfolded it, leaving tiny dots of blood where I touched the paper. I hadn't felt myself getting cut by the miniscule bits of glass but when I looked down my fingers were stained a pale red.

This is Karma you lying psycho witch. Someone needs to lock you up. Permanently.

That's all it said.

I stared at it numbly, frozen in place until the police arrived.

The officers were very sympathetic. Someone made me sit in a kitchen chair and tell them what happened while the other officer went around taking pictures.

They even called in a second car once they saw the note that had been wrapped around the brick.

I just sat there woodenly, watching them while they worked, answering questions accurately and trying not to feel anything. Not terror, not the deep biting sadness that had lodged itself in my chest. The room was full of people but I was so, so alone.

"Okay, tell us what happened one more time," the officer beside me said kindly.

"Maisy?"

I looked up to see Jeremy standing in the open doorway, his eyes locked on me and his expression grim.

I opened my mouth to say something, anything, and then promptly burst into tears.

He was at my side in a second, strong arms wrapping around me while I pressed my face against him and sobbed and sobbed. All the adrenaline of the night flooded out of me.

"You're okay," he said over and over again, his hands rubbing my back. "Maisy, what happened? I saw the lights."

"Why don't you go into the living room?" The officer nearest me said kindly. "We'll take a few more minutes to finish up here and then we can ask a few more questions."

I didn't want to answer any more questions but I let Jeremy herd me to the living room and set me down on the couch.

"What on earth happened?" he said, pulling one of my hands into his and looking at my blood-tinged fingers.

"Some kids threw a brick through my window," I said, numbly shrugging like it didn't matter.

He was looking at me steadily, saying nothing.

"Seriously, it's not a big deal. I can handle it." I pulled my hand out of his, wincing as my pricked fingers scraped across his rough palm.

"I have no doubt about that," he said quietly. "But you don't have to do everything alone, Maisy. Let your friends help."

"It … it's embarrassing," I said finally. "I don't want you to know."

"I've been addicted to gambling since I was sixteen years old." He picked up my hand again gently and studied it. "I told you that my dad kicked me out but it's not the whole story. It's my most painful secret."

I looked up at him in surprise, letting his warm hand stay wrapped around my wrist, waiting for him to go on.

"I owed money to the worst type of people. I tried to get it back by stealing, which shows how stupid I was at the time.

"But when they didn't get their money from me they came to the farm to collect instead. They were bad people, Maisy. And I shudder to think how it could have ended if my dad hadn't paid them off right then.

"As it was, they roughed up my family a little and scared everyone out of their wits. My mom had nightmares about that night for years. I will never forgive myself for the fear they felt that night. Anyway, it was after that that my dad sent me away and said I was never welcome to come home."

"No," I said in shock, turning to look at him. "Jeremy, I'm so sorry."

"Me, too. I had a few bad years there. I did things I'm not proud of. And sometimes, when the stress gets too bad, I have a small relapse like the one I had just before I came to October

Horses. My addiction is under control, but it will never fully go away. Lorne knows. He lends me the truck so I can go to my weekly meetings."

He reached over and brushed a stray lock of hair off my cheek gently.

"Any secret you have to tell me can't be as bad as that, Maisy. You can trust me to help you. And not to judge you. I've been to the bottom, and I know how lonely it can be."

I forced myself to look up and meet his eyes and the kind, open expression on his face nearly undid me again.

"All right," I said finally. "I'll tell you the whole story."

I went through the entire year-long saga for him and the officers, and then reluctantly pulled up the videos to show them.

Jeremy kept his arm tightly locked around my shoulders as we watched them all, his expression getting darker and angrier.

The police actually ended up taking my phone so they could work on tracing the texts and they took the note and the brick away with them, too. Leaving me to clean up the glass and call the insurance company for the second time this summer. I still had to deal with the damage to my poor truck, too.

"You shouldn't be alone tonight," the kind officer who'd spoken to me most, said. "You've had a shock. And, there is a slight possibility that they could come back again."

"I'll stay with her," Jeremy said. "She won't be alone."

"Well, good then. We'll be in touch in the next few days."

"Thanks," I said faintly, ushering them to the door. I sagged back against it as soon as the lock clicked shut and turned to face Jeremy.

"You don't have to stay with me," I said. "I'll be fine."

It was a lie and we both knew it.

"I'm staying," he said firmly. "Let's get this kitchen cleaned up first. Where do you keep your cleaning supplies?"

We worked together sweeping up all the big shards of glass and then went over every inch of the kitchen to find the smaller bits that had scattered across practically every surface. We swept and vacuumed and mopped then wiped down the tables and countertops until everything was a glass-free as we could make it. I was sure we'd be finding bits of glass in hidden places for the next few years.

My next job was to call the insurance company and make the claim for the window. I emailed them the photos and the file number that the police had given me.

"They said they'll get somebody to come out and fix the window in the morning," I told Jeremy. "I guess we'll just have to cover it up somehow tonight."

"Do you have any cardboard lying around?"

"No," I shook my head. "But we could hang a blanket up to cover it for now."

"Good idea."

Together we wrestled the thick comforter off the guest bed onto the curtain rod and pushed some chairs up against it to pin the cover to the wall. It certainly wouldn't keep any criminals out but it would keep bats and bugs from flying in.

I sat down heavily on a nearby kitchen chair, staring at the window and wondering how my life had come to this.

"Have you eaten?" Jeremy asked.

"Yeah." I shook my head to push back some of the lethargy that was falling over me. After the shocks of the evening, I was nearly drooping with tiredness. "I mean, I had some toast earlier. And some cookies."

"Toast and cookies are not food, Maisy. You haven't had anything else since the horse show?"

"No, I don't really feel like eating much lately for some reason. I have lunch with you guys and that seems like enough."

"Well, it isn't," he snapped. "Come on, you're an athlete. You know better than to treat your body like that."

"I'm not an athlete anymore," I shot back. "I'm just a regular person who lives in their parent's basement. I can eat all the junk food I like."

He rolled his eyes and then tilted his head on one side as he studied me.

"You mean this isn't your house?"

"Not the upstairs no. I've been staying up here lately but I belong in the basement."

"Oh, thank goodness. I thought you might have split personalities or something. This place looks nothing like you."

Despite my irritation with him, I started to laugh.

"No, the decorating is all my mom's doing. Come on, I'll show you my suite. There's probably something frozen in the freezer we can eat."

"Processed food isn't—"

"Take it or leave it," I said over my shoulder as I headed toward the stairs. "It's all we've got."

I watched Jeremy out of the corner of my eye as he took in my suite. I'd cleaned it somewhat recently so it wasn't too messy.

"This is nice," he said sounding surprised.

"Thanks. It's got memories of Titan everywhere, though. That's why I've been avoiding it."

"I get that. These paintings and photos are amazing."

I opened the deep chest freezer and peered inside, rummaging through the stacks of frozen meals until I found something that looked edible.

"Lasagna?" I asked, pulling myself upright.

But Jeremy had wandered to the far side of the room and pushed open the door to the gym.

"Holy cow, Maisy. You have a whole fitness center in there. I thought you said you weren't an athlete."

"Yeah, yeah. I forced myself to work out when I was in training. But I always hated it. I did it because I had to."

"It's more fun with other people around, you know."

He looked at me expectantly and I sighed.

"You can use the equipment, Jeremy. I don't mind at all. Just don't drag me into it."

"Hmm," was all he said. Which sounded suspiciously like he wasn't going to let it go without an argument.

"I'm going to pop down the hill to grab some things. I won't be gone longer than ten minutes. Will you be okay alone?"

"Of course," I said, squashing down the stab of panic I felt at the thought of being alone in this house for more than five seconds.

He studied me for a moment and then reached out to tug on my arm. "Actually, why don't you come with me. I can grab my things and you can see Chilly for a few minutes."

I knew that the logical thing was to say no. That I didn't need a babysitter or to hang off Chilly like he was my emotional support animal or something. I was better than this, stronger.

"Okay," I heard myself saying. "I'll just put the lasagna on. It will take about an hour."

Five minutes later we were speeding down the hill and I felt better and better the further we got away from that house.

Jeremy let me off at the barn while he went up to the cabin he shared with Lorne and I slipped inside and flicked on the overhead lights.

"Sorry, everyone," I whispered, making my way down the aisle to Chilly's stall. He didn't come to greet me and I crept up to his door and peered inside.

"Aww, are you sleeping, buddy?"

He lifted his head off the shavings, took a look at me, and then set it back down again. Shutting his eyes with a small, contented snort.

I slid the door back and crept inside, going over and kneeling carefully next to his chest. He didn't bother to look up. He just snored softly as I leaned back against him and ran my hands down his neck, tangling with his mane.

I was struck all over again with how beautiful he was. The

contrasting colors, the elegant neck, and finely chiseled head. He was like a living sculpture.

I wasn't sure how long I sat there beside him. But when I heard footsteps in the aisle, I slowly pulled myself to my feet.

"Are you ready to go?" Jeremy asked, smiling down at Chilly who'd raised his head a few inches and then set it back down again.

"Yeah, thanks for bringing me to see him. That's exactly what I needed."

"I guessed that."

"How?" I asked in confusion but he just shook his head.

"Come on, we have some lasagna to eat. Lorne loaned us a loaf of garlic bread, too."

"You told him what happened?"

"Yeah, he's really worried about you. He says you can always stay here if you don't want to stay at home. He has this idea that I'd be an annoying roommate or something."

I laughed.

"No, if you're really okay with it then I'd like to have you stay. Just until the window is fixed."

"That I can do. But it's more than the broken window, Maisy. These people are disturbed. And it's escalated past videos and online bullying. I don't think it's safe for you to be alone there until they find out who is responsible."

"They might never find them," I said quietly.

"They will, don't give up yet. We're going to take care of this together, okay?"

"Okay." Relief washed over me. I wasn't alone in this anymore. We were going to find a way to make the whole nightmare end.

CHAPTER 38

MAISY

*B*ut the next morning, I had to face a different kind of nightmare.

"No, no way. I'm not ready," I said, glaring up at where Jeremy stood at the end of my bed, a wicked gleam in his eyes. He was wearing a t-shirt and shorts and had a towel draped over one shoulder. "What time is it anyway?"

"Oh, just a little before sunrise. Perfect time to get up and get a little exercise."

"No." I burrowed down under the covers and then squealed as he began to slowly pull them off of me. I gripped onto them as long as I could and then finally sat up.

"You're such a bully. I had a traumatic night last night, the last thing I want to do is work out."

"You might think that now, but afterwards you'll feel like a new person."

"Ha, I think I know my own body, Jeremy. It wants more sleep and less drama. And no exercise."

"I'll make you a deal. You work out with me one time. Just once. Without complaining. And after that, I'll leave you alone. If you don't want to do it again, then I'll keep my mouth shut and not bother you about it. Ever."

I narrowed my eyes at him.

"And," he went on, "I'll make you a real breakfast. Eggs, bacon, hashbrowns and ..."

"Okay," I said, leaping out of bed, "you're on. But this is one time only."

"Of course," he said innocently and then headed to the workout room, leaving me to get changed in peace.

I pulled on some leggings, a sports bra and a tank top, and headed to the bathroom to brush my teeth and pull my hair back. I looked at myself critically in the mirror, noticing for the first time how tired and sort of run-down I looked. There were circles under my eyes and I looked pale, despite being out in the sun all day.

Maybe Jeremy was right about the food thing. I haven't been eating well. And I do look kind of awful.

I felt a shiver of nerves as I pushed my way into the gym, wondering what it would be like to work out with someone who actually liked it.

"Should we warm up with a run?" Jeremy asked from where he was fiddling around with one of the treadmills.

"I suppose," I muttered. "Whatever gets this over with faster."

"It's not supposed to be torture, Maisy. It's supposed to be fun."

I raised an eyebrow at him.

"Seriously. Was there never a time when you enjoyed this?"

"Well, maybe when I was a teenager or something. My parents built this so I could work out with my friends. We used to hang out here all the time. But that was a long time ago."

"Okay, well pretend I'm one of your high school girlfriends then. We can gossip and talk about boys and do our hair."

Despite myself, I started to laugh.

"You think high school girls just gossip and talk about boys?" I climbed onto the treadmill next to his and pushed some buttons until I was walking briskly.

"Um, no? I honestly have no idea."

"I thought you had sisters."

"Yes, but I was younger than them. I didn't get to hang out much. But, you're right. I remember that most of the talk was about horses and destroying the patriarchy."

"That sounds more like it."

We kept our banter going back and forth as we transitioned up to a jog. I was surprised how fast the time flew and how easy it was to spend time on the treadmill. I wasn't bored at all.

Jeremy went on the bike and I went to the rowing machine, something I'd forgotten how much I loved.

We ended the session doing reps on a few of the weight machines. By the end I was dripping with sweat and puffing for breath, but I felt exhilarated, too. Like my body had been missing this for a long, long time.

"See, not so bad?" Jeremy said, tugging on my pony tail.

"Don't you dare say I told you so."

"Wouldn't dream of it. I'll get started on the breakfast I promised, if you want to shower."

"How about we both shower," I said, "and then I can help with breakfast."

He stared at me in surprise and then I suddenly realized what I'd said.

"I mean separate showers," I squeaked, feeling my cheeks flush. "There are two upstairs. I'll use this one. Alone. By myself."

Jeremy's mouth drew up slowly into a smile and I knew that I was in for a world of teasing if I didn't get out of there. I bolted for the bathroom, shutting and locking the door firmly behind me and then stuffed myself under a stream of hot water so I could forget what an awkward person I was.

I was over it by the time I went up for breakfast, though. Jeremy had apparently ordered us some food the night before because a van from the grocery store pulled up with bags of supplies.

There was not a bag of chips or cookies to be seen.

"This is all vegetables," I said, wrinkling my nose.

"Yes, Maisy, meet real food. Real food, Maisy."

"Very funny. I know what vegetables are. I just prefer them more—"

"Processed?"

"Yeah, something like that."

"Come on, you won't be complaining once you taste my breakfast."

He had that right. He minced up vegetables and bacon and made these incredible cheese omelets that just melted in my mouth. Then he made hashbrowns with real potatoes.

"How did you learn to make this stuff?" I asked incredulously.

"I don't know. My mom, I guess."

"My mom never cooked anything like this. Seriously, can you make us more of the omelets?"

He raised an eyebrow.

"I promised you one breakfast for one workout session. If I made another omelet then that would be considered second breakfast. Which would mean you owe me another round in the gym."

"What? That's not fair."

"Those are the kitchen rules," he said, shaking his head in mock sadness.

I stared at the frying pan on the stove and sighed.

"Fine, you win. Just one more session then. Now, start cooking."

～

After all the drama of the night before, the rest of the day was strangely peaceful. I'd taken the morning off work since I had to be there when the guy showed up to fix the window. And then I drove into town to buy myself a new phone, picking a brand-new number that nobody else but me knew.

Why didn't I think about doing this before? I thought, feeling strangely free and buoyant.

I made arrangements to drop the truck off at the garage the next day and called my insurance company to tell them what had happened. I didn't think that too much damage had been done, other than a torn bumper. But I wanted to get it checked out just in case.

I got to the barn feeling refreshed and full of energy. And the happy feeling lasted through all my rides and evening chores.

That night, even though the window had been fixed, Jeremy insisted on staying over to keep me company again.

I was so relieved to not be alone in that house that I didn't argue. It felt right to have him around. So right that he kind of just never left.

I didn't even complain about him dragging me into helping him cook these ridiculously healthy meals. It was almost worth all the work when I tasted how delicious they were. I felt like I was living with a gourmet chef.

Which was good because he also insisted on getting up before dawn to work out. And, though I felt my obligation to put up a fuss about it every single time, I had to admit that it was much for fun to exercise with someone else around to keep me company. Even when that someone had way too much motivation first thing in the morning.

"So, um, are you guys living together?" Bree asked me one morning, a few days in to our new arrangement.

I had already told her about the window incident, but we hadn't discussed much else.

"Yes. I mean, no, not like that. We're just friends. He's keeping me company."

"Okay, if you say so." She arched her eyebrows and grinned. "You look pretty happy together, though."

"We do have a lot of fun together," I admitted. "Movie marathons are much more fun when you have someone to share the popcorn with."

I changed the subject before she could say anything more about it.

But I thought about it over the next couple of days. There was no doubt that I was attracted to Jeremy. And he'd certainly been a good friend to me. But he was hard to get a read on whether he wanted more than friendship or not. It was possible that he just felt really sorry for me and wanted to help.

It was too much of a risk to try and push our boundaries yet. I didn't think my fragile self would be able to handle any more rejection this year.

～

"Blueberry tarts or butter tarts?" Jeremy asked as I padded into the kitchen after my shower.

"Wow, who exactly are you?" I said incredulously, looking down at the already-baked tart shells lined up on the counter. "This is amazing."

"One of my sisters is a caterer. And her love of food started young so she did a lot of experimenting. I was a willing test subject."

He looked down at the battered recipe book in front of him and frowned.

"Yeah, I bet you were. What is this sister's name?"

"Olivia. You'd like her. Don't tell the others but she's my favourite."

"Okay, she is officially my favourite sister now, too. Butter tarts, please."

"Good choice. I'll tell her you said that. How are you at chopping pecans?"

"Do we even own pecans?"

"You do now."

"Okay, hit me up." I pulled out one of the stools next to the kitchen island and made myself useful chopping pecans and raisins and locating missing ingredients. And licking the sugar mixture off the spoon when Jeremy wasn't looking.

I could hardly contain myself as I kept my eyes fixed on the oven door, watching them bake. The smell was incredible.

"Um, you seem to have a little something on your face," Jeremy said as he passed by on the way to the sink. When I turned, he was right there, standing just a few inches away from me. He reached over and ran his thumb gently across my cheek. "And here." He touched a spot over my eyebrow. "Somehow, you are coated in filling."

"Huh, that's strange." I kept my eyes locked on his, my cheeks burning with heat. He was so close to me and I was acutely aware of his hand still resting against my skin. My gaze flicked down from his eyes to his lips.

"Maisy." His voice was low and I felt a hitch in my breath.

Before I could doubt myself, I closed the gap between us, pressing myself against him and brushing my lips against his.

For a moment, he froze, and I started to back away in embarrassment. And then he was right there with one hand tangled in my hair and his mouth crushing against mine in a way that sucked the breath from my body. Every nerve in my body came alive like I'd been zapped with electricity.

A few seconds later we broke apart, panting and staring at each other.

I couldn't read his expression and my first thought that was he must have made a mistake. He already regretted kissing me.

"You're stunning," he said, reaching out and pushing a lock of hair behind my ear. Then he pulled me tightly against him, kissing my neck and the line of my jaw, and back to my mouth again. Each touch sweet and burning. "You're the best thing that has happened to me in a long time."

He pulled back and looked down at me, his eyes troubled.

"What?" I asked. "What's wrong?"

"I care about you, Maisy ..."

And, there it was. The I care about you as a friend but not as my girlfriend speech.

"But I've had a rough past. I come with a lot of baggage. I just want you to be sure."

Oh, that was not what I'd been expecting.

"Jeremy, I know you. I trust you. And I come with my own emotional damage and a full-time stalker. I'm not worried about your past."

"Well, I am. I want to do right by you, Maisy. You're important to me. I don't want to wreck things."

I stared up at him. Surprised at the seriousness in his voice. This really meant a lot to him.

"Okay," I said quietly. "We'll take it slow then. There's no rush."

Before things could get any more serious, the timer for the oven went off and the mood was broken.

But something had shifted between us, in a good way. There was a new closeness that felt completely natural.

When we curled up on the couch to watch our latest movie marathon, it felt right to snuggle up next to him with his arm draped casually over me.

And a few nights later it felt right that he didn't sleep in the guest room. That we woke up sleepily entwined next to each other in the morning, our hearts beating peacefully together.

CHAPTER 39

MAISY

*I*t was two nights later, well past midnight, when the phone call came.

I woke up first, adrenaline shooting me wide awake before I realized that it wasn't my phone. I flopped back down immediately and was nearly asleep again by the time Jeremy stopped the ringing.

"Hello," he said quietly, walking out into the hallway and shutting the door behind him.

He didn't sound anxious at all, and I was so tired that I just burrowed under the covers and fell soundly back asleep.

When I woke up, hours later, I was alone and there was a note on my pillow.

Family emergency to deal with, it said, *I'll be back.*

"Oh no." I sat up, cursing myself for falling asleep on him when he might have needed me. Hopefully it was nothing too serious.

I left him a quick voicemail, just checking if he needed

anything and then hauled myself out of bed. Even though he still wasn't back I forced myself to do an abbreviated workout and ate a revoltingly healthy breakfast. When he still hadn't called or shown up an hour later, I threw on my work clothes and headed to the barn.

"Good morning," I called as Chilly stuck his nose out over his stall door and nickered eagerly. I broke off as Julie stomped out of the tack room, looking crankier than I'd ever seen her.

"What … what's the matter?" I asked, taking a few steps back to get out of her way.

"Jeremy," she spat out his name as if it offended her.

"What?" I felt all the blood drain from my face. Was he hurt? Had he been fired?

"He's gone," she said. "He flew back to Scotland first thing this morning. Nicholas drove him to the airport."

"Gone." Cold shock washed over me and I reached a hand out to touch the wall for support as my legs wobbled. "I thought his dad wouldn't let him go back to visit."

"Well, I guess something changed his mind. I can't believe he'd leave us in the lurch like this. It's so irresponsible."

"No, there must be a mistake. He left me a note this morning saying it was a family emergency. He wouldn't have left without good reason."

"Well, I'd like to believe that," Julie said, "I guess we'll see what happens. In the meantime, we're short a rider. Again. You'll take over some of his horses, won't you?"

"Er, yes?" As long as that didn't include Dragon, then I'd ride whatever they needed me to.

"Great, well, let's get to work."

The morning seemed to drag on endlessly. Julie threw me on horse after horse. I finally got to ride Timely, but I was too bewildered by Jeremy's departure that I couldn't enjoy it properly. I rode Jet, Poppy, and Nugget in quick succession, and it wasn't until the very end of day that I was able to play with Chilly.

Bree rode Ace and Nipper and then dragged me down to the ring to help her work with Follow.

I went through all the motions, but it was hard to feel any of my usual happiness in working with the horses.

I left a couple more messages for Jeremy but there was never a response.

"It's for the best, you know," Chloe had whispered to me sympathetically as she passed by. "He had a hidden side to him, Maisy. You were always too good for him. Better off that he's far away."

I'd resisted smacking her and limited myself to rolling my eyes and stomping away from her. Neither she nor Julie had been Jeremy's biggest fans.

Only Bree seemed to understand my concern.

"He'll be all right," she told me more than once. "He probably can't use his cell phone on the plane. It's a long flight, like eighteen hours. I'm sure he'll be in touch the second he can."

I appreciated her confidence. It was what I needed right then to keep me going.

Especially when I didn't hear from him that night. Or the next night. Or the one after that.

Eventually, I just stopped texting and sending messages. I hoped that he was okay.

Bree asked me again to move into the house with her but I just shook my head.

"Thanks, but I'll be okay, really. So far nothing else has happened."

And I was sleeping through the night for once because Julie worked me off my feet the whole day long and at night I just crashed into bed and slept like a rock.

That week ended up being the longest, busiest week I'd ever had. Julie seemed to take all her irritation over Jeremy's departure out on me for some unfair reason. By the second day, I'd run out of excuses to avoid riding Dragon.

But, although it wasn't exactly pleasant, my ride on her was completely uneventful. She was still uncooperative and stubborn, but she wasn't lethal. And really, that was all I could hope for from her.

As day after day passed, and I didn't hear from him, my faith that Jeremy was planning on ever coming back began to waver. He'd just disappeared off the face of the earth.

The only upshot to the week was that there were no new videos posted and no harassing phone calls. Ever since the night the brick had been tossed through my window, things had been eerily quiet. I didn't trust it.

CHAPTER 40

MAISY

"Hey, Maisy," Julie called, waving me into the barn where she was standing with two people. A mom and what I guessed might be her teenage daughter. The girl was dressed in riding gear, and the older lady was dressed like a mom, not a coach. She had on a pant suit and was carrying her leather purse tucked up protectively against her chest like she was expecting someone to mug her, or the horses to eat it or something.

"Hey," I said cautiously, moving toward them. I didn't like the way they were standing outside of Chilly's stall. Even as I watched, he stuck his big nose out into the aisle.

The girl's solemn face broke into a smile and she stepped forward to scratch his neck.

"Maisy, these folks are here to see Nugget. They filled out an application on him, but we must have crossed wires on when their appointment was. We thought it was for next week."

"Oh," I said, nearly sagging with relief. Not here to see Chilly then. "That's no problem. I can ride him for you first if you like and then you can give him a go."

I chatted with them happily as I led Nugget out and let the girl brush him. She seemed to know her way around a horse and handled him kindly enough. I did notice that she looked over at Chilly a few times, though.

"Do you want to tack him up or should I?" I asked quickly, pulling her focus back to Nugget.

"Oh, you can if you like. That horse over there isn't for adoption, is he?"

I looked around to make sure that Julie had wandered out of earshot.

"Sorry, no," I lowered my voice to nearly a whisper. "He actually has a bad injury. We're not sure if he'll ever be sound."

"Oh," she said, looking disappointed. "Okay."

"But Nugget here is solid and sound. And he can do a bit of everything. He's mellow about cross country, he likes jumping, and he's gotten some decent scores at the local dressage shows he's been to. And he can be trail ridden on his own. I think you're really going to like him."

Luckily for everyone, I was right. By the time the girl, whose name was Charlotte, had ridden him around the ring at a walk trot and canter, and then taken him for a short loop on the trails, she was in love.

"I really like him, Mom," she said winningly. "Can't we get him?"

"He's a very nice colour," the mom said encouragingly. "If you like him, then let's get a vet check done. If he passes then we'll ask your father for a final verdict."

"Great, thank you. I know he'll say yes."

They went off with Julie to talk about all the details, leaving me to untack and groom Nugget on my own.

"She's going to be lucky to have a guy like you in her life, buddy," I told him. "I bet she'll spoil you and dress you in sparkly saddle pads."

Nugget snorted happily, leaning into my brush strokes.

Just then, the phone in my pocket began to buzz and I dove for it, thinking against hope that it had to be Jeremy finally calling me to apologize for leaving so suddenly.

But it wasn't Jeremy, it was an old familiar number that I hadn't seen in a long, long time. I knew I shouldn't answer it but, what the heck, my week had gone sideways anyway. What was one more weird thing?

"Dirk?" I said tentatively, fighting the urge to whisper. I had made the decision, for my career at the time, never to contact Dirk again. I felt a little guilty even talking to him. I wondered how he'd found my new number.

"Hello, Maisy," his voice was warm and charming, which was what Dirk usually sounded like when he was wheeling and dealing. He could be charming when he wanted to be. But he could also be sulky, mean, and a bit spiteful at the drop of a hat. It was always best to treat him with caution.

"How are you?" I asked guardedly.

He laughed jovially, the sound too harsh against my ear.

"Despite having my entire career derailed by spiteful, spoiled little witches, I am doing all right. You know, Maisy, I never had the chance to thank you for not getting involved in that lawsuit fiasco. I owe you one for that. If more people kept their noses out of other people's business, the world be a better place."

"Um, you're welcome?" I said, feeling extremely uncomfortable.

"I'm sorry about Titan," he went on in a softer voice, "he was a great horse. And I'm sorry about Europe. You deserved to be on that team. And that's why I'm calling. I have a horse for you."

"You ... a horse? What do you mean?"

"One of my client's bought a younger horse, a five-year-old, who is loaded with talent. Way too much talent for what she needs. She's rich but pretty dumb sometimes. Anyway, we agreed that we need to find a better rider for it for now. I thought of you right away."

"Me? But why?"

"Because you deserve a second chance, Maisy. You deserve a chance to start over fresh. Sooner or later, all this will be forgotten. My lawsuit, the videos, the rumours. And then it will be our turn to shine again. Just like old times. You're a good rider, Maisy. With the right horse, you could be great. Brilliant. My client has some deep pockets and she's attached to this horse. Play your cards right and it could be smooth sailing for you."

My heart thumped in my chest and for a moment I just stood there, frozen, not answering. Part of me recoiled at the casual way Dirk talked about using his client's money. But another part of me was buying what he was selling, could envision riding this brilliant horse and making all these snotty, vindictive witches eat their words.

A picture of Chilly's kind eyes and sweet expression hovered in front of me and I shook my head.

"It's a nice offer," I said quietly, "but—"

"I didn't tell you the best part," Dirk said triumphantly. "This horse is a half-brother to Titan. Looks just like him."

I sucked in a deep breath, my heart speeding up again.

"Just come meet him. You don't have to make any decisions. We can catch up on old times. No pressure."

"All right," I said finally. "After work tonight. I'll drop by the barn."

The one good thing was that, at the end of the day, I played with Chilly in the ring or took him on longer and longer trail rides. We'd been given the green light to trot further distances on flat ground and he was loving his new freedom. He trundled along on a loose rein with his nose stretched out and his back legs pumping like pistons. Not once did he try and break into a canter or deviate from the trail. He was probably the most trust-worthy horse I'd ever sat on.

When we got back to the barn that night, I got another surprise. Julie was there, all dressed up in soft riding tights and tall boots, a helmet held in one hand. Ace stood dozing in the cross-ties, only blinking his eyes open when Chilly came clop-ping down the aisle toward him.

As I drew closer, I could see that on his back was the strangest saddle I'd ever seen. It looked like one of those Spanish saddles with a high pommel and cantle, but it was made out of black, fluffy sheep wool instead of leather. And there weren't any stirrups.

Bree came into the barn at the same time and stopped to stare at Ace in surprise.

"What are you doing with Ace?" Then she looked at the saddle. "Oh, my gosh, Julie. Is that what I think it is? You got one."

I stared back and forth between them. Not understanding what was going on.

"Okay, okay," Julie said, half irritated and half smiling. "Let's not make a big deal of this. I thought it was time that I gave it a try. I hope you don't mind me borrowing your boy for this."

"No, not at all. I'm so excited," Bree said, practically jumping up and down. "Can I touch it?"

"Sure." Julie laughed. "It's pretty plush."

"What is it?" I asked in bewilderment. "Why?"

"It's called a fur saddle," Julie said. "Basically, it's a glorified bareback pad but with more structure." She hesitated, and then took a deep breath. "I have a lot of scar tissue on my legs that makes riding in a regular saddle painful. Beyond painful, actually. So I thought I'd give this a try. Bree gave me the idea last year but I wasn't quite ready to try it out until now."

"Oh wow. Well, it looks comfy. And beautiful," I said, kicking myself for not realizing how damaged Julie had been in the accident. I'd never put much thought into why someone who loved horses as much as she did, didn't ride anymore.

"We'll see how it works," Julie said. "I have it on trial for a few days."

"Can we help?" Bree asked.

"No, that's okay. I'd rather figure it out on my own," Julie said. "But you can come check on me once you've untacked and put your horses away. Make sure I haven't forgotten how to ride."

"All right," Bree said, looking a bit worried, "have fun. We'll see you in a bit."

We watched in silence as Julie carefully adjusted her helmet into place and led Ace out of the barn toward the ring.

"This is amazing," Bree whispered to me. "I'm so excited. But I'm also terrified that it won't work. Julie practically stopped speaking to me when I suggested that she starting riding again last year. This is a big deal for her. I don't know what she'll do if it ends up being impossible for her to ride."

Bree and I brought the senior horses in from the field and made sure everyone was fed and bedded down for the night. We were torn between wanting to give Julie her privacy and also wanting to see what was happening. We lasted another twenty minutes before we crept out to the ring. But when we got there the gate was open and there was nobody in sight.

"She's not here," Bree said, her voice rising in alarm.

We stared at the ring hard as if we could conjure her up out of thin air.

"Would she have taken him out on the trails?" I asked doubtfully.

"I have no idea. She's never mentioned trail riding but—" She broke off as we caught sight of a familiar horse was coming up from the trails.

Julie grinned and waved when she saw us, her face lit up.

"She's okay." Bree reached out and gripped my arm suddenly and let out a deep breath. "She's able to ride."

Julie rode right up to us and then steered Ace back into the ring and over to the mounting block. Her face contorted for a second in pain as she swung herself carefully off and eased back onto the mounting block with a small groan.

"Are you okay?" I asked.

For a second, she didn't say anything, and then she nodded and straightened upright.

"Yeah, it's going to take some getting used to, but the saddle is great. It's way more secure than it looks and it's very comfortable. I'll be able to ride in this, no problem."

"I'm so glad." Bree strode over to her and, without hesitating, wrapped Julie in a tight hug.

Julie froze for a second and then hugged her back. When they finally broke away both of them had tears in their eyes.

"Thank you," Julie said to her quietly. "You're a great friend. I wouldn't have done this without you."

"Oh, you would have—"

"No." Julie shook her head. "Probably not, Bree. This is all you."

CHAPTER 41

MAISY

*B*y the time my meeting with Dirk finally happened, I was almost looking forward to it, even just to break up the exhausting monotony of my work days.

My car crunched slowly up the white gravel driveway between rows of manicured cedar hedges and I felt my first shiver of unease. I hadn't been back here in over a year, not since Dirk had first been dragged into court. I'd forgotten how manicured the farm entrance was, how cold and impersonal; a sharp contrast to the slightly shabby but friendlier vibe at October Horses.

I'd spent many hours getting lessons at this place but it had never felt like home to me. Even Titan had always been eager to load into the trailer when our lessons were over, as if he couldn't get out of there fast enough.

I pulled up in front of the massive indoor arena and shut off the engine as memories of Titan washed over me.

Finally, I sighed and stepped out.

Voices were coming from the indoor as I made my way inside the big barn.

"Oh," a startled voice said. "Hello."

A woman about my age looked up from where she'd been sweeping the already immaculate aisle, a surprised look on her face. "Can I help you?"

"Hey, I'm here to see Dirk."

I thought I'd spoken pleasantly enough, but the woman startled at his name like I'd poked her with an electric cattle prod.

"Do ... do you have an appointment?" she asked, gulping a few times. Her eyes sort of bulged out and for a second, she looked like a goldfish plucked out of water.

"Yes," I said cautiously, not wanting to alarm her again. "He asked me to meet him here to see a horse."

"Oh," her shoulders sagged in relief and I wondered who on earth she'd thought I was. "Okay, great. Well, he's teaching a lesson right now, but I don't think he'll be long."

"Sure, no problem. I'll just wait in the indoor."

"Um, I'm not sure if—"

The sound of Dirk's booming voice cut her off and I drifted toward the arena door and slipped through before she could stop me. There was no way I wanted to wait around with her when I could be watching a lesson.

But as soon as I sat down on the bleachers, I knew that this lesson was not ending well.

The grey horse was lathered in sweat from ears to tail and every line on his body drooped in exhaustion. The rider didn't look much better. Her arms shook as she cantered past me and I could see that her face was puffy with tears.

"Again!" Dirk bellowed. "Ask right now."

"I am," the girl wailed, "I'm trying."

"You're not. You're giving up like you always do. I want you to bury those spurs in his side. And hit him like you mean it. Now!"

The girl flailed her whip out and then thudded her heel into the grey's side. Hard. He made a grunting sound, more of a groan, and then he rocked back and switched leads into a counter canter.

"There," Dirk bellowed enthusiastically, "now keep it. There. Fine, you can let him walk."

The grey shuddered to a walk, his neck stretched out and his sides rapidly heaving in and out like he couldn't catch his breath. The rider slumped in the saddle and ran her hands down the horse's sweaty neck, whispering something to him that I couldn't hear.

"He doesn't deserve a pat and neither do you," Dirk snapped. "You're both lazy, unfit, and undisciplined. I'm not sure that I want to keep working with you, honestly. You're an embarrassment."

The girl looked up in alarm, her already flushed, blotchy cheeks reddening in shame.

"If you lack natural talent and your horse is useless dog-meat, then you need to make up for that with hard work and ruthless determination. I think you're too weak to be ruthless."

A surge of anger shot through me and I got slowly to my feet and made my way into the ring toward them.

Dirk's gaze shot over to me and his expression changed.

"Maisy!" He called out, his smile wide and his eyes warm. The transformation was so abrupt that I might have laughed out loud if it hadn't been so alarming.

I'd forgotten what a chameleon this guy was. Always shifting himself to suit his audience.

I looked up at the student who was doing her best to silently gulp back her tears and then my gaze fell on her horse's sides, drawn to a ragged patch of red that stained his fur.

"You horse is bleeding," I said sharply, snapping my gaze up to meet hers.

"Is he?" She launched out of the saddle and hit the ground lightly. "Oh no, that's from the spurs. I didn't know …"

She touched his side gingerly and drew back when he shuddered away from her.

"He's going through a rough patch," Dirk said, his smile still firmly locked in place, "he's struggling to understand some basic concepts so we have to be a little firmer with him than we'd like. These thin-skinned horses bleed at the drop of a hat. We'll have to get a spur guard for him next time. Right, Desi?"

The only answer from the rider was a sniffle from where she was inspecting the other side of her horse.

"She's a bit sensitive, too," he said, dropping his voice and leaning toward me confidingly. "Sometimes these girls need to be toughened up."

I took an involuntary step back, not liking how close he was into my space and he frowned, some of the warmth of his expression fading away.

"Go cool that horse out and give him a bath," he snapped, turning back to his student. "And get Francis to put something on those rubs."

Cuts, I thought angrily, *not rubs*. Funny how changing a small word could make an awful thing seem almost normal, just a part of everyday training, when in reality it was far from that.

My thoughts were churning as we followed the young rider and her horse out of the ring into the aisle.

"So, Maisy," he said, all smiles again. "Let's go see this horse I was telling you about."

I followed him dutifully down the aisle and stopped dead when he paused in front of a stall and grinned at me.

"Oh, wow," I said, peering into the stall with my heart thumping.

"I thought you'd say that. Maisy, meet Tiberius."

"Aren't you beautiful," I whispered. "Can I go in with him?'

"Be my guest. Be careful, though. He's a bit nervous around people."

"Hey," I said softly, sliding the stall door open and slipping inside. "Look at you, big guy. You remind me a lot of someone I used to know."

The horse didn't leave the back of his stall but he looked at me with interest and stretched his nose out slightly in my direction. The resemblance between this guy and Titan was striking. Same arching neck and sloping withers, same strong legs and broad chest. Same ears that tipped inwards at the top so they looked like little horns.

But, where Titan had been all black without any markings at all, this horse had a thin white blaze and two white front socks. And where Titan's eyes had been full of love and trust, this horse just looked anxious and a little lost.

"It's okay, big fellow," I said softly. "I'm not going to hurt you. I just want to say hello."

He hesitated for a second and then bopped by hand gently with his big nose, testing to see if I was a threat. When I just kept talking to him, he finally stepped forward with a sigh of relief.

His eye softened and he let out a big sigh and nuzzled my arm gently.

"Good boy," I said quietly, running my hands down his neck and over his shoulder.

"You always did have a way with horses," Dirk said.

The horse jumped at the sound of his voice and took a hurried step backward until his rump hit the corner of the stall, as far away from Dirk as he could possibly get.

"Easy boy—" I started to say.

"Oh, he's always like that," Dirk said, "these upper-level horses are quirky. Pretty and powerful but not much going on upstairs, if you know what I mean. Let's get him tacked up and I'll show you what he can do."

I hesitated, staring at the horse longingly, thinking of how nice it would be to ride a horse like that again. A horse almost like Titan in every way. It was so tempting.

"No," I said finally, turning away from the animal, trying not to feel like I was abandoning him. "I'm sorry but this was a mistake. I can't ride here."

"What?" His face went slack with astonishment as I slid out of the stall. "Why?"

"It's not me," I said simply. Dirk was who he was. I wasn't about to lecture him about humane treatment of horses. I'd known him for long enough to know that he didn't care.

And with Titan, it hadn't mattered so much because I'd been there to protect him. He hadn't liked Dirk, but he'd never been abused by him, either. I would have never let him be mistreated in any way.

But riding a horse here, a horse whose fate I had no control over, and who I had no power to protect, would be torture for me. I knew that now.

"I'm sorry. I have to go," I said, turning down the aisle.

"Maisy," he said sharply. "You're making a mistake."

"What?" I turned slowly to face him.

"Your career is already toast. Do you think that anyone but me will take a chance on you now? Give you a world class horse to ride? Give you any opportunities. I saw the videos; you're a spoiled drunk with no future. That's what everyone thinks."

For a second, I felt a surge of anger and shame wash over me but I shook it resolutely away. I glanced over to see the rider from earlier hosing her horse off in the wash stall. She looked away quickly, turned off the water, and led her horse down the aisle away from us.

"We all make mistakes," I said. "But the difference between you and I, Dirk, is that I learn from mine. You were punished for being cruel to both people and animals. That would be enough to make some people change their lives, to do better. But that's not what I see here, Dirk. I see you running your barn through fear and intimidation like you always did.

"I used to think that was normal. But now I know better."

He bristled in anger, taking a step forward, and for a moment I wondered if I should be afraid.

"I'm a good trainer," he said sharply, "my horses win."

"They do," I agreed. "But they're also terrified of you. That horse over there is bleeding and you're not even ashamed enough to be sorry that you hurt him."

"I didn't hurt him," he said, rolling his eyes. "I didn't touch him."

"No, but you knew what was happening," I said, "and what you did was worse. You made his rider hurt him. Someone he trusts and looks for to protection. You hurt both of them. And I think that's what you wanted. I think it makes you feel powerful to have control over others. That's what I didn't see before. I thought you were only harsh to make me ride better, that you had my best interests at heart. But now I see that it was just a game for you. To see how far you could push us."

"You never complained before," he said, snarling at me, "you never seemed to mind all the ribbons that you won."

"No," I said quietly, "you taught me a lot of things, Dirk. And you're a good coach when you want to be. But you have a darker side, too. And I don't want to be any part of it anymore, even as a bystander."

"Get out," he said, a lethal tone in his voice. "Get out of here and never come back."

"Good idea." I turned away from him and marched down the aisle, feeling his angry stare boring into my back. I half-expected him to throw something at me or stab me with a hoof pick or something. But nothing happened and when I glanced back over my shoulder, he was gone.

All the energy whooshed out of me as I stepped out into the sunshine and I sagged, feeling like I'd run a marathon. I couldn't believe what a mistake I'd made in coming here.

That poor horse, I thought, thinking of the awful way

Tiberius had pressed up against the back of his stall. I was so glad I'd never boarded Titan there.

"Excuse me?" a small voice said behind me, and I turned to see the small rider from earlier, grazing her horse at the edge of the parking lot.

"Hi," I said gently, glancing around to make sure we were alone. "Are you okay?"

"No, not really," she sniffled. "Do you really think that I've broken Molson's trust forever?"

She gulped and glanced back to the tired horse who was busily cropping at the grass.

"You overheard that, hey? What's your name?"

"Desi. Today's lesson was awful. We came here because Dirk is supposed to be the best but ..." her voice broke off and she sniffled again.

"Do your parents know about the lawsuit against him?"

"No?" She shook her head. "I don't think so. Does Molson hate me now? I will never wear spurs again. I threw mine away."

She glanced down at my tall boots where my spurs were latched firmly in place and then looked up at me in confusion.

"They're just a tool, Desi," I said quietly. "But you can't use them in anger or frustration. Only to guide the horse."

"I hate them," she said. "I hate ... I hate me for what I did to him."

I wanted to make her feel better, to tell her it was no big deal, that the rubs would heal fast, and that Molson would have forgotten it all by next week. But I didn't. Maybe making a bigger deal of these things and not normalizing them was the first step to change. And if anger at herself made Desi a better caretaker for Molson, and for her future horses, then I was all for it.

"You're a good rider," I said instead, "and the fact that you care about your horse so strongly means that one day you're going to be a great rider."

"You think?' She asked doubtfully. "Dirk said—"

"Don't listen to him," I said quickly. "There are plenty of coaches out there who can help you better than he can. He's sick."

I looked around; we were still alone but suddenly I didn't like the idea of leaving her here with him after I'd gotten him so angry. I didn't want him to take it out on her.

"My mom's on her way," she said, maybe guessing my thoughts. "She was really mad when I sent her the pictures of Molson's cuts. She's coming to pick me up now."

"Want me to wait with you?" I asked.

"Could you?" She sounded so relieved. "Aren't you worried that he'll come out and yell again?"

"Nope," I said, leaning up against my car. "I'm not scared at all."

"You're lucky," she said.

"It doesn't always feel that way."

"Do you have a horse?"

An image of Chilly rose up in front of me; his kind eyes, his goofy expressions, the way my heart lightened the second I was around him.

"Yeah," I said finally. "Yeah, I guess in a way I do."

Instead of going home after my visit to Dirk's place, I drove right back to October Horses. The barn was peacefully filled with the sounds of horses crunching on their dinner hay.

I didn't bother turning the lights on as I made my way down the aisle to the stall I knew the best.

"Chilly," I whispered, and he popped his head up with a surprised nicker.

He pushed forward and nuzzled my face, lipping at my hair and then dropping his head down over the side of the stall so he could gently search my pockets.

"Here's your cookie," I said, fishing one out and feeding it to him. He took it gently, crunching it slowly as if savoring every bite.

I kissed him goodbye and then went back to my car, driving it up to Julie's house before I could change my mind.

"Maisy," she said in surprise as she answered the door. "Is everything okay?"

"Yes," I said, "or at least it will be. Can I come in? I want to talk to you about adopting a horse. And then I need to speak to Chloe.

It took twenty minutes to convince Julie that I was the only home for Chilly.

But in the end, after I'd convinced her that I had enough in my savings account to keep Chilly living the life he was accustomed to, and that I needed this horse in my life more than anything, she finally handed over his paperwork and gave me a tight hug.

"I hope you won't come to regret this," she said sighing.

"I won't. No matter what happens next in my life, Chilly and I are in this together."

I'd tucked his papers carefully away in my purse.

"Now, I need to speak to Chloe."

She must have somehow sensed what I was there for. Because when she came into the room, her face was pale and anxious.

"I'm so sorry, Maisy," she said before I'd even opened my mouth. "I had nothing to do with it. I told her you were a good person and that she should stop. She wouldn't."

"Who is it?" I asked firmly. Not giving her any room to wriggle out of this conversation.

"Peyton. She's a good person, she was just ... so angry with you."

"Who the hell is this Peyton person anyway?"

"She's young. Like sixteen. Her sister rode with you. With ... Dirk. He was really bad to her. And she was part of the lawsuit. They were really mad that you wouldn't testify."

"So, did this Peyton break my window in my house, too? Smash into my truck?"

"No," Chloe said miserably. "That was an accident. Well, she paid some kids she knows to drive around and throw the brick on your driveway with a note. But she didn't mean for them to break anything. Or wreck your truck. Or scare you so badly. She's really sorry about that."

"All right, I'm going to need this kid's address. This ends right here."

Chloe didn't even argue. She just pulled out her phone and texted the address to me.

"I'm really sorry about all of this," Chloe said miserably. "I should have told you earlier that it was her, but I thought she'd come to her senses and stop on her own. I didn't want her to get into more trouble."

I looked down at her tear-stained face and tried to feel something. Anger, sadness, some compassion. But there was nothing there.

Then I turned around and headed toward my truck.

The low-slung rancher wasn't quite what I'd expected. It looked cozy; not like it was harbouring a little psychopath with mad internet skills.

I knocked on the front door, then rang the bell when there was no answer. Then rang it again. It was getting late, but I was hoping that maybe her parents were home, too. I'd love to tell them exactly what their precious kid had been up to.

"I'm coming, hold your horses," a voice grumbled from inside and then the door flung open, and an irate teenager with her blonde hair in two braids on either side of her head glared out at me.

Her expression changed the second she realized who it was

and she leapt backward, grabbing at the door to try and slam it closed.

"Not so fast, Peyton," I said, "I just want to talk to you."

"I don't have anything to say to you," she said, her voice coming out a terrified squeak. "I'm going to call my dad right now. And the police. And a lawyer. You're trespassing."

"Well, that sounds like a great idea," I said calmly. "Here, I'll dial for you. Should we try the police first? I don't think they look too kindly on cyberbullying and stalking, Peyton. Not to mention paying some thugs to break into my house."

Her face dropped, then she made one last lunge to slam the door. She was surprisingly strong for such a little thing, probably all those hours spent doing barn work, but I was able to shoulder my way inside and shut the door firmly behind me.

"I'm sorry," she said quickly, looking like she was about to keel over with terror. Was I really that scary? I sure hoped so. "I didn't mean it. I'll take the videos down."

"Yes, you will. Now, I'd like to know why the hell you made them in the first place. Why are you angry with me?"

Her face flushed beet red and she looked down at the floor, her lower lip trembling.

"My sister is Ingrid Feldman," she said shortly. "You used to ride with her."

"Oh," I said suddenly, the breath whooshing out of me. "Ingrid. Is she … is she okay?"

"No," Peyton said sharply, "she's not. She tried to hurt herself again and she's in the hospital. And it's all your fault."

This last part was said though a flood of tears as she turned and fled down the hall.

I hesitated and then followed after her. She'd made it as far as the living room couch where she'd thrown herself down to continue her cry.

"Go away," she said, sensing me standing there. "I don't want you here."

"Peyton. I'm really sorry about your sister. I always liked Ingrid. She was a talented rider and a great person."

She sniffled a little and then sat up, wiping her eyes.

"Yeah, she's the best. But Dirk ruined her. He destroyed all her confidence, he nearly killed her."

"He is an awful person," I agreed.

"You're just as bad," she cried out. "You lied for him. You protected him. It's your fault we lost the lawsuit. We didn't have enough evidence because not enough people would testify. Ingrid felt … she felt like nobody believed her, like everyone was judging her. I just wanted to you to feel like she did. Like you were nothing."

"Oh," I said sadly, "I'm so sorry. I know you believe that I could have helped your lawsuit but really, I couldn't have. I just kept to myself and got out of there. Yeah, I knew Dirk wasn't a nice man, but everyone knew that. I never saw anything that I didn't consider normal day to day life at the barn."

"But it wasn't *normal.*" Peyton half-shouted. "That creep almost killed my sister. She's still suffering for what he put her through. And you were his accomplice. Everyone there was."

"Peyton I …." I broke off, a sudden memory flooding over me. Me finding a sobbing Ingrid shut up inside one of the lockers one afternoon. It was one of the big lockers where the boarders kept their tack; big enough for saddles, bridles, and boots, but not big enough for a person to be in there for any length of time. She'd been hysterical when I'd found her, but when I'd tried to go get help she'd refused to let me tell anyone.

"They'll think I'm stupid," she'd whispered. And she'd refused to tell me who'd done it, either. I'd figured it was one of the other working students, but I'd guessed it was her business and if she didn't want me to tell anyone then I wouldn't.

I'd seen bruises on her before too, and the haunted look in her eye. But I'd never had any reason to believe it was Dirk, not really.

"Does Ingrid still ride?" I asked and Peyton looked up at me in surprise.

"No, she's too depressed to do much. She only comes home from the mental health center on weekends. But I get her to visit my horse with me sometimes. I board with Lauren."

Ah, so that explained it all. She'd been at the casino that night for Lauren's party. She must have filmed every minute of my drunken spree.

"I'll take down the videos," she said quietly. "I was going to anyway. Ingrid figured out what I was doing and she told me to stop. She's not angry with you like I am."

"You're a good sister," I told her, surprising her again. "I wish I'd someone like you in my corner when I was young."

She sighed and smiled at me a little.

"I just hate that Dirk wins," she said grimly. "I hate that he can just go on hurting horses and people with zero consequences."

"Well, he did do some jail time, so there's that. His reputation is pretty shaky. But, you're right, he shouldn't have horses under his care anymore. A six-month ban wasn't long enough. He shouldn't be working with animals."

"So, what do we do about it?" Peyton asked.

"I think I might have an idea," I said slowly. "But I'll need a list of all his current boarders."

It was actually pretty easy once we'd set our plan into motion. It only took a few days.

Peyton had lots of old photos and videos of Dirk being mean to horses at local shows. And it wasn't hard to track down Desi to get her to send photos of the spur marks on Molson's sides. She'd already moved him to his new barn so she wasn't so worried about offending Dirk anymore.

With the list of all of his current boarders in hand, we put together a long email stating all the crimes listed against him, including the worst of the videos. We also included a list of other farms who were accepting new boarders.

I added a personal note to Tiberius's owner, telling her that I'd owned Titan and how much the two reminded me of one another. And she and her horse deserved much better.

Peyton had wanted to keep running with it, to make Dirk's life a living hell, but I wouldn't let her. It was time for both of us to let go of the past and move on.

"Thanks again for not pressing charges," she'd told me. "I owe you for that. And I told Ingrid everything. I hope it's okay that I gave her your number. She wants to talk to you about maybe volunteering sometime at that thoroughbred place you ride at."

"Oh, that's great. I'd love to see her again. And I think she'd really like October Horses. It's a magical place and it sure helped me to heal."

"Well, maybe we'll see you around sometime then. Thanks again, Maisy. I'm sorry for… you know, everything."

I looked into her earnest face and felt the last vestiges of my own hurt and anger fade away.

"Don't worry about it," I said, "it's already forgotten."

CHAPTER 42

MAISY

I sat up as tires crunched on the driveway and went to the front door, hoping against hope that Jeremy had come back. It was a few days after my confrontation with Peyton and I still hadn't heard from him.

I peered at the strange rental car that pulled up next to the house and then flung open the door.

"Mom, Dad, you're home."

I had never been so glad to see them.

"Maisy," my mom said in surprise as I caught her in a tight hug. We'd always been a close family but not the type to be overly affectionate or throw around hugs.

She stiffened and then wrapped her arms tightly around me.

"We missed you," she said in my ear. "It's so good to see you."

I broke away to hug my slightly perplexed father who was just staring at us in bewilderment.

"I have so much to tell you," I told them. "I hope we can put off selling the farm a little longer. I just bought a horse."

"Oh," my mom said, her face falling. "Oh dear. Darling, I'm so sorry. We got an offer. We've already sold it. That's why we came home a bit early. The new owners want to move in next month."

"We should have told you sooner." My dad put a hand on my shoulder.

I stood in shock for a minute. I'd known it was coming but it still felt too soon.

"Maisy," my mom said quietly and I shook my head.

"No, you know what guys. It's okay. I'll be fine."

They both still looked stricken so I took the keys from my dad's hand and pushed the button that popped the trunk.

"I'm so glad you're both home," I said again. "Let's get your stuff inside. We have a lot to catch up on."

It took the rest of the afternoon for us to get caught up. They told me about their travels and showed me about a million pictures from their cruise and from their road trip afterwards. And I told them about riding at the farm and all about Chilly.

I didn't tell them about the videos, my confrontation with Peyton, or about Jeremy. Some things were still too painful for me to talk about.

That evening I started to organize my suite, deciding on what I wanted to keep. I wasn't sure if I wanted to find an apartment somewhere or take up Bree on her offer to move in upstairs at the farm. But, either way, I was in need of some serious downsizing.

"Honey, you know you don't have to pack up everything right now?" my mom said from the doorway. "We have some time before the new owners take over."

"I know. But I'd like to get some of the things in storage now so I won't have to rush around later. It feels like a good time to start over."

"Yes, but darling, what does that mean?" she said, sitting down on my bed. "You're being so cryptic all of a sudden. Your father and I are a bit worried."

"I'm not trying to hide anything," I said, reaching out and squeezing her hand. "I don't have a clue what I'm going to do next. But I'm not worried about it. I'll figure it out. Julie says I can stay on the farm too, if I like."

"You could go to university," my mom said hopefully.

"Maybe. Possibly. I do think I want to do something with horses long-term, but I'm going to give myself some time to just think it through."

"Well, your father and I trust you dear; you always make good, practical decisions."

That was nice of her to say, if completely inaccurate.

"Thanks, mom. I'm trying, anyway."

"And, you're happy dear? You're doing all right?"

"I'm happy," I said. And for the most part that was true. I was still sad about the loss of Titan, and of Jeremy. Both of them had left big holes in my life that would take a while to heal. But I knew that I would be okay eventually.

I picked up the framed jockey club certificate on my desk, the one with Chilly's name on it, and then placed it back down next to a photo Bree had taken of me and my new horse. It was the same one she'd used on her blog when she'd announced that I'd adopted him.

The doorbell chimed suddenly through the house, making both of us jump and then start laughing.

"I won't miss that horrible thing," she said, "the new condo won't have any bells."

"Maisy," my father called down the stairs. "You have a visitor."

"For me?" I trotted slowly up the stairs and then froze when I caught sight of the figure at the front door. "Jeremy?"

He smiled at me wanly and I took in the dark circles under his eyes and the pale skin.

For a second, I hesitated, wondering what I was walking into. Had he been drinking? Had he spent time in jail? All those thoughts flitted through my mind, and then he opened his arms to me, and I knew only that it was my friend there, more than a friend maybe, and that he was hurting and that he was home.

I moved quickly then, closing the distance between us until I practically crashed into him, my eyes stinging with tears as the familiar warmth of him closed in around me. He pulled me in tightly, pushing his face into my hair.

I didn't know how long we stood that way, but the sound of someone clearing their throat brought me back to reality.

"Uh, Jeremy," I said, taking a deep breath and pushing back slightly so that I could see his face. "This is my dad."

Things were a little less intense after that, but not much. Jeremy kept a tight grip on my hand as I introduced him to my parents and he said all the right things as they eyed him up suspiciously, their slightly disapproving stares drawn down to our clasped hands.

"I was just about to start packing Titan's stuff up to put in storage," I said finally so we could get away. "Come help me in the barn and we can catch up."

As soon as we were in the barn, he pulled me against him again. "Maisy, I'm so sorry. I should have contacted you. I was dealing with some really heavy stuff, but that's no excuse."

"No, it isn't." I pulled away. "You left without saying a word of goodbye. I thought we were friends."

"We are," he said solemnly. "You're the best thing I have in my life. My dad died."

"Oh." I inhaled sharply. "I'm sorry."

"It was intense. But I got to say goodbye at least. So that was good. I think in the end, he forgave me. It was a bit of closure anyway."

"That's good."

"I just had to be sure, Maisy. Before I contacted you and came home again. I had to make sure that I had this thing beat. That my addiction wouldn't catch hold of me again when I was in a weak moment. I'm sorry, but I had to know."

"And … did it catch hold of you."

"No." He shook his head. "I'm okay. My family invited me to come back home, to take over my part of the inheritance again."

"Oh." My heart sank. Even if I'd half-predicted this was coming, it still hurt. "Why did you come back here then?"

"Maisy, I came back for you. And for the horses."

"Me and the horses?" I said, half laughing to be lumped in with the livestock.

"I want you to come with me. I'm going to talk to Lorne about taking Timely and Dragon when I go."

"Aren't there horses in Scotland?" I asked.

"There are. But these are very good horses. They deserve a chance to compete properly and they won't be able to get it here in such an isolated place. The big shows are just too few and far between."

"All right, fair enough." I nodded. "That explains the horses, but why would you want to take me? Aren't there other girls in Scotland, too?"

"They are nothing compared to you," he said, smiling at me. "It was pretty bleak there without you. I spent the whole time wishing you were there beside me."

"Oh, Julie would have loved that," I said, trying to joke my way around this conversation. "If we'd both up and left out of the blue."

"Maisy, I'm serious. I want you to go with me, to meet my family. The farm is huge and they breed good horses. There is a cottage there we can use and you would be able to show in Europe just like you'd always wanted to."

I stared at him with a mixture of hope and terror. It was too good to be true. Everything he was saying was exactly what I wanted to hear; there must be a lie or a catch in there somewhere. If he could go away once and leave me then he could do it again.

He was watching me so earnestly that I had to look away.

"What if it doesn't work?" I asked, my voice tight with emotion. "What if we end up hating each other and then I'm stuck there overseas all my own without a place to live or a—"

"Maisy," he said patiently. "That's not going to happen. And if it does then you'll just buy a ticket and come home. I know that I just launched this at you out of the blue. I'm not trying to force you to do anything you're not ready for. Just promise you'll think about it."

I stared out over the empty paddock, across the woods and to the tips of the mountains beyond. This place had been my home for so long, it felt terrifying to think about leaving it.

But here was an adventure calling to me; the thing I'd always wanted was being placed in my lap.

What else is holding me here? I thought. *Here is my chance to start over again. And to experience the world. I would be a fool not to jump at this.*

Jeremy was looking out over the fields, too. And, even though he'd said that he didn't want to pressure me, I could see the strain, and the hurt, in his eyes.

"Okay," I said quietly.

"Okay?" He turned and clasped both of my hands in his, his face lighting up. "You'll go? Seriously?"

"I'll go. But there's probably one thing you should know."

"What?" He frowned down at me.

"We're going to need a bigger airplane. Timely and Dragon aren't the only horses going on an adventure."

"What?"

"I bought a horse."

"You…" he wiped a hand across his face and when he looked up, he was grinning from ear to ear. "I knew it. You bought Chilly, didn't you?"

"I did."

And then he pulled me into another tight hug that nearly crushed the air out of me. Strangely enough, I didn't mind a bit.

CHAPTER 43

BREE

"So, that's the story," Jeremy said, looking at Lorne and Julie with serious eyes. "We'd give the horses a great home and a chance to live up to their full potential. I'll pay you fair-market value for them. I have a little spending money now that my inheritance has been freed up. Enough for two horses, anyway."

"Well," Lorne said in astonishment. "This is a lot to take in. But, yes, taking Timely is no problem. You'll do well with him. But, Dragon ... that's another story."

"And Maisy, what are you planning to do about Chilly?" Julie said, looking at her a little disapprovingly.

"I'm taking him, of course," Maisy said, rolling her eyes. "You didn't think I was going to dump him somewhere, did you?"

"Ah, no, of course not," Julie said, backtracking in the face of Maisy's obvious anger. "It's just so sudden. I want to make sure you've thought everything through carefully. It's a big decision."

"Nope, I'm done overplanning things," Maisy said, looking

over and sharing a smile with Jeremy. "I'm going to try being spontaneous for a while. I have an exit plan, though. I'll always keep enough in savings to make sure Chilly and I can get home if things don't work out. I mean, if Jeremy turns out to be horrible, or tries to make me eat haggis or something."

She winked at him to show she was kidding, and he just shook his head.

I looked at them in wonder, so happy to see them both with the weight of the world off their shoulders. But also sad because I was really, really going to miss them both. Especially Maisy, who had become like a sister to me.

"You'll come visit us, right, Bree?" Maisy said, catching my eye. "You and Nicholas will come for the summer or for Christmas holidays."

"Yeah," I said smiling. "Nicholas has always wanted to travel. I think that would be fun."

"Good, because I'm going to miss you like crazy. I don't know how I would have made it through these last few months without you. I've never met a nicer, kinder person than you, Bree. You are one in a million."

My eyes welled up with tears, and in a second, Maisy had jumped up and wrapped me in a hug, both of us crying and sniffling.

"So, what about Dragon?" Lorne asked slowly once we'd both composed ourselves. "Jeremy rides her well. She finished her first event without too much embarrassment. But then there's Chloe."

"Yes," Julie said, sighing. "Jeremy, I think we're going to need a few days to think about Dragon."

Jeremy nodded. "Sure, take all the time you like. Another option is that we could …"

He was cut off by the sound of something clattering down the stairs.

"Stop, don't sign anything!" Chloe said abruptly, spilling out onto the landing and lurching through the kitchen to stand before us.

Her face was pale, and her eyes wild-looking. She glared at Jeremy furiously and then looked away. "He's not who he says he is. You can't let him take Maisy and the horses to Scotland. He's fooling you all."

Everyone looked at her in astonishment.

"Chloe, don't do this," I said in a low voice. I wasn't sure how I was going to reason with her when she was in this state but I had to stop her. Whatever random conspiracy theory that she was about to say was going to hurt everyone.

"Don't stop me, Bree," Chloe said. "Everyone should know who he really is. Especially Maisy. Before it's too late."

I looked over at Maisy, who had sat up straight and put a hand protectively over Jeremy's. He was watching Chloe with a strangely calm expression. Out of everyone in the room, he looked the least disturbed by her outburst.

"He's a thief and a gambler," Chloe said loudly. "And probably an alcoholic. His own family kicked him out."

A heavy silence fell over the room.

"It's true," Chloe said, looking around wildly. "Ask him. Go on, ask him. He's been lying to everyone."

"Chloe, that's enough," Maisy said evenly. "It's none of your business. You don't know what you're talking about."

Jeremy reached out and patted her arm soothingly.

"I do. He's fooled all of you but not me. But I have proof that he betrayed his family and they disowned them. It's all on the internet if you dig deep enough. If he sold out his own family, then who's to say that Lorne isn't next? Or any of us? He could be lying about everything he told us."

"Chloe, I think you had better sit down," Lorne said firmly. "You're making a fool of yourself."

"What?" she asked him, her expression falling. "But I'm trying to protect you all. Wait until you see what I found out."

"I don't need to see it," Lorne said quietly. "Jeremy told me the whole story a long time ago. Everyone has their struggles, Chloe. It doesn't mean that he's a bad person."

Another silence fell over the room.

"Jeremy is a good rider and has always been trustworthy," Julie said. "I admit that I had my doubts at first, but he has proved me wrong. He's the right rider for Timely and Dragon."

Jeremy looked at her in surprise and then smiled.

"Chloe, I'm not an alcoholic," he said, turning back to her, "although I'll admit that I've come close. But I do have trouble with gambling. And I did lose a good chunk of my family's money. Something my father never forgave me for, at least not until I returned home and made peace with him right before he passed away. Gambling is an addiction for me. But I've been getting help and I will have a good support system back home. Sometimes I mess up, but that's just part of the journey. And even when I do mess up, it will never affect how I treat the horses. Or Maisy."

"But ... you, I saw you go into the community center for those meetings. And I followed you when you went to the casino. I saw you go inside."

"Chloe, Lauren's family *owns* the casino so that's where her office is. But, you're right. It wasn't a good idea to go there. I told her that I wouldn't meet her there anymore. I know my limits now."

"You followed him?" Lorne asked, looking at Chloe with such a disappointed expression that she flinched her gaze away.

"I had to know what he was up to," she said stubbornly, "I had to protect you."

"Don't you think this anger and vengeance thing has gone on long enough?" Julie asked. "First Maisy, and now Jeremy. Think of all the harm you could have caused. Look what it's doing to you, Chloe."

"But I … I …" Suddenly Chloe burst into tears. "I just don't want to lose anyone else."

With that, she turned and hobbled up the stairs as fast as she could, leaving us all a bit stunned in her wake.

"Well, that solves that," Lorne said heavily. "I'd put money on Jeremy doing exactly what he says he will. He has the facilities there, and access to world class shows. And Maisy will be there to keep him in line. Dragon and Timely should go with them to Scotland."

"Then I suppose we should sign these papers and get these two horses off to their new careers."

"Actually, can you hold off on that for a few minutes?" Jeremy asked. "I want to go talk to Chloe first."

"Are you sure?" Lorne asked, frowning. "You don't owe her anything."

"I know. But I'd like to mend one bridge if I could. I'll be right back."

We all watched as he walked away.

"What's he doing?" I whispered to Maisy.

"I'm not a hundred percent sure," she said slowly. "He had this idea before but I'm not certain if …"

She broke off at the sound of something crashing to the floor upstairs, and then the thudding of feet. Then just silence.

Julie stood up uncertainly and then sat back down again.

Five minutes later, Jeremy came back downstairs whistling under his breath.

"You didn't strangle her, did you?" Maisy asked.

"Nope, she is alive and well. She'll be down in minute. We have come to a sort of business arrangement if you're all right with it."

"Business arrangement?" Lorne asked in bewilderment. "Don't you want Dragon now?"

"Yes, I do. Next year when she's had more conditioning. This will be a busy time getting everything set up the way we want it there. And winter is coming. I propose that we leave Dragon here until next spring. Chloe will be able to start riding next month and she can keep her toned and fit. She's promised to take regular dressage lessons with you, Julie. And then in spring, she can choose to send Dragon over to us or to come stay with us as a working student."

"You'd do all that for her after she's been so awful?" Julie asked.

"Yes," Jeremy said. "She reminds me of myself when I was about that age. I threw myself against every door that closed on me with a vengeance. I was bitter and angry for longer than I needed to be. Hopefully, this will be the chance she needs to find her old self again."

"Thank you," I said, nearly starting to cry again. "You have no idea how much this will mean to her."

"Oh, I have a pretty good idea. She nearly knocked me over thanking me."

Chloe came down later, her face radiant even though it was still puffy with tears.

Another year, I thought, *we have another year together at least before things change again.*

But I'd learned that change wasn't always bad, even though it felt that way at first sometimes. Usually, it ended up leading to something better.

EPILOGUE

MAISY

"*T*here they are," I said, waving out the window in excitement to where everyone stood clustered on the tarmac next to the small runway. I drank in their faces eagerly, memorizing every last detail. "I'm going to miss them so much."

"Me too," Jeremy said. "We'll visit, though. I've already invited them to come watch the horses compete. And, we'll see Chloe next year when she comes to stay."

"I know."

Lorne had his hat off and was waving it back and forth in the air like he was an air traffic controller. Chloe, still wobbly without her crutches, had one arm linked through Bree's and the other raised in a final wave. Her gaze met mine and she gave me a watery smile.

Chloe and I had talked a lot in the weeks leading up to my departure and I'd gotten to know her much better. It was like a weight had dropped right off her shoulders, returning her to the fun, kind girl she was supposed to be.

I'd been busy teaching her and Bree everything I knew about liberty work, which honestly wasn't that much, and they'd both promised to send me videos and updates on how they progressed.

I couldn't wait to see what Follow would look like in another three months. Bree had been working with her hard and the little mare was steadily emerging from her shell and becoming more confident.

The little plane rumbled to life and I sucked in a nervous breath. We were taking a small plane over to Vancouver where we would then catch our international flight out.

The horses had left the day before and were probably half way to their new home in Scotland by now.

I gulped as the plane gave a lurch and began to move very slowly down the runway. I reached out to touch the window with my fingertips, already feeling homesick for my life at October Horses. I'd made some real friends there and I missed them already.

"You're not having second thoughts, are you?" Jeremy asked, sounding a little worried.

"No," I reassured him. "I'm not. But it feels like this whole door on my life is closing shut tight, and I have no idea what's in front of me. It's scary but, you know, exciting, too."

"This is sort of like your destiny, you know.

He reached out and took my hand. "You were knocked down and then you got up and brushed yourself off, and here you are. Off to Europe to ride horses just like you'd planned."

Not quite like I'd planned, I thought, squeezing his hand. I wasn't going to compete on Grand Prix horses anytime soon, but maybe I'd found something better. Friends, family, and a new beginning with Jeremy. And a whole other side of horses to explore with Chilly.

But I liked the sound of following my destiny. There was no telling where it would lead me if I just sat back and enjoyed the ride.

The End

ACKNOWLEDGMENTS

Keeping Chilly was written in memory of my best guy, our stallion Image of Champions (Champ), who passed away suddenly last year. There is no feeling worse than losing a great friend and heart-horse. You will always be missed, big guy!

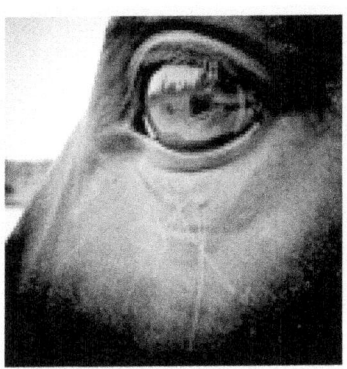

Big thanks to Helen Cartwright, Helen Yeo, Honey Johnston, Mariko Brown, Marti Oltmann and the rest of the fantastic Advanced Reader team. Your insights are always invaluable.

Always thankful for the current ponies in my life, Messenger and Fiona, and to all the past horses and ponies who taught me so much.

ABOUT THE AUTHOR

Genevieve McKay is the author of over a dozen books, and most of them are about horses. She is an avid reader, baker, eater of snacks and a tea-drinker. She lives on the west coast of Canada with her family, her horses, and an assortment of barnyard animals like dogs, cats, sheep, chickens and two half-tame ravens.

ALSO BY GENEVIEVE MCKAY

I hope you are enjoying the October Horses series, Defining Gravity series, Three Sisters series or any of my other books. I'd love if you'd take a moment to write a review on Amazon, Goodreads or any of the platforms where they are sold.

The October Horses series

The October Horses

Facing The Fire

Keeping Chilly

Defining Gravity series

Defining Gravity

Flight

Freefall

Riding Above Air

Touching Ground

Three Sisters Farm series

Everyday Horses

Short Stories and Collections

The Horses of Winter

Greystone Manor Mysteries

The Curse of the Golden Touch

The Sting of the Serpent's Blade

The Wayfarer's End Series

The Opposite of Living

Good Bones

Wayfarer's End

Visit my website at www.genevievemckay.com

Follow my pics on Instagram: @mckaygenevieve

Or join my Facebook author page: www.
facebook.com/authorgenevievemckay

If you're interested in learning more about adopting a retired racehorse then here are some great resources to get you started!

The Retired Racehorse Project

https://www.retiredracehorseproject.org/

Greener Pastures

https://greenerpasturesbc.com/

Retraining of Racehorses

https://www.ror.org.uk/

And New Track, New Life is a fantastic resource to have:

New Track New Life

Printed in Great Britain
by Amazon